THE DISINTEGRATING CONSCIENCE
AND THE DECLINE OF MODERNITY

CATHOLIC IDEAS FOR A SECULAR WORLD

O. Carter Snead, series editor

DE NICOLA CENTER
for ETHICS AND CULTURE

Under the sponsorship of the de Nicola Center for Ethics and Culture at the University of Notre Dame, the purpose of this interdisciplinary series is to feature authors from around the world who will expand the influence of Catholic thought on the most important conversations in academia and the public square. The series is "Catholic" in the sense that the books will emphasize and engage the enduring themes of human dignity and flourishing, the common good, truth, beauty, justice, and freedom in ways that reflect and deepen principles affirmed by the Catholic Church for millennia. It is not limited to Catholic authors or even works that explicitly take Catholic principles as a point of departure. Its books are intended to demonstrate the diversity and enhance the relevance of these enduring themes and principles in numerous subjects, ranging from the arts and humanities to the sciences.

THE
DISINTEGRATING CONSCIENCE
AND THE DECLINE
OF MODERNITY

STEVEN D. SMITH

University of Notre Dame Press
Notre Dame, Indiana

Library of Congress Control Number: 2023937786

ISBN: 978-0-268-20691-8 (Hardback)
ISBN: 978-0-268-20693-2 (WebPDF)
ISBN: 978-0-268-20690-1 (Epub)

To the grandkids.

CONTENTS

ACKNOWLEDGMENTS

I'm very much indebted to friends, colleagues, and critics for help in preparing and refining this book. Those who read and commented on all or part of the book include Larry Alexander, Jim Allan, Helen Alvaré, Stephanie Barclay, Mary Anne Case, Nathan Chapman, Marc DeGirolami, Bruce Frohnen, Rick Garnett, Craig Harline, Paul Horwitz, Andy Koppelman, Sandy Levinson, Michael Moreland, Luis Coutinho Pereira, Jeff Pojanowski, Micah Schwartzman, Maimon Schwarzschild, George Wright, and participants in the Annual Law and Religion Roundtable. Elizabeth Sain was a wonderful editor, and Sasha Nuñez and Liz Parker provided much appreciated assistance with the citations and index.

PROLOGUE

How Did We Get Here?

Mire' los muros de la patria mia,
si un tiempo fuertes, ya desmoronados
de la carrera de la edad cansados
por quien caduca ya su valentia.

I gazed upon my country's walls,
So powerful once, now a withered ruin,
Weary with the passage of the years,
Their valor now by age outworn.

—*Francisco de Quevedo, "Miré' los muros de la patria mía"*

Modern Western civilization is finished. Done. Or at least so declared the eminent historian Jacques Barzun, possibly the most learned human being then residing on the planet, in a hefty book timed to align with the start of the new millennium (or, more apropos, with the close of the old millennium). The twentieth century is ending, Barzun said, and "in the West the culture of the last 500 years is ending at the same time."[1]

1

The previous glorious and exciting half-millennium—the "modern era"—had blessed humankind with a rich endowment of unprecedented achievement and progress, scientifically and politically and economically. "[T]he peoples of the West offered the world a set of ideas and institutions not found earlier or elsewhere," Barzun observed.[2] But the project had run its course. "[T]he culture is old and unraveling,"[3] he intoned mournfully.

Barzun elaborated on this doleful assessment for eight-hundred-plus pages in a lively history covering a vast and sometimes bewildering panorama of people, ideas, and movements. These people, ideas, and movements had advanced a number of exhilarating principles and causes, including—Barzun put the major themes in capital letters—EMANCIPATION, INDIVIDUALISM, and SECULARISM.

Lofty causes, these. *We* may think so, anyway. And yet

> now these purposes, carried out to their utmost possibilities, are bringing about [the civilization's] demise. This ending is shown by the deadlocks of our time: for and against nationalism, for and against individualism, for and against the high arts, for and against strict morals and religious belief.[4]

Whether or not Barzun was right about the demise of Western culture, it seemed that he himself, at the age of 93, must surely be nearing his own demise. And yet, perhaps like the civilization he admired, and lamented, the venerable historian lingered on—not departing until 2012, after a respectable tenure in this mortal realm of 104 years. As of this writing, Western culture with its commitments to emancipation and individualism and secularism—and to rule of law and democratic governance and human rights—likewise lingers on.

Or at least staggers on. And yet it would be premature to declare with any confidence that Barzun was mistaken. Against the backdrop of centuries that the historian was working from, after all, what is a decade or two? A few grains of sand in the hourglass. And surely the "deadlocks" that Barzun noted would seem to be if anything more intractable now than they were when he wrote.

So the institutions of contemporary Western democracies—electoral politics, capitalism, the rule of law—lurch along clumsily at best. Polarization has intensified; it increasingly seems to be both toxic and irremediable. In America, the major political parties seem categorically incapable of perceiving their opponents as anything other than vile and mendacious. Unable to work together constructively, they instead offer rationalizations for adopting Shermanesque "scorched earth" policies on one or another issue—a tax bill, a judicial nomination, an impeachment. In surveys, startlingly high percentages of citizens anticipate an imminent civil war.[5] As of the time I write this sentence, the nation along with much of the world is in "lockdown," and large-scale protests sometimes accompanied by rioting, looting, and shooting have been regularly breaking out around the country—in Minneapolis, Seattle, Portland, New York, and elsewhere.

And with a fraught election upcoming, things look to get worse. Who knows what the situation will be by the time the book is finished and you read these words, if indeed that ever happens?

Still, who can say? If anything can be learned from history, it is that history is unruly, hard to reduce to secure generalizations and predictions. Even for the most learned historians (like Barzun)—that is why they are historians, not prophets. History's contours are discernible, if at all, mostly in hindsight. Things will seem to be following a definite trajectory, which a decade or so later will have been forgotten, replaced by a different trajectory, which will in its turn be replaced by still another one. The population is growing at an unsustainably rapid pace. Population growth is too low for sustainability. Religion is destined for imminent extinction. Religion is taking over the world. Liberalism is dead (after the 2004 American election). Conservativism is dead (after the 2012 election). And so on.

Unlike Barzun's tome, therefore, this book will be both much shorter and more tentative: it will offer no confident pronouncements on the death of Western civilization. Still, his title—*From Dawn to Decadence*—seems apt, whatever the future may hold. Ideas and movements that were fresh in the sixteenth century, and that have had in some cases a glorious run, do seem to be floundering or decrepit today. Maybe they will recover—who knows?—but they seem in deep trouble at the moment.[6]

So, how did we get from there to here?

That is what this book aims to consider, in a limited way. It is what Barzun considered as well, of course, but there will be no attempt here to duplicate his scholarly achievement. For one thing, his book has already been written, so there is no need to write it again. And even if Barzun had, let's say, decided in a fit of frustration to chuck his manuscript into the fire without publishing it, an author with scarcely a smidgeon of Barzun's erudition could hardly undertake a similar project. Rather than attempt to canvas the field, therefore, the much more modest effort here will be to discern and ponder the transformative changes in several smaller, discrete episodes.

In three episodes, to be precise, or three chapters. These three episodes, I will suggest, reflected in microcosm decisive turning points at which Western civilization changed from what it had been in premodern times to what it is today. Just in themselves these episodes may not seem to have carried any epic significance. And yet by focusing in on them (and, yes, by projecting onto them), we can discern what have turned out to be major transformations.

Instead of offering the panoramic cast of characters that Barzun discussed—a cast that makes the list of figures in a Tolstoy novel seem paltry by comparison—we will focus instead on three main characters, one for each chapter or episode. To anticipate: our principal protagonists will be Thomas More, James Madison, and William Brennan. Other supporting actors will appear as well, of course: none of our protagonists performed on an empty stage. But we will center our inquiry on one character per episode. The hope is that through this "up close and personal" perspective we may discern and appreciate possibilities and tendencies and contradictions—and slowly developing dangers—that would be left in fuzzier focus if we tried to survey the entire historical landscape.

The treatment here will be more modest than Barzun's in two other ways as well. First, Barzun tried to trace and develop about a dozen themes. Here we will focus on only one—conscience—and not even one that showed up explicitly on his list, although it has been very closely associated with several of his themes, including the ones noted already: emancipation, individualism, and secularism. A commitment to something called "conscience," I will suggest, has been a central and in some ways defining feature of modern Western civilization. Reflecting on the changing meanings and importance attributed to conscience can thus provide a revealing perspective on fundamental developments that gave rise to the "modern era" Barzun presented, and that may now be bringing that era to some sort of close.

There are of course other themes that might have been chosen—changing ideas about God, for example, or the nature of the human person—that may seem more fundamental and potentially more revealing. Conscience has the advantage, however, of being concrete and profoundly practical: it has often been at the core of live political or legal controversies with existential consequences that have forced participants to articulate their assumptions and commitments not just in abstract or academic ways but in situations where a good deal—life or death, freedom or imprisonment—has been on the line. Nor is conscience a matter independent of arguably more fundamental issues like God and human personhood; on the contrary, it is in a sense a practical or as-applied implementation of those fundamentals.

But, second, although our first chapter will be international in the scope of its reflections, our second and third chapters will be more particularly focused on the political experiment that nearly everyone will agree has played a leading role, for better or worse, in the unfolding of modernity. Namely, America. In the 1830s, Alexis de Tocqueville contended that the emergence of democracy and egalitarianism in America was leading and presaging a transformation that would spread through the civilized world. In that he was surely correct. So examining the development of conscience in America is no parochial undertaking. Still, there is no reason to suppose that events have followed exactly the same course—or that they must necessarily follow exactly the same course in the future—in other regions and countries as they have done and will do in America. (This is an observation, I trust, that carries with it a measure of hopefulness.)

So much for the preliminaries. And now . . . let us raise the curtain on chapter one, in which a paragon loses his head.

CHAPTER ONE

Lost World, New World

Thomas More and His Troublesome Conscience

I

"Sir Thomas More," the presiding judge pronounced,

> you are to be drawn on a hurdle through the City of London to Tyburn, there to be hanged till you be half dead, after that cut down yet alive, your bowels to be taken out of your body and burned before you, your privy parts cut off, your head cut off, your body to be divided in four parts, and your head and body to be set at such places as the King shall assign.[1]

Thus was sentence rendered on the internationally renowned lawyer and Renaissance man; "the most avant-garde humanist north of the Alps";[2] "undoubtedly the cleverest and most learned Englishman of his generation";[3] lately lord chancellor of England; longtime friend, confidant, and adviser to King Henry VIII; future saint but scourge of the emerging Protestants; and by one later distinguished observer's assessment "the person of greatest virtue that these [British] islands ever produced."[4] A man extravagantly revered—and also reviled—in his own century, and in ours.[5]

Though ungentle, the sentence was standard in cases of treason, which was what Thomas More had been convicted of. And how had he been a traitor to the realm? By being relentlessly, resolutely silent. In the three years since More had resigned as chancellor, the king had broken with the Roman Catholic Church, had ended his marriage to Catherine, his Spanish wife of twenty-four years, and had married Anne Boleyn. Henry had sought to manufacture support for these controversial actions by requiring all subjects to swear an oath affirming their legitimacy. For his part, More had refused to swear, and had remained firm in his refusal during fourteen months of close confinement in the Tower of London. At the same time, he had adamantly declined either to criticize the king or to explain *why* he would not take the oath—except to say that he was acting from "conscience."

On that point, he had been adamant. "How be it (as help me God) as touching the whole oath," More had insisted, "I never withdrew any man from it nor never advised any to refuse it nor never put, nor will, any scruple in any man's head, but leave every man to his own conscience. And me thinks in good faith that so were it good reason that every man should leave me to mine."[6]

At his trial before the King's Bench, More had contended that mere silence could not constitute treason. It was a solid enough legal argument, and his case had been presented by the foremost lawyer in England—namely, himself. Even so, the verdict had been foreordained. That was because, on the queen's insistence, an impetuous and increasingly imperious king had demanded that his friend must choose: swear, or die. The jurors at More's trial knew what they must do; had they voted to acquit, they might themselves have been imprisoned.[7] Only an extraordinarily courageous jury could have stood up to the king's demand, and More's jury did not distinguish itself for courage.[8]

Indeed, through the whole royal and ecclesiastical crisis, few in England exhibited anything that looked conspicuously like courage.

The most prominent exceptions were More himself and his friend John Fisher, bishop of Rochester, who had likewise refused to take the oath, and who had already been executed for treason. (Though partners in treason and martyrdom, More and Fisher had conducted themselves differently: whereas More had steadfastly guarded his silence with respect to the king's divorce and Anne's succession, Fisher had been outspoken, writing no fewer than seven books defending Queen Catherine's position.)[9] Less prominent examples included a handful of obscure but determined Protestant dissenters whom Lord Chancellor Thomas More had caused to be executed — a troubling complication that we will need to consider more closely.

Following the pronouncement of the sentence, More was taken back to the Tower to await his execution. During his final five days on earth, he collected himself and, as was his habit, composed prayers. His last prayer pleaded with God to strengthen him ("Good Lord, give me the grace in all my fear and agony to have recourse to that great fear and wonderful agony that You, my sweet Savior, had at the Mount of Olivet before your most bitter passion"), to unite him and his fellow Christians ("Make . . . us all living members, sweet Savior Christ, of Your holy mystical body Your Catholic Church"), and to forgive him together with those who had opposed and condemned him:

> Almighty God, have mercy . . . on all that bear me evil will and would
> harm me. And by such easy, tender, and merciful means as Your in-
> finite wisdom can best devise, grant that their faults and mine may
> both be amended and redressed; and make us saved souls in heaven
> together, where we may ever live and love together with You and
> Your blessed saints.[10]

Perhaps this last plea for reconciliation was at least partially answered, after a fashion anyway, because in a last gesture of clemency, the king relented by softening the sentence for his friend. And so as it turned out, Thomas More was not carted through London on a hurdle, or disemboweled and deprived of his genitals while still alive, or drawn and quartered.

Instead, he was led out to nearby Tower Hill and directed to ascend the axeman's scaffold. Feeble from months of confinement in a dank cell and suffering from kidney stones, but always ready with a joke, the condemned man asked the attendant guard to help him up the steps, "and for my coming down, let me shift for myself."[11]

From the platform, More briefly addressed the onlookers, declaring himself to be the king's loyal servant but God's first. Then, "with a cheerful countenance," as his son-in-law reported,[12] and after a moment of banter with the executioner about the shortness of his neck, he placed that diminutive neck on the block. A moment later, picking up the now autonomous head from the straw where it had fallen, the executioner waved it before the crowd, shouting "Behold the head of a traitor!"[13]

The spectacle completed, More's head was posted on a spike on London Bridge for passers-by to ponder. On the same spike, it seems, that had lately supported his friend and fellow traitor-martyr Bishop Fisher; to make room for More's head, Fisher's was taken down and tossed into the Thames.[14] More's final disposition was more dignified: when the time came to retire him from the bridge, his head was retrieved by his devoted daughter Margaret, or Meg, a formidable scholar in her own right,[15] who packed the head in spices to preserve it for the duration of her days.[16]

And thus ended an extraordinary life—and also, we can say in retrospect and with only a little historical license, an extraordinary age. Even a world. Or, in a less morose tone, and looking forward rather than backward, we might say that thus began a new era, or a new world. Thomas More was living in what historian Derek Wilson calls a "fulcrum moment in human destiny."[17] The title of a history of the period by Susan Brigden expresses the idea: *New Worlds, Lost Worlds.*[18] Thomas More was exiting along with the world—the lost world—that he had valiantly but futilely struggled to preserve. His removal was part of the clearing away needed for the emergence of a new world ruled by "new men,"[19] as More described them.

And yet in fact (a word invented by More) there was a paradox (another word invented by More):[20] both Thomas More and the "new men" who brought about his demise wrapped themselves in the mantle of something called "conscience." Thus, More was hardly alone in professing a profound commitment to fidelity of conscience. His nemesis—the rebel former monk Martin Luther, who bore the blame in More's view for the events that had led up to his own condemnation and demise—did the same.[21] Indeed, Luther's celebrated declaration rejecting the Church's authority to dictate his theological views—"Here I stand! I can do no other!"—had been if anything even more clarion in its affirmation of conscience than More's more sedate "it were good reason that every man should leave me to [my conscience]." Biographer Heiko Oberman thus reports that "Luther's appeal to conscience as the highest authority made an extraordinary impression on later generations."[22]

More's good friend and deadly foe—Henry, the king—likewise insisted on the sanctity of his conscience. Henry had justified his divorce of Catherine and his marriage to Anne Boleyn as a course commanded by conscience. In this vein, Henry's counselor and chancellor Cardinal Thomas Wolsey reported that the king "considers it would be offensive to God and man if he were to persist in [his marriage], and with great remorse of conscience has now for a long time felt that he is living under the offense of the Almighty."[23] Historian Richard Marius describes how "Henry, sitting under a canopy of cloth of gold, spoke at length about the matter he said was dearest to his soul—the state of his own conscience. Catherine protested that his conscience had taken a very long time to awaken."[24]

Conscience, it seems, had a ubiquitous, versatile, chameleon-like character. It had the conserving power to confirm and unite—but also the radical power to divide and disrupt. Its versatility equipped it for various forums and various functions, and endowed it with a perduring quality. Although all of those who invoked it in connection with the events in which Thomas More was fatally implicated would inevitably pass from this world within a few years' time, conscience itself—as an authoritative ideal, and as a potent rhetorical trope—would survive them, and would flourish. Inherited from the old world that was in process of being lost, conscience—or at least something or some (perhaps disparate) *things* often described as "conscience"—would provide a segue into the emerging new world, where that thing or those things would play an even more prominent and at times defining role. Indeed, the new era that was beginning with the passing of Thomas More might aptly be christened as "the Age of Conscience."

Thus, conscience would become a central and cherished theme for the Protestants who (despite More's efforts) would take control of England, and then would colonize America, and would go on to establish a republic on American soil.[25] And conscience would remain a respected theme in twentieth-century America and into the new millennium. Commenting on the concept's "astonishing persistence," Paul Strohn observes that

> [t]oday, [conscience] is embraced with equal conviction by non-religious and religious alike. It enjoys a privileged place in theology and devotion, but no less in art and philosophy. Politicians claim to act on its behalf, and occasionally do. Equally striking is the breadth of its appeal among all kinds and classes of persons: a subject of rarified academic inquiry that works at street level too, and is confidently cited by people in all walks of life as a basis for their actions.[26]

And yet if conscience was there with Thomas More and his world, and was helping to bring the man and his world to an end, half a millennium later conscience may be playing a role in bringing our own age to an end as well (if, as the eminent historian Jacques Barzun thought, our age is in fact coming to an end).[27]

Or maybe not. We will consider the possibility in a later chapter.

So we need to examine and reflect on that utterly familiar, eerily elusive, humbly majestic, potently protean thing. Conscience. And there is perhaps no better way to do this than to remember Thomas More, and try to figure what conscience meant to him, and what part conscience played in his own and his world's demise.

MORE'S ENIGMATIC CONSCIENCE

Not that this will be any straightforward task. Historians—and others, including playwrights from William Shakespeare to Robert Bolt of *A Man for All Seasons* and novelists like Hilary Mantel of the *Wolf Hall* series—have pondered More's actions and fate and have tried to fathom why he did what he did. They have produced as many questions as answers. More's own contemporaries likewise found his stance baffling. No one—not his enemies, not his friends, not his daughter Meg who knew his mind best and whom he loved more than anyone else in the world,[28] certainly not his wife Alice—seemed able to understand what he was doing, or what he was saying (or refusing to say). A sympathetic twentieth-century Catholic historian, Hilaire Belloc, observed that "[t]o his own family as a whole probably, to his wife certainly, to nearly all his friends and to the mass of Englishmen of his time, his position was not heroic but absurd." [29]

Consider the basic pertinent facts.

As noted, More was arrested because he refused to take an oath affirming that Anne Boleyn was the rightful queen and, by implication, that Henry was the head of the church. Over the next fourteen months, from the time of his arrest up to and even on the very day of his trial, More was assured, over and over again, that he could regain his freedom and eminent position simply by affirming the words of the prescribed oath. He didn't have to *believe* the words; he only needed to affirm them. The king's men urged him to do that. So did his friends, and his family, in a "vehement piteous manner," as he put it.[30]

Some of the arguments that were pressed upon him addressed his position, insofar as it could be discerned, on the merits. Others emphasized the catastrophic consequences of his intransigence. Taken together, they added up to a weighty case for taking the oath.

Start with the consequence-oriented arguments. The most immediate adverse consequence of More's stance was obvious enough: by refusing to take the oath, he faced the present certainty of indefinite imprisonment, to be terminated (as seemed likely, and as in fact occurred) by a public trial and painful execution. The history of Christianity has, to be sure, featured heroic or perhaps perverse souls who have eagerly sought martyrdom,[31] but Thomas More does not belong in that select company. On the contrary, he dreaded "the terrible prospect of death," as he put it in one of his last meditations.[32]

Actually, it was not exactly dying itself that principally concerned him but rather the intense pain that would accompany that transition. Or so he said. "[A] man may lose his head and have no harm,"[33] he quipped, and he professed himself "well content to go, if God call me hence tomorrow."[34] He looked forward to "the bliss of heaven."[35] "[I]f anything should hap to me that you would be loath," he counseled Meg, "pray to God for me, but trouble not yourself: as I shall full heartily pray for us all, that we may meet together once in heaven, where we shall make merry for ever, and never have trouble after."[36]

Was he as calmly confident as he sounds in these pronouncements? Maybe, maybe not: Who can say? Either way, he trembled before the agonizing prospect of pain associated with his execution. After all, torture—an art that had been refined by the Tudor period—was a real possibility. "[H]e envisaged torture upon the rack and terrible pain inflicted by more ingenious instruments," biographer Peter Ackroyd explains; "he envisaged death by disembowelling, his heart torn out of his body and shown to him while he was still alive."[37] And even if he could have counted on the king's clemency commuting his sentence to mere beheading, there was no assurance that the job would be completed with one swing of the axe: when the Duke of Buckingham had suffered a like fate a few years earlier, three strokes had been needed to finish the job.[38] More's writings from the Tower were thus filled with meditations and prayers pleading with God to strengthen him so that he could endure the ordeal (or, should he flinch, to forgive him).[39] His commentary-reflection on *The Sadness of Christ*, written while he was imprisoned in the Tower, is essentially an extended meditation and prayer on this theme. More confessed at one point that he found "my fleshe much more shrinkinge from payne and death, than me thought it the part of a faithful Christen man."[40]

There was also the matter of his good name, or his reputation. Meg reported to him that even his friends looked upon him (as his wife Alice openly did) not as some paragon of courage and integrity but rather as a pig-headed fool.[41] In fact, More was already well aware that people regarded his stance as reflecting, as he put it, mere "stubbornness and obstinacy."[42]

Nor was it only More himself who would suffer for his silence: his refusal and likely conviction for treason placed his family in grave danger of losing their property, or worse. It was one thing to accept the personal consequences of his silence, but was it right of him, standing stubbornly on his supposed integrity, to bring possible punishment and likely disinheritance on his family?[43] Alice, More's wife, certainly didn't think so, and she told him as much—emphatically, accusing him of being a "fool."[44] And indeed, More confessed to Meg that it was "a deadly grief unto me, and much more deadly than to hear of mine own death . . . [to] perceive my good son your husband, and you my good daughter, and my good wife, and mine other good children and innocent friends, in great displeasure and danger of great harm" because of his stance.[45]

Other arguments appealed to More's character, and to his judgment. He was repeatedly reminded that all of the learned men and clerics in the realm (except Fisher) had deemed it proper to take the oath. This number included prelates whom More respected, including Cuthbert Tunstall, bishop of London and a longtime friend and ally in the fight against heresy.[46] His own family had also taken the oath. "Why should you refuse to swear, Father?" Meg pleaded, "For I have sworn myself?"[47] More regarded pride as the basest and most dangerous of sins. But wasn't it prideful of him—arrogant and presumptuous—to set up his own opinion against that of so many learned and pious men and women?

And not only prideful but also ungrateful, because he was spurning his friend, Henry the king, who had done him so much kindness, taking a lowly London undersheriff and raising him up to the highest legal office in the land. Meg reminded him of his debt to Henry, and cautiously suggested that in remaining obdurate he might actually be incurring "peril unto your own soul also."[48]

She also tried to use his own teachings to soften him. He had believed and taught that what matters to God is what a person believes in his heart, not what he says with his lips. The playwright Robert Bolt reconstructed the exchange when he had Meg say to More: "'God more regards the thoughts of the heart than the words of the mouth.' Or so you've always told me." Based on this principle, Meg urges her father to "say the words of the oath and in your heart think otherwise."[49]

Perhaps, we might suppose, Thomas More was one of those rare individuals who believe that truth-telling is an absolute or categorical obligation, without possibility of exception. If your innocent Jewish friend is hiding in your attic and the Nazi gestapo show up at your door and ask if you are concealing any Jews, you have to say yes.[50] Kant would later take this categorical view.[51] So had Saint Augustine[52]—the Church father whom More most admired.[53] And yet it seems that More was not in fact so rigorous, or so rigid, in his commitment to truth-telling. He was after all a lawyer. He had long been a government minister. And in performing his lawyerly and ministerial duties, he had demonstrated the necessary ability, on appropriate occasions, to . . . let us say, fudge and finesse the truth.[54] Peter Ackroyd notes that "as he admitted himself, on occasions [More] did not shrink from '*mendaciolum*' or a small lie."[55] So then why on this occasion did he find himself utterly unable to recite some slippery words to avoid catastrophic consequences?

Indeed, would it even have been necessary to lie, exactly? Surely, brilliant lawyer that he was, More could have come up with some construction, however strained, or some mental reservation, that would have permitted him to avoid the dire consequences that his refusal entailed? Ackroyd notes that More was adept at "putting a lawyer's gloss upon ambiguous circumstances."[56] Could there have been a more opportune time to employ this lawyerly skill?

And what would have been the harm anyway? After all, in taking the oath More would not have been misleading anyone: everyone would have known that he was opposed to the divorce and even more opposed to the king's assumption of authority over the Church. Conversely, his dying did no earthly good;[57] it amounted to a kind of personal retreat and surrender in what he perceived to be a desperate "battle for the soul of England," as one historian has described it.[58] If the defense of the Church's position in that battle was so imperative, wouldn't it have been more prudent—more virtuous, really, even more unselfish—to take the oath (with mental reservations if necessary) and live on to defend that cause, a task for which More was uniquely qualified? He couldn't have known it, but within less than a year Queen Anne with her seductive wiles and her Protestant impulses would follow him to the Tower and the scaffold. And Henry, though infatuated, was still fundamentally Catholic, attending three masses a day on hunting days, sometimes five on other days.[59] If only Thomas

More, whom the king loved and admired, had still been around to guide him.

Or let us stipulate that no meliorating construction was available, so that in taking the oath More would unavoidably have been affirming something he did not actually believe. Even so, wasn't there something grossly disproportionate about his stance? Was the wrongfulness of uttering a few words at variance with his belief really so weighty as to justify the loss of his life and the serious risks and deprivations he was imposing on his family? Was his stance really one of conscience, we might ask? Or rather, as his family and friends hinted and more than hinted,[60] was it more in the nature of a finicky, unmoored, perhaps even self-indulgent scrupulosity (which in Christian tradition has been regarded as a sin)?[61]

So, which was it? Integrity? Or scrupulosity?

MORE AS HYPOCRITE?

And perhaps also hypocrisy?

The question arises because in More's particular case, there is an additional and troubling complication—one that historians and novelists and interested spectators have debated endlessly in the centuries since. We have already seen that in defending his refusal to take the oath, More repeatedly and eloquently invoked the idea of conscience. One of the prison letters describing a conversation with Meg has been compared to a Platonic dialogue on the subject of conscience.[62] And More had indicated that conscience creates reciprocal obligations. Once again: "I . . . *leave every man to his own conscience. And me thinks in good faith that so were it good reason that every man should leave me to mine.*"[63] And yet in his career as a government minister and especially as lord chancellor, More had seemingly shown little enough respect for the consciences of Protestant dissenters. On the contrary, as we will see, he had vigorously pursued them, hounded them, burned their books, and sometimes burned *them* if they refused to recant what he regarded as their heresies.[64]

So, wasn't it hypocritical of More, now that *he* was the one in the dock, to pronounce piously on the sanctity of conscience when in more felicitous times he had shown so little respect for the consciences of his opponents?

In asking what conscience meant to More and why it was so imperative as to lead him to his death, we have thus come upon a number of questions. What did More understand conscience to be? Why was it so imperative? And how, if at all, could he square his proclaimed respect for conscience with his persecution of Protestants?

In attempting to answer these and related questions, our hope will be to get a clearer understanding of that portentous idea or faculty that helped to bring More and his world to an end, and that helped to usher in a new world—our world—but that may now in turn be contributing to that new world's decline and demise. We will be trying to get a clearer understanding of that portentous and paradoxical thing—conscience.

First, though, we need to take a closer look at the man himself. Who was Thomas More? How did he come to embody the world that he was desperately struggling to save?

II

THE MAN AND HIS ENEMIES

So we begin by asking: Who was Thomas More? And sometimes one can understand a person by asking what and whom he hated, or who hated *him*, so we should ask about More's opponents as well.

Thomas More was born in 1478 to a moderately prosperous family living in London. His father, John More, was a lawyer who would eventually rise to be appointed to the King's Bench, one of the highest courts in England (and the court which would later convict More of treason). Young Thomas received a varied education. Five years at St. Anthony's grammar school on Threadneedle Street, just a few minutes' walk over mud and cobblestones from his family's house on Milk Street. Then two years' service at Lambeth Palace as a page in the household of Archbishop and Lord Chancellor John Morton. Then, at age fourteen, More became a scholarship student at Oxford. The year was 1492; while Thomas (Tommy?) pored over his books,

Christopher Columbus was en route to the New World—thereby preparing the stage for the events in our next chapters. More was a precocious student, but after two years at Oxford he acceded to his father's wishes and returned to London to train in the Inns of Court for a life in the law.

As he began his legal career, More was also undergoing a different type of intense experiential learning. In his early twenties, he went to live at the Carthusian Charterhouse of London, where for almost four years he joined in the monks' strenuous spiritual exercises. He observed the frequent fasts. Every night around midnight he would rise and join the monks to chant prayers and celebrate mass—an exercise that was repeated early each morning and again each evening.[65]

This varied education prepared More for more than one distinguished career. With the benefit of his Oxford education, he might have gone on to be a scholar—and he did. With his legal education in the Inns of Court, he might have gone on to be a lawyer and government official—and he did. His training with the Carthusian monks might have prepared him to become a man of the cloth and the crucifix. He did not do that, exactly, but he came close.

First, the scholar. More was a master of Latin and Greek, with an intimate knowledge of classical literature. He hung out with humanist thinkers and writers. One of his closest friends—and one who would occasionally stay for weeks on end as a guest in his house (to the consternation of More's wife)—was the celebrated humanist scholar Erasmus of Rotterdam, who dedicated his most famous work, *Praise of Folly*, to More. And although More's other duties left him little time for purely literary work, his own scholarly output was nonetheless impressive. He wrote poetry that, though not much read today, was at one time highly admired: in Samuel Johnson's eighteenth-century *History of the English Language*, More's poetry received more than twice as much space as Chaucer's.[66] He translated a biography of the renowned Italian renaissance humanist Pico della Mirandola. He wrote a chilling history of the murderous King Richard III, from which Shakespeare derived his own terrifying play on the same character. More's most noteworthy and lasting literary accomplishment, though, was his book *Utopia*, published in 1516, using a fictional island society to explore questions of what an ideal government and culture would consist of—and also to present some cutting criticisms of his own society.

But these literary endeavors had to remain mostly an avocation. More's bread-and-butter profession was the law. He handled cases and gave lectures to law students. He served as an undersheriff in London—basically a part-time judge with jurisdiction over low-level criminal cases and commercial or property disputes.[67] From there his considerable legal and administrative abilities led to increasingly important offices, including member of Parliament, then diplomat in the king's service, then member of Parliament again and speaker of the House of Commons, then councillor to the king and member of the king's inner circle. (This last position was both official and unofficial: it seems Henry and Catherine greatly enjoyed More's company and conversation, and often insisted when business was done that he stay late into the evening to "be merry" with them.)[68] Finally, he became lord chancellor of England. In that office he discharged his duties with integrity, "dispensing justice with equity," Peter Ackroyd reports, "in a manner which the prelates of the Church, his predecessors, had never been able to achieve."[69]

More's monastic internship together with his profound piety would have seemed suited to a priestly vocation, but instead he opted to become a family man, in a major way. In his mid-twenties he married sixteen-year-old Jane (or Joanna)[70] Colt, eleven years his junior. Over the next six years, Thomas and Jane became the parents of four children—including his favorite, the precocious Meg. Then Jane died. Thomas, left as a single parent with four young children and a demanding career to maintain, almost immediately remarried: the widow Alice Middleton, three years his senior, became stepmother to More's children, and More became stepfather to Alice's two daughters. The household later grew to include an adopted daughter (a neighbor girl whose mother had died), sons-in-law and daughters-in-law, as well as a variety of exotic pets: monkeys, foxes, ferrets, weasels, and birds.[71]

But although More was never ordained a priest, he maintained throughout his life the rigorous spiritual discipline he had learned from the monks. His commitment was apparent in his daily routine. Rising in the dark at two a.m.—the quiet of night was better than the "noisy bustle" of day, he thought, for receiving "divine consolation"[72]—he would devote five hours to prayer and study. Then, when the children were awake, the family would gather for a recitation of psalms and the Litany of the Saints; scriptures would also be read and discussed at meals. More attended mass daily, and on Fridays he would retire to his private chapel to spend the entire day and often the night in prayer and spiritual exercises.[73]

To instill humility, beginning perhaps in his mid-thirties, he wore a prickly hairshirt beneath his lawyer's robes. He occasionally practiced self-flagellation.[74] And although he is best known for humanistic works like *Utopia*, the largest portion of his writing was devoted to religious topics: meditations on heaven, hell, and purgatory[75] and on Christ's passion,[76] for example, and lengthy treatises refuting what he took to be emerging Protestant heresies.

All of which might lead us to expect to find in More a dreary, morose, insufferably pious and censorious soul. Remarkably, the reality seems to have been just the opposite: the king and queen did not crave his company for nothing. Thus, as a young page in the house of John Morton, More had excelled as a player in the household plays and revelries.[77] As an adult he was known for his wit—often, it seems, deadpan[78]—and his love of jokes and banter.[79] "A funny story," he confessed, "never comes amiss to me."[80] Peter Ackroyd records that "it was reported of More that he could make even the most solemn colleague burst into laughter."[81] At home, family meals might begin with scripture reading and discussion, but afterwards attention would turn to jests and jokes, led by Henry Patenson, a live-in jester or "fool" retained by More to entertain the household.[82]

His son-in-law William Roper reported that he had lived in More's household for sixteen years and had never once seen More angry or "in a fume."[83] Erasmus described him as "so polite, so sweet-mannered, that no one is of so melancholy a disposition as not to be cheered by him." "There is nothing," Erasmus observed, "from which he does not extract enjoyment, even from things that are most serious."[84]

And indeed, Thomas More was a man of many enjoyments. He loved learning and literature and, more generally, language. He was a linguistic innovator: words or phrases attributed to More's invention include "fact," "taunt," "shuffle," "anticipate," "paradox," "pretext," "obstruction," "monosyllable," "meeting," "not to see the wood for the trees," and "to make the best of something."[85] In addition, he loved music, astronomy, and meteorology. And he loved animals: recall the aforementioned menagerie of family pets.[86]

Nor did his professional obligations and private devotions keep him from commingling with his community. Although a poor singer (according to Erasmus), More nonetheless joined in the choir of his small parish church; he also accompanied his fellow parishioners in processions, and walked with them from services.[87] He often personally visited the poor of the parish and offered financial support, and he invited the sick and needy into his home, for shelter and to join his family for dinner. Eventually he established a separate house for the poor, infirm, and elderly. Learning that a woman of the neighborhood was in labor, More would promptly kneel to pray for mother and child.[88]

Despite these varied pursuits and interests, however, in his later years More's scholarly, legal, and spiritual gifts were mostly devoted to one all-consuming purpose: the combating of what he viewed as cancerous, world-threatening heresy.

The Hounder of Heretics

Though he could not have known it at the time, this phase of More's life began in 1517. More, now almost forty, was on a diplomatic mission to France. He was assisting the formidable lord chancellor and cardinal, Thomas Wolsey, who had risen from origins even humbler than More's—Wolsey's father was reputed to have been a butcher—to become the most powerful man in the realm below the king himself, and one of the wealthiest. Although More's diplomatic assignment was a mark of career advancement, the waiting and inactivity were not to his liking. He fretted and pined for home and family.[89]

Meanwhile, in neighboring Germany, a then virtually unknown Augustinian monk was nailing a sheaf of ninety-five theses or debating points to a church door in Wittenburg.[90] Luther's theses were mostly a challenge to the Church's tawdry practice of raising revenue through the sale of indulgences. Over the next several years, though, while King Henry was becoming increasingly dependent on Thomas More for counsel and company, Luther's disagreements with the Church would escalate.

By the early 1520s, a now notorious and defiant Luther would be excommunicated, and would disseminate a series of provocative writings declaring the papacy to be not merely corrupt and misguided but indeed the Antichrist.[91] In 1521, summoned to the Diet of Worms (Diet meaning convocation and Worms being the city in Germany where the gathering was held), Luther refused to recant and instead made his famous "Here I stand!" declaration, thus announcing his unwillingness to accept the Church's authority over himself or his opinions.

Devoted English Catholics like More—and, at least for the moment, Henry—saw in Luther and his ideas a more serious threat to the Church's authority, and to Christendom, than smaller-scale heresies of past centuries had been.[92] And they were right, for reasons that we will consider more closely. Confronted with what looked to be an existential threat, the Church's defenders responded vigorously, and on more than one level.

With the assistance of More and others (including More's friend and later companion in treason and execution, John Fisher), the king wrote a tract, *The Assertion of the Seven Sacraments*, attacking Luther's doctrines, and earning for himself a papal commendation as "Defender of the Faith." In addition to assisting with Henry's apologetics, More himself wrote strident criticisms of Luther. And Luther responded in kind. Although conducted in proper Latin, these were not polite academic disputes. Luther was known for, as one historian puts it, his "tirades of ungovernable verbal abuse heaped upon his enemies";[93] More reciprocated by calling Luther an ape, an ass, a drunkard, a lousy little friar, a piece of scurf, a pestilential buffoon, and a liar.[94]

Later, in the late 1520s and early 1530s, More wrote longer treatises comprehensively denouncing and refuting Luther and his English sympathizers, including especially William Tyndale, the translator of the Bible whose work would significantly inform the later King James Bible that has been cherished in the Anglo-American tradition.[95]

Beyond issuing polemics, English authorities employed the force of law. They attempted to prevent Lutheran literature from being imported into the country, and they also sponsored public burnings of Luther's writings. When these measures failed to stop the contagion, the authorities began enforcing criminal sanctions against the disseminators of heresy (as they regarded it)—including the death penalty for heretics who refused to acknowledge their errors, or who recanted but then reverted to their disfavored views.

Thomas More was intimately involved in these repressive measures, especially in his role as lord chancellor, a position he held between 1529 and 1532. He was criticized for these activities in his own century, and modern observers are likely to find his repression of Protestants even more troublesome. So, why did he do these highly illiberal things?[96]

Some standard excuses are less than satisfactory. It is said that heresy was against the law, and that in enforcing that law, More was simply doing his job.[97] Louis Martz points out that "More was 'personally involved' in prosecuting only three out of the six cases of heresy in all of England that led to burning during the three years of his chancellorship," and Martz contrasts this number with the more than sixty-five people executed as traitors for supporting the papacy under Thomas Cromwell, who succeeded More as Henry's right-hand man and was instrumental in securing More's own execution[98] (and who—partly for that reason?—has been elevated by Hilary Mantel to the position of hero in a recent series of popular novels and television series).

Or, conceding that More was not acting as modern liberal principles would prescribe, admirers suggest that he could hardly be expected to do that: after all, John Locke and John Stuart Mill and John Rawls were still centuries in the future.[99] It was not until the mid-seventeenth century, historians tell us, that the concept of "toleration" gradually came to be viewed as a virtue. Before then, to say that someone was tolerant was to insult them—to accuse them of being weak or waffling.[100] It was *intolerance*, not tolerance, that was thought to be the virtue in those days (as it is once again today, actually, with respect to some offenses—sexual harassment, for example, or perceived racism). And Thomas More was a most determinedly virtuous man. So, could we really expect anything different from him?

These defenses are cogent up to a point, and yet less than satisfying. More himself would likely have waived them. Thus, More did not merely inherit the laws against heresy and the attendant duties: he embraced those prohibitions—vigorously, enthusiastically. At times he pursued suspected Lutherans more relentlessly than his now wavering sovereign would have wanted.[101] "[H]e cried for heretics to be burned alive, and he rejoiced when some of them went to the fire," Richard Marius asserts. "This fury was not a bizarre lapse in an otherwise noble character; it was almost the essence of the man."[102] Marius exaggerates,[103] but even so. . . .

Moreover, it is not as if John Locke or John Stuart Mill invented the idea of religious toleration: prominent Christian thinkers going back to Tertullian in the early third century or Lactantius in the fourth had advocated it, along with a host of less celebrated figures through the centuries.[104] Surely Thomas More, thoughtful and learned as he was, might have done the same? And he surely would have been familiar with Bede's celebrated *Ecclesiastical History of the English People*, in which Bede had reported that the seventh-century King Aethelberht, who accepted Christianity in response to Pope Gregory the Great's missionary embassy to Britain, "compelled no one to accept Christianity." Aethelberht adopted this policy, Bede had explained, because he "had learned from his teachers and guides in the way of salvation that the service of Christ was voluntary and ought not to be compulsory."[105]

Indeed, it may seem as if More not only *could have* appreciated but *did* appreciate the value and virtue of religious toleration. Toleration is praised in More's *Utopia*, in which More seems to anticipate Locke. Thus, the fictional Utopian legislator is "quite certain that it was stupid and arrogant to bully everyone else into adopting one's own particular creed." And the Utopians "doubt if God will be at all pleased to see someone who, instead of running gladly to answer His summons, has to be dragged into His presence by force." Consequently, they "made a law, by which everyone was free to practise what religion he liked, and to try and convert other people to his own faith, provided he did it quietly and politely, by rational argument."[106]

Moreover, as noted, even as More was vigorously pursuing and sometimes executing Protestants, he was also speaking eloquently on the sanctity of conscience. He implored other people to respect *his* conscience. Why then could he not respect *theirs*?

Which brings us back to the central questions we noted earlier. Why was conscience such an imperative authority that it would lead Thomas More to sacrifice his own life, to incur the serious risk of torture and loss of reputation, and to put his own family at risk, rather than swear an oath that he did not believe? And was More being hypocritical in professing the profoundest respect for conscience even though he had vigorously persecuted and even executed Protestants for adhering to and acting on their own consciences? Having taken a closer look at the man and his situation, we can now turn to those questions.

III

Conscience as Tautology, as Paradox

What is this "conscience" that More and Luther and many others have regarded as so mandatory? It will become apparent in the course of our examination that not everyone who has used the term has meant the same thing by it.[107] Sometimes they have attached almost opposite meanings to the term. Thus, Thomas More did not understand conscience in the same way that Martin Luther did, but More's and Luther's understandings had more in common with each other than they had with some common modern usages.

And yet running through most references to conscience, it seems, is a sort of persistent, pregnant tautology. We should appreciate that tautology before considering how different invokers of conscience have nurtured and directed it in different ways.

By the time Thomas More invoked the concept of conscience, that concept was already firmly established in Christian teachings: both medieval canon law and the great Thomas Aquinas had taught that it was a mortal sin to violate one's conscience—even if the conscience was in error, and even if one's conscience contradicted a teaching or directive of a church authority.[108] You should do what you believe to be right even though you may be mistaken, and indeed even though you may incur excommunication for doing so.

This may seem an audacious teaching, as indeed it turned out to be, but in its essence it is little more than a humble tautology. Or perhaps a simple fact—an unavoidable fact about mortality, or about human finitude—superimposed onto a tautology.

The tautology is the proposition that if something is the right thing to do, then you ought to do it. That is just what it means for something to be "right." As some modern philosophers barbarously put the point, moral rightness has the feature of "have-to-be-doneness" built into it[109] as an essential or defining property. Or you can appreciate the force of the tautology by considering the contrary proposition: What sense would it make to say, "X is the right thing to do and you should not do X"? If you shouldn't do it, then it isn't the right thing to do. Right?

Now add in the limiting and perhaps lamentable fact, inherent in the human condition, that as much as you might wish to, as a choosing agent and a fallible human being, you lack the power to just simply and automatically do what is right. You are not an automaton, nor are you infallible; on the contrary, you act as the result of choice, and your choices are connected to the right only through the medium of your fallible judgments about it. So the best you can aspire to is to do what *you believe* to be right. There is always an implicit qualifier: the tautological "You should do what *is* right" has to be practically understood as "You should do what (*you believe*) is right."

The qualifier—the (you believe)—gives us conscience. Conscience refers, basically, to your beliefs or convictions about what it is right and wrong to do.[110] The qualifier also points to a paradox that would in later centuries prove to be a powerful source of unity—and also division, and also confusion. Given human fallibility, to say that it is right to act in accordance with conscience entails, paradoxically, that it can sometimes be right to do what is wrong.

In this way, conscience contains a sort of capacity to cover for— even to consecrate—error. Suppose I am convicted of having acted improperly in some respect—even wickedly, or criminally. It is still open to me to say, "Alright, maybe I did the wrong thing, but in a more basic sense I did the right thing. Because although what I did was wrong (as I now understand), I *believed* it was right. And so I was obligated to do what I did. In that sense, I did what was right (even if it was also wrong). And I merit praise and approval for doing the right thing, not condemnation for doing the wrong thing."

Or, refusing to concede my error, I might argue in the alternative: "I believe I did the (objectively) right thing, but even if I'm mistaken, I still did the right thing, because I did what *I believed* to be right. Either way, right or wrong, I did what was right." Conscience thus appears to offer us a win-win situation: if I do what *is* right, I do right;[111] and if I do what is wrong, I still do right—provided that I do what *I believe* to be right.

This "whether right or wrong, I'm right" construction might arouse suspicions; it seems too good to be true. And notice how audacious—or how implausible—this sort of stance would seem in many contexts. Suppose, for example, that the school teacher tells the pupils, "On this exam that I am handing out, you should read the questions and write down the correct answers." The teacher's instruction has the same implicit qualifier that gave us conscience: given the pupils' fallibility (which is after all why they are being instructed and then tested in the first place), the instruction can only mean that they should write down what *they believe* to be the correct answers. So suppose that, confronted with the question "2 + 2 =?," arithmetically challenged Johnny, in obedience to the teacher's instruction, writes down "5." The teacher marks Johnny's answer wrong and docks his grade. And Johnny protests: "But I did exactly what you told me to do. I wrote down what I believed the correct answer was. How can you punish me for doing what you said to do and what I believed to be correct? Are you saying I should have given an answer that I believed to be *incorrect*?"

Or, at the horse race, you bet on Gold Digger. Gold Digger finishes last. You attempt to collect on your bet and are refused. And you indignantly complain: "But I really did believe that Gold Digger was the fastest horse in the race. Should I be punished for betting as I sincerely thought was right? What more could I have done?"

In most contexts, these pleas will seem frivolous. You are rewarded for doing what *is* right. True, as a fallible human being, the best you can do is to do what *you believe* to be right. That is simply a lamentable fact from which nothing much follows. If you make your best judgment but get it wrong, you will be punished, or denied the reward. You did what you thought was right, but you were mistaken: You bet on the wrong horse. Too bad for you!

And yet if we can bring your choices and judgments within the domain of "conscience," the outcome somehow mysteriously changes. Now, even if you did the wrong thing—"objectively" wrong, so to speak—you still also did the right thing, warranting approval, if you really and sincerely acted from conscience.

Anticipating, we can appreciate how this capacity of conscience to excuse or even consecrate error might be highly valuable in some contexts. In contexts of pluralism, for example. Suppose that on some vital matter—a matter of faith or salvation, for example—people hold a dozen incompatible opinions, or a hundred, or a thousand. Just as a matter of mundane logic, it would seem that most of these people, and possibly all of them, must be mistaken. They are embracing and acting on opinions that are, to be blunt, . . . false. But now let us ascribe to this diverse throng, not infallibility (that would be preposterous), but at least sincerity, and let us drag their disparate opinions into the category of "conscience." Suddenly it seems that all of them are acting rightly (even if they are also in a different sense still acting wrongly). If our objective is to find a way in which all of these differently minded, diversely acting people can be treated with some sort of mutual respect, conscience may turn out to be an indispensable aid.

We will need to wait until the following chapter and our examination of James Madison to see this possibility begin to be realized. And yet the possibility was already beginning to appear in the circumstances of Thomas More's world, and in the events leading to his execution. Conscience, which in medieval thought was mostly a sort of realistic concession to human finitude (ideally, people should do what *is* right, but the most that can actually be expected of them is that they do what *they believe* to be right),[112] was becoming an instrument for justifying and even consecrating controversial beliefs and choices, and for dealing with the challenges and uncertainties of a fragmenting Christendom. (And also—most clearly with Luther, but perhaps even with

More?—conscience was an instrument for fomenting and exacerbating that fragmentation.)

THE AUTHORITY OF CONSCIENCE

While noting its tautological core and anticipating some of its possible uses, we have not yet discovered why conscience was or is so imperative—why it might carry such weight for people like Thomas More or Martin Luther. Just by itself, a tautology cannot tell us how to live. All else being equal, you should do what is right, no doubt—that, once again, is what it means for something to be "right"—but how weighty is that desideratum, really? After all, any petty pickpocket might cheerfully acknowledge that in the abstract and other things being equal, so to speak, you should do what you believe to be right, but sometimes moral rightness competes with other valuable goods that might be gained by doing wrong. Your neighbor's wallet, for example. Or it competes with serious evils that may be incurred by doing right—death, for example, as in Thomas More's case. In such circumstances, why is it so imperative to follow conscience?

For Thomas More—and also for Martin Luther—the answer to that question might be framed in terms of two convergent propositions. One of these propositions amounts to a gloss on the core tautology; the second embellishes on the implicit qualifier that, superimposed on the tautology, gives us conscience.

The first proposition is that, for these men, to say that you should do what is right is practically equivalent to saying that you should do God's will.[113] God is the ultimate authority and the source of all goodness and indeed of being itself. Without God, nothing—including you—would even exist. So no consideration could outweigh the imperative of obedience to the divine will.

The second proposition observes the fundamental duty, as Shakespeare would put it, "to thine own self be true." To act with integrity, as we might say—or perhaps (to invoke a later locution that we will see in our final chapter) authenticity.

In other contexts, these propositions might seem to be potentially in tension, even in fundamental opposition. Which of the imperatives takes priority? The injunction to obey God? Or the mandate to be true to yourself? In much contemporary thinking, as we will see, the second proposition (Be true to yourself) breaks free from the first (Obey God). The first proposition may even disappear altogether in modern understandings of conscience. But if one believes, as Thomas More surely did, that God is our creator and sustainer, that God knows and loves us better than we know and love ourselves, and that it is only in God that we "live and move and have our being,"[114] the propositions converge to form a united and overwhelming injunction. To obey God *is* to be true to yourself. Conversely, to turn away from God is to depart from the very source and foundation of your own being. Of yourself, or of your self. The soul that turns from God is like the spark that flies away from the fire, to be momentarily extinguished.

No reward, or no avoidance of suffering, could justify such a self-defeating deviation. After all, what shall it profit a man if he shall gain the whole world and lose his own soul?[115] Which is what a violation of conscience, unless repented of, would lead to.

And thus the imperatives of conscience come to have surpassing weight. "The glory of a good man is the testimony of a good conscience," declared the popular devotional writer Thomas à Kempis, whose *Imitation of Christ* More frequently consulted.[116] "Therefore, keep your conscience good and you will always enjoy happiness, for a good conscience can bear a great deal and can bring joy even in the midst of adversity."[117] Thomas More demonstrated his commitment to this teaching by his insistence on fidelity to conscience even at the cost of his freedom, his reputation, and his life, not to mention danger to his family. To adhere to conscience might lead to dire consequences (as it did for More). But to depart from conscience, and thus from God, would be to betray and renounce the very ground of one's being—a consequence that More described as "perpetual damnation."[118]

Things worked out more favorably for Martin Luther, temporally speaking at least. His bold invocation of conscience at the Diet of Worms did indeed lead to his condemnation, but Luther managed to escape the grasp of Church and emperor. He took refuge for a period in Wartburg Castle (where he stoutly resisted the devil's wily devices and translated the Bible into German),[119] and then he proceeded to live a relatively long and prosperous life with his wife, the former nun Catherine of Bora. Still, he could not have known when making his defiant declaration that this would be the outcome. He might well have suffered More's fate: arrest, imprisonment, execution. Thus, in many respects, Luther's commitment to conscience parallels More's. Both men accepted that they should do what they believed to be right; both equated doing right with doing God's will;[120] both understood God to be the very source of their being; and both demonstrated the courage of their convictions even at considerable risk to themselves.

So then were these bitter adversaries, More and Luther, identical in their understandings of conscience? The query brings us back to a pressing problem noted earlier: was More inconsistent or hypocritical in demanding respect for his own conscience even as he supported persecution of Luther's followers for acting in accordance with *their* consciences? The question will allow us to appreciate a fundamental difference in the adversaries' conceptions, which will in turn shed light on More's actions in his later years both in persecuting Protestants and in resisting Henry's takeover of the Church.

THE INDIVIDUALIST VS. THE COMMUNAL CONSCIENCE

Our discussion to this point has not identified any disagreements between More's and Luther's understandings of conscience. Both men would have agreed that one should act in accordance with what one believes to be right, and both would have identified what is right with God's will.[121] But now we come to a crucial point of divergence. The separation is not as straightforward as it first appears. Our best approach will be to state the disagreement simply, and then amend our statement later to account for complications.

Here then is the simple statement: to Luther, conscience had an individualist or subjective (and hence, potentially, radical or socially disruptive) character.[122] Whereas for More conscience had a primarily communal (and hence conservative) quality.

Thus, to Luther, conscience evidently meant something like "private judgment," as the issue would come to be framed in future centuries.[123] As an individual person you study a matter and judge for yourself what you think the truth is, and then you act on that understanding. A subjectivist or individualist emphasis was evident in Luther's famous declaration. "Here *I* stand! *I* can do no other!" Unless you can convince *me* that *my* judgment or *my* interpretation of the scriptures is incorrect, *I* must stand by *my* opinion. I, I, I.

This individualist or "private judgment" understanding was destined to become so closely associated with the idea of conscience that we have difficulty imagining that the term could have any other meaning.[124] The right or duty of acting on one's private judgment resonates with Kant's later insistence that if you are a mature individual you must "think for yourself"[125]—a precept that has become so platitudinous that it has been routinely (unthinkingly?) recited by countless people and generations since. And yet this individualist interpretation does not capture what medieval thinking, and Thomas More, understood by conscience. On the contrary, a man did not form his judgments of conscience "upon his mind alone,"[126] as More explained to Meg.

So then how *did* he form his beliefs? In his most lengthy discussion with Meg, More explained that one should form one's convictions according to "the common faith of Christendom," or "the general council of the whole body of Christendom evermore," or "a general faith grown by the working of God universally through all Christian nations."[127] He was merely reiterating a position that he had articulated before: "I lean and adhere," he had insisted, "to the common faith and belief of Christ's church."[128]

More was not far removed from monumental debates within Christendom about "conciliarism." Was the final authority within the Church, and thus the ultimate earthly judge of theological truth, the bishop of Rome—the pope? Or was it rather a general council, like the Councils of Nicaea and Chalcedon that had formulated Christian creeds in the early Church, and the Council of Constance that had resolved the papal schism early in the fifteenth century? Scholars debate exactly where More's opinion fell with respect to that issue.[129] In his most extended discussion with Meg, More referred to councils, not to the pope.[130] Still, in this context he does not appear to have been taking a deliberate position on the question of papal versus conciliar authority.[131] Rather, his overall meaning seems to have been that the truth is established not so much by the pronouncements *either* of a particular pope *or* of a particular council but rather by the judgment of Christians generally and across the centuries—a congregation that includes the dead as well as the living.[132] The "common faith"—that which "from the apostles' time to now . . . has been practiced, taught, and approved"—was to be ascertained, he said, based on "experience in my own time" together with "the consistent talk of other respectable people from all other places of Christendom" and "also by books and memoirs left from long ago, together with the writings of the old Fathers, now saints in heaven."[133]

In this respect, More's understanding of conscience was consistent with the received Christian tradition. "The view that individuals could read the Bible and make judgements about religious doctrine and the Church was a Protestant position," John Guy explains. "Catholic 'conscience' was to be anchored to the 'consensus' or 'common faith' of Christendom."[134]

We can use the matter of the king's divorce to illustrate the point. Before marrying Henry, Catherine had been the bride of Henry's brother Arthur, who had died almost immediately—perhaps without consummating the marriage: the point was contested. Was it permissible to marry a deceased brother's wife? The validity of Catherine's subsequent marriage to Henry hinged—or so it was assumed—on the answer to that question, which in turn hinged on the proper interpretation of scriptural passages in Leviticus and Deuteronomy, each of which was subject to various interpretations that appeared on their face to be conflicting. How were these seemingly incongruent texts to be understood and reconciled?[135]

The question was being fiercely debated throughout Christendom. J. J. Scarisbrick reports that once the issue was mooted,

[s]oon English agents were abroad, in France and Italy especially, quizzing and cajoling, ransacking libraries, interrogating university faculties, drawing up lists of signatories in this or that friary, urging canonists and Scripture scholars to take up the pen. . . . Meanwhile, of course, the other side had been no less energetic. Men great and small rallied to defend Queen Catherine, meeting tract with tract, opinion with opinion. By 1529–30 the king's divorce had occasioned

an international debate as violent and swift-moving, though on a much smaller scale, as the contemporary conflict between Catholic and Protestant polemicists. . . . One can only come away marvelling at the learning of so many of the contestants; at their ease with the Fathers, with the remoter Councils, with minor scholastics; at their dialectical acumen; at their energy.[136]

Henry, and most of the nobles and prelates of England, had concluded that the controlling text was the one in Leviticus, and this meant that the marriage to Catherine had been invalid from the start. These interpretations, of course, had hardly been disinterested: Henry's hermeneutics were swayed by organs other than the brain,[137] and the nobles and bishops were in turn strongly influenced by Henry's imperatives and threats. More remarked to Meg that most of these men had previously held the contrary view, and he wondered what had happened to change their opinion. The heavy penalties imposed on anyone who refused the oath—the penalties he himself was experiencing firsthand—"might hap make some men . . . frame their consciences afresh to think otherwise than they thought."[138]

But he quickly added that it was not for him to judge what was in another man's mind and heart. The important point was that, for More, it was not the opinion of English leaders that was determinative of the truth or of the requirements of his own conscience. Nor was it simply a matter of reading the verses and deciding for himself what those verses meant (well practiced though he was in reading both law and scripture). That was the approach that Luther had stood for at Worms. Under More's conception of conscience, by contrast, what mattered was the opinion of faithful Christians generally, including not only those outside of England but also "them that are dead before, and that are I trust in heaven."[139] And under this criterion, he implied (still without explicitly declaring or explaining), the marriage to Catherine had been valid.[140]

If Luther's conception of conscience was strongly individualist in character, therefore, More's was more communal. Conscience was not something that would lead you to challenge or defy the received body of opinion, as Luther and his English sympathizers were doing, but rather something that would bind you more closely to that body. Whereas Luther's conscience was potentially revolutionary (as events testified), More's was inherently conservative.

Once again, this description oversimplifies; it glosses over one crucial respect in which More's conscience was likewise individualist in character—and necessarily so. We will return to the point, but for now the "communal vs. individualist" distinction does seem to capture an important difference. And for More, the individualist conception was hubristic—"proud, insane folly."[141] Who was Martin Luther—or, for that matter, who was Thomas More—to set up his own puny opinions against the collective judgments of Christians through the centuries?

In addition, the Protestant conception was self-contradictory. Or so More believed. After all, in the very scripture that Luther and company purported to treat as the sole authority, Christ had promised to send the Holy Spirit to guide His Church.[142] In effectively denying the efficacy of that promise by setting their own opinions against those of the Church, More thought, the Protestants were betraying and undermining what they themselves purported to hold up as authoritative.[143]

IV

MORE'S CONSISTENCY

This contrast between the individualist and the communal conscience allows us to give a clearer answer to one question that we noticed at the outset, and that has troubled historians ever since: Was Thomas More being inconsistent and hypocritical in claiming respect for his own conscience even though he had enthusiastically persecuted Protestants for acting on what they believed to be right?

The answer turns in part on a semantic point. If we limit the meaning of conscience to its tautological core—doing what (you believe) is right—then it seems most plausible to conclude that the Protestants *were* acting on conscience, and More was therefore acting inconsistently in claiming respect for his own conscience while punishing the Protestants for exercising theirs.[144] But if we understand conscience more substantively as acting on beliefs based on the collective understanding of Christendom, as More did, then it seems that he was not being inconsistent after all. That is because, sincere or not, the Protestants were not acting on conscience—not *as he understood it*. Rather they were acting *against* conscience.

Indeed, they were openly and unapologetically acting against conscience by setting up their own personal judgment in opposition to and in defiance of the doctrines held by the Church and by Christians generally. Once again, Luther had been proudly explicit at Worms on exactly this point. Whereas for More, this course was not only hubristic and reckless and self-contradictory: it was precisely the opposite of what it meant to act on conscience.

But in More's view the Protestants were acting against conscience in an even more basic and threatening way. They were not merely acting against conscience themselves; they were working to make it impossible for Christians generally to act on conscience.

How so? As we have seen, for More, to act on conscience is to act in accordance with the collective understanding of Christians through the centuries. But this is a possibility only if there is a united Christianity to which you can look in shaping your beliefs and actions. Conversely, if Christianity is split into two contending factions—or three, or a hundred—the very possibility of acting on conscience will tend to disappear. How can you shape your beliefs by what Christians have everywhere and always taught when it becomes painfully apparent that Christians have been and are in fact teaching very different things on even the central matters of the faith? Now it seems you will have little choice except to look to the sources—scripture, perhaps, or personal intuition or inspiration, or whatever—and make your own independent judgment about what the truth is. That sort of private personal judgment might become necessary, but it is not *conscience*.

This prospect—the prospect of a world in which private judgment in something like Luther's sense is pretty much the only option—may seem exhilarating or it may seem terrifying. Either way, it will not be a world in which acting according to conscience *as More understood*

conscience will be easy, or perhaps even possible. But this was just the
kind of world, as More perceived, that the Protestants were bringing
about. That is, they were actively and knowingly working to break
Christianity into pieces. Into many pieces. Because it would soon be
apparent—indeed it was already apparent—that "Lutheran" and
"Catholic" would not be the only alternatives.[145]

Right from the outset, Luther had quarreled with his even more
radical colleague Andreas Karlstadt over their "profound theological
differences," as a recent history explains.[146] Then there had been the
so-called Zwickau prophets, who came to Wittenberg claiming to have
learned directly from the Holy Spirit that infant baptism, the mass,
confession, images, relics, and oaths were all to be abolished.[147] And
there was Thomas Muentzer, who took Luther's teachings and example in a radical political direction and led a bloody rebellion in the
mid-1520s, leading to an immense destruction of property and the loss
of thousands of lives.[148] (We will revisit Muentzer's rebellion again
shortly.) Luther vehemently denounced these would-be reformers,
and he got into an angry shouting match with Ulrich Zwingli when
the various Protestant leaders attempted in vain to reach a consensus
about the Eucharist in a meeting at Marburg Castle.[149] And even as
More languished in the Tower, an Anabaptist insurrectionist group
was establishing theocracy, communism, and polygamy in Münster,
Germany, before being crushed by an army supported by both Catholics and Lutherans.[150]

Observing these developments, More commented caustically that

> these modern men who have sprouted up overnight as theologians
> professing to know everything not only disagree about the meaning
> of Scripture with all those men who led such heavenly lives but also
> fail to agree among themselves concerning the great dogmas of the
> Christian faith. Rather, each of them, whoever he may be, insisting
> that he sees the truth, conquers the rest and is in turn conquered by
> them. But they are all alike in opposing the Catholic faith.[151]

In short, Protestant positions and factions were already proliferating.
And this fragmentation was inevitable, really, and obviously so. It is

fine to say that every person should interpret the Bible for himself or herself, unbeholden to the Church. But the Bible is a big and complicated book,[152] and individual Christians are endlessly diverse in their hermeneutical capacities, perspectives, and inclinations. It is utterly predictable that if people are left to interpret the Bible for themselves, as individuals, they are going to interpret it in a thousand different ways. Which is just what was already happening[153]—as Thomas More perceived.

To More, as we have seen, conscience meant acting in accordance with the uniform opinion of Christendom. But the Protestants were acting to ensure that there would be no uniform opinion of Christendom. Indeed, they were threatening Christianity itself. Languishing in the Tower, More wondered whether "the time approaches when . . . the mystical body of Christ, the church of Christ, namely the Christian people, will be brought to ruin at the hands of wicked men."[154] That would be a world in which the conditions for acting in accordance with conscience would no longer obtain. Conversely, in attempting to preserve the unity of Christianity,[155] More was struggling to hold onto a world in which acting from conscience would be a real possibility.

The End of the World as He Knew It

But it was not just the possibility of acting on conscience that the Protestants with their private judgments were undermining. They were acting to bring about the end of a world that had endured for a millennium. A world that was worth preserving, More thought, because even though it was shot through with injustice and iniquity and general shabbiness, it was also in a deeper sense a unified and consecrated world in which people and things large and small had a sacred meaning, and in which God's purposes could be carried out. Whereas the world that was coming into existence would be a divided world bereft of consecration. A desecrated world.

The common one-word term for More's world is "Christendom," a generic term often used to describe Europe during the thousand or so years from the last stage of the Roman Empire up until the Reformation.

For our purposes, we can explicate that term by asking about the ties that bind. What is it that holds the world together? More specifically, what holds a *society* together? Indeed, we can go farther: what holds an *individual life* together—allows us to think of the baby and the octogenarian as the same person living the same life that somehow is bound together as a whole? The simple answer for Thomas More's world was that things both large and small—society, the political order, the individual person—were held together as unified components of an overall unified whole by being grounded in and consecrated by God. By God as understood in Christian teaching and as implemented and administered by a single Church. That was what Christendom meant.

This summary answer needs elaboration. We can begin with an individual life, then consider society, then the larger political order. What was it that held these things together, kept them from falling apart, from fragmenting into a thousand personal and social and political pieces?

The Individual Person

William Wordsworth began a well-known poem with the observation that "[t]he child is father of the man," and he added that "I could wish my days to be / Bound each to each by natural piety."[156] But how can "piety" bind a person's days together to make them into a unified whole, rather than just a succession of separate and contingent events— "one damn thing after another,"[157] so to speak? Charles Taylor notes the question—"whether our lives have unity, or whether one day is just following the next without purpose or sense."[158] What is it, beyond the continuing name, that allows us to regard the Solomon Grundy who is born on Monday and christened on Tuesday as the same person, in a meaningful sense, as the Solomon Grundy who dies on Saturday and is buried on Sunday?

The answer, in More's period (as in the preceding millennium), was through Christianity, and more specifically through the sacraments, administered by the Church. These rites served to consecrate and connect the events of an individual's life. Thus, christening and baptism consecrated the commencement of life. Important life transitions were marked and consecrated by confirmation, marriage, or ordination. And the end of life, and hence the transition to the next world, was consecrated by the sacrament of last rites, or extreme unction.[159] "Every important event for the individual," Kevin Madigan explains, "from birth to death (including, from the ninth century, marriage) was marked by ecclesiastical ritual."[160] Beginning was tied to middle, and middle to end, and this life to the next life, by being grounded in a divinely instituted and consecrated pattern.

To be sure, no human life (except one—Jesus's) follows undeviatingly the path laid out in Christian precepts: to one degree or another, every mortal departs into sin and rebellion. And yet even these ubiquitous departures were themselves recognized, and redeemed within the Christian framework, by the sacrament of confession.

Social Ties

The sacraments that served to tie an individual's life events together into a consecrated whole also bound the individual to the community.[161] Historians including Eamon Duffy and John Bossy have shown how, in what Bossy describes as "the social miracle," late medieval piety worked to bring Christians together in the "body of Christ"—a body that for believing Christians was more than metaphorical and that extended not just to the living but also to the dead (and, for that matter, to the yet unborn).[162] This ideal was imperfectly realized, to be sure, but it was more than just an abstract teaching. And the ideal was implemented in practice by means of the sacraments and concretely embodied in a variety of ways and forms.

Thus, baptism was a public event, connecting the baptized infant to godparents who were likely not of the baptized person's family.[163] Marriage was likewise a communal event, commemorated with public ceremony and feasting.[164]

But the sacrament that was most important in sustaining community was the mass, celebrated on a weekly and indeed daily basis.[165] Carlos Eire explains that "the Mass brought communities together for prayer, instruction, and celebration. . . . [It] allowed the laity to experience repeatedly a synthesis of the ultimate Christian values they ostensibly shared."[166]

Those Christian values included, as Susan Brigden explains, "the seven corporeal works of mercy (feeding the hungry, giving drink to the thirsty, clothing the naked, housing the homeless, visiting the sick, aiding prisoners and burying the dead)."[167] Brigden observes that

> [i]n London neighbourhoods loyalties could transcend the divisions between rich and poor and sustain friendships between families who otherwise moved in different social spheres. People remembered poor neighbours in their own parishes in their wills; paupers whom they knew by name, like 'John with the sore arm'. John Stow, London's chronicler, recalled the great summer festivals of the 1530s, of his youth, when wealthy citizens set out tables with food and drink and invited their neighbours to 'be merry with them in great familiarity'. Bonfires were lit; '*bon fires*', according to Stow, because of the 'good amity' amongst neighbours they engendered. But Stow remembered this social unity half a century later with the nostalgia of one who thought it lost and hardly to be recovered.[168]

Nor was this communion limited to a particular time or locality. "Because every Mass was believed to transcend time and space," Eire explains, "and to link all Christians, past and present, to Christ's sacrifice on the cross, this liturgy also assumed a practical spiritual and social function connecting the living and the dead."[169] The connection to departed forebears was embodied in the practice of saying prayers and celebrating masses for the dead, on the premise that such performances would ease the condition or shorten the tenure of souls in purgatory.[170]

This community of living and dead was perhaps most vividly manifest in the celebration of All Souls' Day, "one of the great festivals of traditional Christianity," as Bossy explains. In the late Middle Ages,

> the Christian was reminded with increasing insistence of 'all the faithful departed', those who had nobody to pray for them, all those buried in the churchyard, all of the souls of the parish. On the feast itself

the formal business consisted of a requiem for the souls of the parish; a procession around the churchyard, and the blessing of the graves. . . . On the vigil of All Souls in the fifteenth century, the church bells rang through the night.[171]

Similar processions and parades and passion plays,[172] together with celebratory feasts, marked other holy days, which were liberally sprinkled throughout the calendar. Some such days were especially cherished: Epiphany, Good Friday, Easter, Pentecost, Christmas, Corpus Christi, All Saints' Day.[173] By the late fifteenth century, the feast of Corpus Christi had become especially popular, celebrating (as the name suggests) the union of all Christians, living or dead, young or old, male or female, prosperous or poor, in the body of Christ. The processions that marked such days—including, as we have noted, those in which Thomas More joined with his fellow parishioners—were communal affairs, as priests and parishioners rich and poor would mingle in the celebratory march, "filling the streets and squares through which they moved with prayers and sacred music."[174]

Political and Institutional Ties

Nor was it only the local community that was brought together in the body of Christ. That body was thought to extend to all of Christendom. By Thomas More's time, the divisions of the fourteenth century—the so-called Babylonian Captivity and Western Schism, in which rival popes had asserted themselves, excommunicating their rivals and issuing conflicting claims on the rulers and peoples of Europe—had been overcome, so that all of the lands west of Russia and north of Greece were under the jurisdiction of a single Church headed by a single pope.

To be sure, this unity was neither simple nor uniformly peaceful, but it was nonetheless real. Although the pope was in principle the head of the Church, papal authority might be resisted or defied by obstinate rulers or prelates. And as Alisdair McGrath points out, Christendom on the eve of the Reformation was a scene of rich pluralism in theology and doctrine.[175] The late medieval Christian world was, as

Brad Gregory explains, a "combination of unity and heterogeneity." And yet this "almost riotous diversity [was] held together in an over-arching unity by a combination of ingrained customs, myriad institutions, varying degrees of self-conscious dedication, and the threat of punishment."[176]

Western Europe's rambunctious ecclesiastical unity entailed also a sort of political communion, of two different kinds. First, there was if not a unity at least a harmony, as an ideal and often as a practical reality, of two things we have since learned to regard as inherently separate—namely, church and state. To be sure, it was a distinctive Christian commitment going back to Jesus's "Render unto Caesar"[177] and Pope Gelasius's "Two there are" that church and state, or church and king, were independent authorities.[178] And sometimes these two authorities could clash, even violently: in England, the twelfth-century conflict between Archbishop Thomas Becket and King Henry II, leading to Becket's assassination in Canterbury Cathedral by Henry's men, was probably the most dramatic instance. Even so, church was integrated into state and state into church: churchmen (like Cardinal Wolsey) sat in the councils of government, and secular rulers had a say in the appointment of prelates. Moreover, the ideal and often the practice was for princes and prelates to cooperate in pursuing the common good as they perceived it. We have already noticed one leading example: in the repression of heresy, it was for the Church to judge whether a man or woman was a heretic, and the government would then proceed to discipline and punish that person.[179]

Ecclesiastical unity also entailed a kind of international political unity. Benjamin Kaplan observes that "[b]efore the reformations, from the boot of Italy to the fjords of Norway and from the Emerald Isle to the plains of Lithuania, Europe had formed a single spiritual community—a 'catholic' one, in the sense of universal—united, if only loosely, under the aegis of Rome."[180] Because all of the princes and emperors were themselves members of the Church, and indeed were consecrated as princes or emperors *by* that Church, they were all in some (often contested) sense subject to its jurisdiction. The pope could and did hear and adjudicate disputes that might arise among the various kingdoms. And if secular rulers disobeyed the pope's edicts, he could and sometimes did excommunicate them, releasing their subjects from any obligation of obedience, or issue interdicts suspending the administration of sacraments in their lands until they acquiesced to his judgments.[181] It was just such papal jurisdiction, encompassing as it did the matter of King Henry's marriage to Catherine, that eventually led Henry to break the ties of the English church to Rome.

Papal jurisdiction was sometimes effective and sometimes not (as Henry's revolt dramatically demonstrated). Wars among the various princes and kingdoms, against each other and sometimes against the pope himself, were common enough. We might then ask: Was the supposed unity of Europe under the Church and the pope a reality, or a disingenuous facade?

The question calls for a subtle rather than a simple answer. In a much-lauded book, a modern scholar has explained that whether people constitute a "community," as opposed to an atomized mass of individuals living in proximity to and bouncing around and off of each other, is not so much an empirical fact as a matter of how these people conceive of themselves, or imagine themselves.[182] If they imagine themselves as a community, they *are* one; if not, not. So what we today call the "United States of America" consists of three hundred million–plus differently minded and sometimes raucously antagonistic individuals, of different races and ethnicities and religions and socio-economic classes, acting within a whole variety of different legal and governmental entities (cities, counties, states, etc.) and often gathering (or not) into contending political parties that can be badly split within themselves and that in recent years appear to have nothing but contempt for each other. There is no person and no institution—not Congress, not the Supreme Court, not the president—that realistically has the power to make these teeming millions fall into line. Even so, if and as long as they *think of themselves* as a nation, they are one.

In the same way, if the human beings living in early sixteenth-century Europe thought of themselves as a community under the jurisdiction of the Roman Catholic Church, then they *were* one, however fractious and unruly that community could sometimes be. And it seems that they did think of themselves—imagine themselves—in this way. Many of them did, at least.[183] Thomas More surely did. And that imagining mattered. It gave the rulers and subjects in the various lands a way of working together, and disputing, and resolving their disputes, and in general of relating to each other.

Thus had Europe existed, more or less, for the past thousand years—bound together politically and socially, temporally and spiritually, by Christianity and the Church. The eminent historian Robert W. Southern observed that "[o]ne of the greatest achievements of the Middle Ages was the detailed development of this idea of a universal human society as an integral part of a divinely ordered universe in time and in eternity, in nature and supernature, in practical politics and in the world of spiritual essences."[184] Heaven knows—and Thomas More certainly knew—that the unity of Europe in Christendom and, more generally, the unity of society in the body of Christ, was in some ways more an ideal than a practical reality. Anyone who supposes that More innocently believed either politics or society to be deeply Christian in actual practice need only read his *History of Richard III* or his social criticisms in *Utopia*.[185] And yet an ideal, embraced, is itself part of the practical reality.

SEVERING THE TIES THAT BIND

Protestantism was now dead set on annihilating all of this. Or so Thomas More believed. The Protestants, he thought, were "destroying Christ's holy sacraments, pulling down Christ's cross, blaspheming his blessed saints, destroying all devotion, forbidding people to pray for their parents' souls, flouting fast days, setting at naught the holy days, pulling down the churches, railing against the Mass, villainously demeaning the Blessed Sacrament, the sacred Body of Christ our Savior."[186]

Most conspicuously, in denying the authority of Rome and the pope, the Protestants were negating the institutional force that held the Christian world together.[187] At least in this respect, he was surely correct: over the next decades, what had been a turbulently unified Christendom would fragment into a jarring collection of national and dissenting churches housed within an array of nation-states, each claiming "sovereignty" in a new and more absolutist sense that would be expounded by theorists like Bodin and Hobbes. Even more important for the ordinary Christian, perhaps, was that Protestantism was dissolving the bonds that had connected the people in local communities to each other, to the wider congregation of Christians, and to their ancestors and descendants, and indeed that had consecrated every person's Christian life into a unified whole.[188]

In part this fragmentation was the consequence of particular Protestant doctrines. Luther and his fellow Protestants reduced the sacraments from seven to two or three. And even the vestiges of those sacraments, More believed, were reinterpreted in ways that deprived them of their mystical or metaphysical unifying force. The holy mass gave way to the church service centered on a homily that, even if well delivered (as it often was not), spoke to the intellect of individual parishioners but did not consecrate the soul and the community in the way the Eucharist, in which the body of Christ was actually brought into the midst of the body of Christians, had done. Protestants, to be sure, retained the practice of communion, but they disagreed among themselves about its status or significance. To Thomas More, at least, those who continued to partake of the bread and wine while denying that Christ was truly present in these emblems were depriving the ordinance of its consecrating and unifying force. He compared them to Judas, who had betrayed Christ into the hands of sinners.[189]

Other Protestant doctrines were likewise corrosive of social unity and order, at least in More's understanding. If salvation came by faith alone (*sola fide*), what was the motivation to engage in good works and to care for the poor?[190] If every man and woman could be their own priest in a "priesthood of all believers," what was the incentive to come to church as a community to join in the priest's celebration of the sacred rites?

In a similar spirit, the Protestants dismissed as superstition and idolatry the images and relics that in late medieval piety had served to consecrate and unify the people and the land. And the Protestants ended the processions and communal feasts that had sanctified the social order. Rejecting the doctrine of purgatory, they negated the whole basis of and reason for masses and processions linking living Christians with those who had gone before.

Eamon Duffy describes the change in terms that would have resonated with More's perception:

> Whatever else the Reformation was, it represented a great hiatus in the lived experience of religion. It dug a ditch, deep and dividing, between people and their religious past, and in its rejection of purgatory and of the cult of the saints, of prayer to and for the holy dead, it reduced Christianity to merely the company of the living. Overnight, a millennium of Christian splendour—the worlds of Gregory and Bede and Anselm and Francis and Dominic and Bernard and Dante, patterns of thought and ritual and symbol that had constituted and nourished the mind and heart of Christendom for a thousand years—became alien territory, the dark ages of popery. Protestantism was built on a series of noble affirmations—the sovereignty of the grace of God in salvation, the free availability of that grace to all who seek it, the self-revelation of God in his holy Word. But in England it quickly clenched itself around a series of negatives and rejections; as it smashed the statues, whitewashed the churches, and denounced the pope and the mass.[191]

At the core of the Protestant dissolution of Christendom, however, and beyond the specific doctrinal divergences, was the very faculty or instrument that More invoked on his own behalf as he jealously guarded his silence in the Tower. Namely, . . . conscience. So long as every man and every woman insisted on his or her own right to believe as he or she wished based on his or her own interpretation of scripture, how could the communal ties that bound society together hold?

In sum, Protestantism was heedlessly slashing the cords that had held society together since the breakup of the Roman Empire. And once those cords were cut, what would keep the social order from falling to pieces in the same way that the Christian world was already visibly doing?

Perhaps nothing. "[M]y increasing experience with those men," More wrote to Erasmus in 1533, "frightens me with the thought of what the world will suffer at their hands."[192] Looking out on the world that was passing and the alternative world that was coming into existence, Thomas More the poet might have concurred in the assessment of a later poet: "Things fall apart; the centre cannot hold; / Mere anarchy is loosed upon the world, / The blood-dimmed tide is loosed, and everywhere / The ceremony of innocence is drowned."[193] In severing the ties that bind, Luther and the Protestants were turning the world into chaos—into a world "thrown into confusion and fallen into a wildness," as More put it.[194]

The possibility seemed more than a prediction: it was actually being realized in real world events. Or so it appeared to Thomas More. Thus, in 1524 and 1525, thousands of peasants and others in German-speaking lands and beyond had risen in revolt against their lords, creating, as one historian puts it, "Europe's most massive and widespread popular uprising before the 1789 French Revolution."[195] Pillaging, burning, murder, and rape were unleashed on the lands. The revolt was swiftly put down—peasants armed with pitchforks were no match for the princes' professional armies—but as many as one hundred thousand rebels were slaughtered in the process.

Thomas More blamed the massive violence and disorder on Luther,[196] and not wholly arbitrarily. Although the grievances asserted in what has come to be called the Revolution of 1525 were mostly social and economic in nature, the complaints were pervasively framed in religious and indeed Lutheran terms. A manifesto asserting twelve demands was thoroughly interlaced with scripture, and the twelfth article, sounding very much like Luther at Worms, demanded that all of the proposed reforms be judged by the Bible alone and rejected if and only if they were found to be contrary to scripture. The rebels offered a list of theologians to be consulted in such assessments: Martin Luther was at the top of their list.[197]

To be sure, an alarmed Luther denounced the rebels and implored secular rulers and "everyone who can [to] smite, slay, and stab, secretly and openly" in order to put down the revolt.[198] Nonetheless, the revolution was thoroughly imbued with Lutheran ideas. Or at least so the rebels themselves believed—and so Thomas More perceived.

And then just two years later a second outrage against order had occurred: unruly troops of Charles V, including many German Lutheran soldiers, had invaded and sacked Rome,

> wreak[ing] such havoc within the city that the details were not forgotten for a hundred years. Old men were disembowelled and young men castrated, women raped and tortured, children tossed onto the point of swords before being butchered. The corpse of Pope Julius II was dragged from its ornate tomb and paraded through the streets. The living pope fled to the castle of St. Angelo, where he remained a prisoner.[199]

Geoffrey Elton observes that "the sack was rightly seen at the time as the end of a great age. The Rome of the Renaissance was no more."[200]

Two such cataclysmic and bloody events occurring in such close succession, and both seemingly connected to Luther's theological revolution, sustained Thomas More's assessment that the new heresies were not only theologically disastrous, they were threatening the very foundations of the social and political world. That was more than sufficient reason, he thought, to use force to try to stop the subversion.[201] Thomas More was, as Peter Ackroyd observes, "fighting for the life of his world."[202]

V

LOST WORLD, LOST CAUSE

And yet by the time he was imprisoned in the Tower, More perceived that the battle was lost.[203] With benefit of hindsight, we may say that he was right; indeed, we may suppose that More's world had been lost even before he himself discerned the threat and acted to oppose it. More blamed the catastrophe on men like Martin Luther. But suppose that Luther had been of a more docile bent—that he had cowered before the emperor's imposing authority of the Diet of Worms—or perhaps that in his defiant feistiness he had been apprehended and executed before managing to inspire a new religious movement. Or suppose that Henry had never laid eyes on Anne Boleyn—that Anne had died as a young girl of a fever, maybe—and hence the king had remained a steadfast royal defender of Catholic orthodoxy and the church. Would the ultimate outcome have been different?

Martin Luther, after all, was only the latest in a series of would-be reformers who had challenged the hold of the institutional church. Carlos Eire reports that "[c]alls for reform were endemic in the Middle Ages, as were confrontations over the supremacy of the pope and his clerics."[204] A century before Luther, Jan Hus had similarly attacked the sale of indulgences (and had been condemned and executed as a result). Hus had drawn upon writings of the earlier English reformer, John Wycliffe, who had sharply criticized corruption, opulence, and worldliness in the church.[205] Even earlier, in the fourteenth century, Marsilius of Padua strongly criticized papal worldliness and claims to temporal authority, suffered condemnation by the church, and took refuge with the emperor Louis of Bavaria.[206] Although the church had managed to put down these challenges, with benefit of hindsight it seems only a matter of time before one of these movements would escape such suppression. If it hadn't been Martin Luther, wouldn't it have been someone else?

And then remember two events that had occurred, perhaps without More's notice, in 1492, when the young Thomas More was taking up his studies at Oxford. Christopher Columbus had sailed for America. And the Jews had been expelled from Spain, and had thereby been forced to migrate and make a place for themselves in other lands, including the Low Countries, just across the Channel from England. These events would inevitably wreak changes on the world. Could the Church's monopoly on authority have maintained itself through those changes?

Thus, the discovery and colonization of the New World would result in the thrusting together of peoples from the various nations of Europe, along with those native to the new continent, under conditions in which long-established Christian structures were not already securely in place. To be sure, some of these colonizers would do their best to reproduce Christian society. The Spaniards would attempt, with some success, to impose Catholic Christianity in their lands; the Puritans would seek to create their own version of the Christian city on a hill. (By then, of course, the Protestant Revolution had already left Christianity in fragmented condition.) Could these efforts to maintain Christendom have persisted indefinitely?

Nor would the presence of the Jews be conducive to the sort of society in which Christianity provided the acknowledged framework for community and governance. Christian rulers had understood the point, consciously or intuitively, and so had acted in the preceding centuries to marginalize and exclude Jews, either through ghettoization or through outright expulsion: the exile of 1492 was only the latest of such exclusions. This sort of segregation and subordination could be maintained for a period—for a very long period, actually. But could it have gone on forever? From our perspective, with benefit of hindsight, the mistreatment of Jews, like slavery, appears to be a gross violation of Christian principles. Might not the practice eventually have provoked opposition even from within the Christian community, as would happen with slavery?

As it happened, Thomas More did not have to confront this particular challenge. The Jews had been expelled from England centuries earlier, in 1290, under Edward I. There was still widespread antisemitism: recall Shakespeare's Shylock. More himself seems to have been peculiarly free of such prejudice[207]—which is admirable, perhaps, but not an answer to the basic dilemma. The question of the Jews was bound to arise sooner or later. Could More's cherished Christendom have responded satisfactorily to that challenge?

THE SUBVERSIVE CONSCIENCE

But beyond these particular historical events and developments, it may seem that the world of Christendom was inherently threatened by the very faculty or instrument that More invoked as he attempted to preserve that world. Namely, conscience.

How so? We have already seen that conscience as More conceived it was thoroughly grounded in—and conservative of—medieval Christianity. You should do what you believe is right—which is what the Church itself had long taught—and you should form your beliefs about what is right not on the basis of your own private judgment but rather according to what Christians have always and everywhere believed. We have seen as well how Martin Luther's more individualistic conception of conscience—"Here *I* stand; *I* can do no other"— departed from this inherited understanding. Which was why More perceived Luther's notion as subversive and also hubristic; indeed, he did not regard it as conscience at all. And yet there was a sense in which Luther's conception was more faithful to the core tautology than More's was. In which case, we may suppose, More's more communal conscience harbored an innate tendency to dissolve itself into the more individualistic (and subversive) conception that would come to prevail in later times and today.

Thus, we have already seen how conscience comes out of the inescapable qualifier: even if you are committed to doing right, the best that you can do as a fallible mortal is to do what *you believe* is right. And the "you" in "you believe" is, inescapably, . . . you. You, the individual. Upon reflection, it may thus seem that you have no choice but to trust in and act on your private judgment. You *are* an individual, for better or worse—even if you wanted to there is simply no way you could dissolve yourself into some organic Christian mind—and so at some point you simply have no choice except to declare or act on what you think. On what you think *as the individual* that you inescapably are.

With Luther, you might take scripture as the criterion of truth; with More you might instead embrace the received Christian tradition. Either way, it will in the end be *you*—you the individual—who has to judge. Wasn't the inevitability of private judgment already manifest in the Thomistic teaching that you should follow your conscience even in defiance of the authority of the Church?

Consider once again the issue that proved fatal for More: the validity of Henry's marriage to Catherine. More thought that rather than just read the pertinent scriptures and decide what you think they mean, you should instead be guided by the collective understanding of Christians over the centuries. Fine. But then what if there is a disagreement about *that*, as there might well be (and, arguably, *was*)—a disagreement, in other words, about what the collective Christian understanding has been? What are you supposed to do in that case? Try to ascertain what the collective understanding of the collective understanding has been? And what if there is disagreement about *that*? The regress can go only so far, and at some point it seems you will need to exercise your private judgment.

Or consider this: how did the collective understanding of Christianity get constituted in the first place? How, for example, did the first Christians form their opinions on some difficult and disputed question—the necessity of circumcision, maybe, or the reality of the universal resurrection,[208] or the relation between the Father and the Son, or the relation between Christ as God and Christ as man—when there was not yet any received and official collective understanding to appeal to? It seems that they must have acted on their own personal interpretations—of scripture, or of Jesus' received teachings, or of the whisperings of the Holy Spirit, or whatever. What else could they have done?

And indeed in his extended conversation with Meg, More repeatedly acknowledged the inevitability of what amounted to private judgment—and the obligation of following that judgment. Thus, the prelates of the realm (minus Bishop Fisher) had made the judgment that the content of the oath was true and acceptable. More thought their judgment was mistaken; even so, he explained, as long as they were sincere they were bound to follow *that* judgment.[209] Conversely, More himself had studied the matter and had come to an opposite conclusion (on the basis, to be sure, of his understanding of Christian teaching), and he was bound to follow *that* judgment. If he were to act against his judgment by taking the oath, he would be risking damnation—even if his judgment turned out to be in error and the contents of the oath were perfectly acceptable and true.

In sum, it seems that however communal we may be in our commitments, personal or private judgment just inevitably comes creeping back in. Whether we like it or not, private judgment is not so much our right—or our privilege, or our duty—as our unavoidable fate. In this respect, Kant's "*Think* for yourself" is not so much either ennobling or misguided as simply gratuitous: the great philosopher might as well have urged us to *"Digest* for yourself," or to *"Defecate* for yourself." What else could we do?

If private judgment is inevitable, so are the corrosive or subversive effects that More perceived and dreaded in the Lutheran conscience. Indeed, More's own case starkly and tragically illustrated the point. More feared that the individualistic conscience would set itself up against, and thus undermine, the political and social order. It was a valid concern. And yet what was he himself doing if not setting himself and his own beliefs against virtually the entire realm of England?

In short, it seems that the medieval Christendom that More cherished was doomed, not only by historical developments, but by the very individualistic subversiveness buried in the concept of conscience. Conscience was a sort of ticking time bomb, so to speak, waiting for the right (or wrong) circumstances and occasion to explode Christendom. Without Martin Luther and Anne Boleyn and Henry VIII, the end of that Christian world might have been deferred—for a long time, perhaps, but surely not forever. Thomas More was invoking a conscience grounded in the older Christian world, and he was invoking it in his attempt to preserve that world. But the attempt was futile. Like it or not, that older world was passing.

And whether self-consciously or intuitively, More was also taking a concept from the old world—conscience—and reshaping and repurposing that concept for use in the world that was irresistibly emerging.

More and the Modern Conscience

Our discussion thus far has presented Thomas More as the defender of the older world—the world that was in the process of being lost—deploying a communal conception of conscience that was harbored in and that strove (in vain) to uphold that world. Conversely, More's nemesis, Martin Luther, has been presented as a force disrupting that older world in favor of a newer emerging world, and endorsing a more individualistic conception of conscience that would become almost axiomatic in that newer world. In *our* world.

Thomas More, defender of the old order. Martin Luther, prophet of the new world. This is a relatively straightforward, easily graspable depiction that seems accurate up to a point. And yet it also provokes suspicions.

Notice, to begin with, that the characterizations are at least curious. Just looking at the two men, we might easily take More—the Renaissance scholar, the lawyer, the author of utopian speculation—to be the more modern figure. Luther, conversely—Augustinian priest, insistent on the all-encompassing authority of an ancient religious text—might seem to be the more hidebound, backward-looking character.

Historians have sometimes dealt with the first of these incongruities by imagining two Thomas Mores—the forward-looking, humanist More who would join with Erasmus in reforming the Church, and the later reactionary More who doubled down to defend the Church and the medieval world.[210] Thomas More: reformer and Renaissance man . . . turned medieval inquisitor. And yet in fact More remained a church reformer to the end: even in his last days of imprisonment in the Tower, he continued to denounce priestly corruption.[211] And, conversely, there is a sense in which it was not Luther but rather More, and indeed the later More, who anticipated and helped to usher in the modern world—albeit contrary to his own intentions. Moreover, it was the very thing he used to defend himself and his world—namely, conscience—that worked despite himself to foreshadow and facilitate the world he dreaded.

We can notice two respects in which this was so.

Conscience as Concealment

Recall that in refusing to swear the oath, More persistently declined to give his reasons (at least until after he had been convicted) except to say that he was acting on "conscience." The king's men found More's persistent silence on this point infuriating. They wanted him to be more forthcoming, of course, mostly because they wanted evidence that they could use to convict him of treason. But even a detached but curious onlooker, or a devoted admirer (like Meg), might have found More's reticence vexing—because it did not actually reveal anything. Saying "I won't do it because of conscience" was offering a reason that was not really a reason at all, or at least not a reason that provided any illumination.

More was a man of deep convictions who was hiding those convictions behind an obfuscating tautology. He was saying, in effect, "It would be wrong for me to do it because (I believe) it would be wrong for me to do it." How helpful is that?

It is easy enough to understand why More refused to elaborate, of course: he was trying to avoid doing or saying anything that might aid the prosecution against him. That was at least part of his motivation. Put more abstractly: More was using the vocabulary of "conscience" not to reveal but rather to conceal his deeper convictions, and he was doing this for prudential purposes.

In this respect, he was quite unlike both his friend, Bishop Fisher, and his nemesis, Martin Luther. Those men did not hold back in explaining what they believed and why they did what they did. Unlike Fisher and Luther, in using "conscience" as a device for concealing or cloaking fundamental beliefs that it would be imprudent to make public, More was anticipating one of the central devices that would come to be deployed in the modern world to deal with the diversity of conflicting religious and political opinions.

In the world that was in process of being lost, rulers dealt with conflicts of belief in a straightforward way: they picked the set of beliefs that seemed to them true, or "orthodox," and then declared and acted on those beliefs—if necessary by repressing opposing beliefs as heretical or "heterodox." But in the world that was emerging, pluralism of belief would proliferate, and the expedient of simply declaring an orthodoxy and repressing dissent would eventually (following some horrific "wars of religion") come to seem inefficacious and unacceptable.[212] So then what to do?

This has been the central problem for modern liberalism—a problem addressed by theorists we have noticed earlier as having been unavailable to Thomas More: John Locke, John Stuart Mill, John Rawls, and many others. And a common strategy has been to camouflage or conceal the welter of conflicting beliefs, for public purposes anyway, under some generic and unrevealing rubric. Something like "public reason." Or "equality."[213] Or "neutrality." Or . . . "conscience."

We will look at this strategy of concealment more deliberately in our next chapters. For now it is enough to notice that within the confinement of his cell, Thomas More was already practicing the modern liberal strategy of concealment—under the cover of "conscience."

Fitting his Family for the Future

Not only was Thomas More putting conscience to a modern use; he was preparing those he loved—his family—to do the same. And it seems he must have been doing this deliberately and self-consciously.

Thus, one abiding question that has sometimes puzzled historians is why Thomas More refused to reveal his reasons for opposing the oath even to the members of his own family, including Meg, whom he dearly loved. In this vein, Richard Marius observes that

> a certain insoluble mystery hangs over [More's martyrdom], a mystery that baffled his contemporaries and confuses moderns. . . . What kind of martyr is it who will not make a strong, clear statement of the reasons for his martyrdom? His entire family swore the oath that he would not swear because he thought it would damn his soul. He did not reproach anyone in his family for what they all did. In his view of the world, fathers were supposed to be instructors in virtue to their households. Yet More refused to instruct his family about the oath.[214]

Part of the answer to that puzzle is obvious enough, of course. If More had told Meg or others why he believed the oath to be so egregiously and dangerously wrong, he would have been giving exactly the evidence that the king's men were seeking in order to convict him of treason. And Meg might have been forced to testify against him (or have been punished for refusing). Moreover, he might actually have persuaded her—he was after all a very persuasive man—so that she would have taken the same position that he did and suffered his same fate. Surely a loving father would not want this for his daughter.

Even so, this answer does not fully satisfy. Or at least it exposes the paradoxical power of conscience to consecrate error. More believed the contents of the oath to be contrary to the truth. He himself believed—or he believed *for himself*—that it was more important to adhere to the truth than to avoid punishment in this life, even if the punishment is death. And yet he stood silently by and watched as those he loved affirmed what he believed to be gross error. How could he do this? Of course he did not want them to die, but then he himself did not want to die either. For himself, nonetheless, it was better to die than to speak against the truth. Why did those same priorities not apply to his loved ones?

The answer, if there is one, must seemingly lie in the paradoxical idea of "conscience." More was no relativist: if the contents of the oath were false, they were false for him and for everyone else. Even so, someone who did not understand the oath's falsity could take it without acting against conscience. They could live in a world of error, and could even embrace and solemnly affirm that error, while still in a sense acting conscientiously and in accordance with God's will.[215]

And this was precisely the kind of world, More foresaw, in which his family would be consigned to live. A world full of error that was officially tolerated, and approved, and even forcibly imposed. In failing to explain to his family why what they were doing was wrong, he was fitting them to live in that world. To live in good faith—in good conscience, we might say—even as they supported what was wrong and solemnly affirmed what was false.

GRIM PROSPECTS

This kind of world—a world in which error abounds, and is accepted and acted on, and legally protected and even imposed: this was obviously not an ideal world for Thomas More. Nor one in which he wanted to live.[216] And yet he perceived its imminence.[217] And though he himself chose to go to the scaffold rather than enter into that unpromising land, he foresaw, grimly, that this would become the homeland for his descendants.

Years after More's head was chopped off, his son-in-law and Meg's husband, William Roper, recalled a conversation that had occurred in happier days, perhaps when More was still lord chancellor and Henry was still on the side of Catholic orthodoxy. How fortunate they were, Roper had remarked, to live in a realm united in the Christian faith, with "so catholic a prince that no heretic durst show his face, so virtuous and learned a clergy, so grave and sound a nobility, and so loving obedient subjects all in one faith agreeing together." More concurred, but then added:

> "And yet, son Roper, I pray God," said he, "that some of us, as high as we seem to sit upon the mountains treading heretics under our feet like ants, live not in the day that we gladly would wish to be at a league and composition with them to let them have their churches quietly to themselves, so that they would be content to let us have ours quietly."

Roper assured his father-in-law that no such thing could happen, but More was not so sure. "Well," said he, "I pray God, son Roper, some of us live not till that day."[218]

Religious believers of various conflicting faiths, all living and worshiping "quietly" in their own churches under the "league and composition" of a sort of mutual nonaggression pact. That sounds much like what More had described in *Utopia*. And like what *we* might call "religious freedom." More anticipated the possibility—and implored God that he would not live to see the day.

And he didn't. But he lived to see the new and dreaded world beginning to emerge. He saw that his own family would not be destined to live in the unified, consecrated Christian world that his son-in-law described, and that had been approximated in the world that was in process of being lost. And More anticipated, it seems, that what would be needed to negotiate the difficulties of the coming pluralism would be that paradoxical instrument with the power to lift up individuals against Church and society ("Here I stand!"), to bury and conceal troublesome truths, and to consecrate error.

The instrument of . . . conscience.

CHAPTER TWO

Disestablishment
and the New Establishment

James Madison and the Gospel of Conscience

I

May 1776. In a sort of local precursor to the revolutionary convention about to convene in Philadelphia, and also to the nation-
constituting convention that would deliberate in Philadelphia eleven
years later, prominent Virginia politicians — and some not-so-prominent
ones — are meeting in Williamsburg to declare independence for their
commonwealth and to frame a government for it.[1] After voting in
favor of independence from England, the delegates take as their first
order of business to ensure that no new tyranny will arise to replace
the old tyranny (as they view it) from which they are intent on freeing
themselves. And so they promptly turn their attention to drawing up
a Declaration of Rights.[2]

The delegates begin with general principles, framed in accordance with the forward-looking political wisdom of the day. Anticipating (and possibly inspiring)[3] the celebrated pronouncement in the not-yet-written Declaration of Independence, article 1 proclaims "[t]hat all men are by nature equally free and independent and have certain inherent rights." Article 2 declares that "all power is vested in, and consequently derived from, the people." Corollary propositions—namely, that government exists for the benefit of the people (not the other way around), and that the people possess "an indubitable, unalienable, and indefeasible right to reform, alter, or abolish it"—are set forth in article 3. After article 4's prohibition of hereditary offices, article 5 provides for the separation of executive, legislative, and judicial powers.

In the following sections the delegates get down to particulars. Voting rights. No suspension of rule of law. Protections for people accused of crimes, including the right to jury trial and a ban on "cruel and unusual punishments." Freedom of the press.

Article 15 reverts to majestic generalities. The article piously declares "[t]hat no free government, or the blessings of liberty, can be preserved to any people, but by a firm adherence to justice, moderation, temperance, frugality, and virtue."

This might seem like a fitting finale. But it isn't. There is still one article to go.

Is the last article—article 16—a sort of tacked-on afterthought? Or have the delegates deliberately saved the most important matter for last? In any case, the article declares

> [t]hat religion, or the duty which we owe to our Creator, and the manner of discharging it, can be directed only by reason and conviction, not by force or violence; and therefore all men are equally entitled to the free exercise of religion, according to the dictates of conscience; and that it is the mutual duty of all to practice Christian forbearance, love, and charity toward each other.

And then the delegates move on to other matters, scarcely suspecting how portentous the wording of this provision will turn out to be, or at least to seem.[4] And yet that wording has been the product of careful thought—not by most of the delegates, probably, but by one of them.

The original phrasing, written by George Mason (or so most historians will report),[5] was different. You will have to pay close attention to notice what the significant difference is, exactly. And even if you do read the versions closely, and compare and reflect on them (as we will do together, in due course), you might still conclude that the changes are mostly cosmetic. Be advised, though, that if you draw that conclusion, you may be in accord with most of the delegates at the time, but you will also be placing yourself at odds with a consensus of later observers and scholars who will consider the difference to be substantive, momentous, transformative. Even, perhaps, prophetic. The initial proposal for what became article 16 was this:

> [R]eligion, or the duty which we owe to our divine and omnipotent Creator, and the Manner of discharging it, can be governed only by reason and conviction, not by force or violence; and therefore . . . all men should enjoy the fullest toleration in the exercise of religion, according to the dictates of conscience, unpunished and unrestrained by the Magistrate, unless, under colour of religion, any man disturb the peace, the happiness, or safety of society, or of individuals. And . . . it is the mutual duty of all, to practice Christian forbearance, love and charity towards each other.[6]

Stirring words, no doubt—and yet one of the delegates is dissatisfied. A boyish James Madison ("Jemmy" to his friends) is making his first trip to the capital from his backstate home at the base of the Blue Ridge Mountains.[7] At age twenty-five, he is one of the youngest delegates; at a little over five feet in height, he is engulfed in a company of towering men, most of whom happen to be six feet tall or more.[8] Spindly, sickly, feeble of voice, lacking any political or other notable accomplishments to speak of: in a gathering of luminaries and seasoned political leaders, Jemmy is distinguished if at all by his conspicuous unimpressiveness[9]—and perhaps by his curious conical hat imported from England and modeled after the fashions of the Cromwellian Protectorate, more than a century previous.[10]

Looks can be deceiving, of course. Delegates who get to know the diminutive young man are struck by his erudition—remarkable in one so young—and by the carefulness of his thought and expression.[11] Edmund Randolph, a fellow (and even younger) delegate at the Williamsburg gathering, will later recall that Madison maintained a steadfast silence in the debates, "except to some member who happened to sit near him." But "he who had once partaken of the rich banquet of his remarks did not fail to wish fairly to sit within the reach of his conversation." Madison "delivered himself without affectation," Randolph will remember, "upon Grecian, Roman, and English history from a well-digested fund. . . . [H]e never uttered anything which was not appropriate and not connected with some general principle of importance."[12]

And as it happens, the precocious neophyte is quietly unhappy with the wording of article 16. Conscious of his own lack of stature (political or physical), and already manifesting the political shrewdness that in due course he will repeatedly exhibit, Madison refrains from voicing his objections. Instead, he persuades a more famous and flamboyant colleague and relative, Patrick Henry—he of "Give me liberty or give me death!" celebrity—to introduce an amendment.[13]

Among other alterations, the proposal provides that "no man or class of men ought, on account of religion to be invested with peculiar emoluments or privileges." Delegates read this language to mean that Virginia's longstanding support for the Anglican (later renamed Episcopal) church and its clergy would be ended; they read the words to mean this because . . . well, it is what the words pretty plainly say. A clergyman's salary is surely an "emolument." Isn't it?[14] And wouldn't the authority to perform marriages—an authority not shared with clergy of dissenting faiths—count as a "privilege"? Henry's amendment—in actuality Madison's amendment—would eliminate all of this.[15]

But this kind of disestablishment would be a radical step that Virginians are not prepared to take. Nor is it something that Patrick Henry himself favors. (A decade later, as governor, Henry will be the leading obstacle to Madison's and Thomas Jefferson's efforts to accomplish such disestablishment, leading Jefferson at one point to write to Madison that "What we have to do I think is devoutly to pray for his death.")[16] So then why did Henry agree to sponsor the amendment? Did he even read it?[17] In any case, Henry protests that no such disestablishment is intended.[18]

Henry is a formidable figure—the convention will shortly be selecting him to be the newly independent state's first governor[19]—but in this instance the delegates are more impressed by the plain words of the amendment than by Henry's feckless disclaimer. They vote the amendment down.[20]

Madison then orchestrates a second amendment—this time through Edmund Pendleton, another relative and a steady supporter of the established church—containing the words that are ultimately approved, and that we have quoted above.[21] A casual reading might lead one to suppose that this version is basically the same in substance as the original Mason proposal except more succinct in its articulation. Succinctness is a virtue—right?—in general and *a fortiori* in legislation. In any case, Madison's revised wording is adopted with little or no discussion,[22] and the convention moves on. It is doubtful that anyone supposes that anything of significance has just happened in the adjustment of wording.[23] Anyone other than Madison, anyway.

And yet there *is* a difference in substance. Or at least Madison thinks there is, and in later years most scholars will agree—and applaud.[24] The eminent nineteenth-century historian George Bancroft will describe Madison's amendment as "the first achievement of the wisest civilian in Virginia."[25] In a recent biography, Richard Brookhiser declares that "Madison's language . . . lifted the Declaration of Rights from an event in Virginia history to a landmark of world intellectual history."[26] Jack Rakove is even more effusive: he discerns in Madison's tersely conveyed conception of religious freedom "the true beginning of the liberal project" and even "the birth of the modern self."[27]

Who would have guessed that the alteration of a few words could accomplish, or at least portend, such an earthshaking, self-birthing transformation? Not Madison's fellow delegates, surely, including Edmund Pendleton, the traditionalist who actually sponsored the amendment. So then how exactly have Madison's changes conveyed this revolutionary new understanding?

Answers are more elusive than many have supposed. Upon closer reflection, the standard explanations of what Madison did will turn out to be less than satisfying. Could it be that the bulk of the delegates are right to suppose that nothing except a minor change of wording has just occurred?

And yet, once again, Madison evidently thinks—and later commentators and historians will enthusiastically agree—that something momentous has happened. We will try in this chapter to figure out what that something was (and what it *wasn't*) and what sort of major change it portended in the career of conscience. And in the emerging liberal or democratic societies for which a commitment to conscience would be a central and even defining feature.

First, though, we should finish the immediate story by briefly recalling the celebrated *denouement* of Madison's 1776 maneuvers. And then we need to circle back to become a little better acquainted with the maneuverer himself.

So, fast forward to 1784. After years of bloody back-and-forth struggle, independence is now a fact and not merely an audacious aspiration. After the chaos of war, it is time to regularize the relations between church and state.[28] To that end, Patrick Henry, once again governor, is pushing a proposal for subsidizing Christian clergy, albeit this time on an ecumenical basis: citizens will be permitted to designate which Christian churches should be the beneficiaries of their (legally mandatory) contributions. Baptists will be able to support Baptists; Presbyterians, Presbyterians; but everyone will support *some* religion. Now more experienced and politically self-assured, this time Madison openly leads the resistance to Henry's proposal, employing both his political skills and his analytical and rhetorical powers. His "A Memorial and Remonstrance against Religious Assessments,"[29] penned as part of that resistance, will come to be revered as a classic in the American constitutional tradition.[30]

And when the political smoke clears two years later, Henry's bill has been defeated, the Virginia religious establishment has been terminated (thus realizing Madison's original plan to banish "emoluments" and "privileges"), and the legislature has adopted Jefferson's seminal "Virginia Statute for Religious Freedom" with its prohibition of coercion in matters of religion and its eloquent preamble.[31] *"Almighty God hath created the mind free."* To compel anyone to support the propagation of "opinions which he disbelieves" is "sinful and tyrannical." Coercion in matters of religion is *"a departure from the plan of the Holy Author of our religion,* who being Lord both of body and mind, yet chose not to propagate it by coercions on either, as was in his Almighty power to do."[32] Did any politician ever surpass Jefferson for a resonant turn of phrase?

These reverberating propositions now express the official position of the Commonwealth of Virginia. Nor is their appeal limited to Virginia; on the contrary, Madison's and Jefferson's propositions will be quoted again and again, in and beyond the American constitutional tradition. (Thanks in part to Jefferson himself, who was at pains to have his statute translated and distributed throughout Europe.)[33]

These are not exactly the kinds of assertions one would have heard from, say, Thomas More. So it seems we are now squarely in the world that More foresaw—with dread.

Or are we? What exactly has happened, and how? How did Madison's subtle amendments in the 1776 legislature help to foreshadow, and articulate, and effectuate the transformation—if that is what it was?

But first things first: Who exactly is this James Madison anyway?

II

Young Mr. Madison

With Thomas More, we began at the end—with his trial, sentence, and execution. With Madison, we have begun near the beginning—with the fledgling politician on his first trip to Williamsburg. His later illustrious career, whereby he became "one of the great lawgivers of the world" (as one biographer puts it),[34] will already be familiar to most readers. How he helped to draft and enact the United States Constitution, and indeed earned the unofficial title of "Father of the

Constitution." Then served in Congress, then as Secretary of State—
an office in which he gave his name to the most celebrated of all Supreme Court decisions.[35] (Albeit unwillingly: summoned, he had
refused even to make an appearance in court.) Then was elected the
nation's fourth president, to serve during the fraught period of the
War of 1812. These facts are known to most educated Americans, and
to many who are not Americans, and are recited in an abundance of
biographies. We will not be rehashing these accomplishments; for the
most part they lie beyond the scope of our particular concern here.

But we do need to take a closer look at the man himself—in particular at the man in his formative stage. Who was that man? Or at least
who was the boy, and the young man, who brought about the inconspicuous but portentous change dimly inchoate in article 16 and consolidated a decade later in the "Memorial and Remonstrance" and the
"Virginia Statute for Religious Freedom"?

Born in 1751, James Madison was the son of a father of the same
name, owner of a four-thousand-acre plantation at Montpelier near
the Rapidan River in Orange County, Virginia, looking westward toward the majestic Blue Ridge Mountains.[36] Although backstaters, the
Madisons were nonetheless part of the Virginia aristocracy. Thus,
James was related by blood or marriage to many of the leading men
and families of the state—to George Washington, and to Patrick Henry
(who introduced Madison's first amendment to article 16), and to Edmund Pendleton (who introduced his second amendment), among
others. A cousin, also named James Madison, would become the president of the College of William and Mary and later the first Episcopal
bishop in Virginia. (Bishop James would preside over the church
during a period of decline in stature and influence brought about by
the work of his politician cousin.)[37] Another cousin would become
governor of Kentucky.[38]

The Madison plantation required considerable manual labor for its
cultivation and upkeep. But there were slaves to do that work—a hundred or so of them[39]—as well as the household chores.[40] And in any
case, young James was not well suited to such work. Slight and not at
all robust—he suffered from what may have been epilepsy[41] and perhaps hypochondria, and throughout his life he was described as "pale,"

"feeble," and "sickly"[42] — master Madison was better equipped for mental reflection and study.

And study he did. His early education in a local plantation school was probably limited to the essentials — reading, writing, arithmetic, and of course dancing (an indispensable skill among the Virginia gentry).[43] But at age eleven, the precocious boy was sent to board and study with Donald Robertson, a Scottish immigrant and (as Madison would later describe him) a "a man of great learning, and an eminent teacher."[44] Under Robertson's tutelage young James learned Latin, and probably some Greek, and read the classical authors — Cicero, Virgil, Horace, Sallust, and company. He also studied math and logic, and he learned a little Spanish, Italian, and French.[45] Enough French to be embarrassing, anyway. Later in life, Madison still vividly recalled the painful incident when a French visitor showed up at the home of John Witherspoon, president of the College of New Jersey, in Princeton, where James had enrolled as an undergraduate. Witherspoon happened to be absent, and no one else claimed to know any French, and so James was called upon to entertain the visitor. It seems that communication failed utterly, and so the two passed an awkward morning until Witherspoon returned.[46]

With that anecdote, we have already moved Madison forward to his college days. His enrollment in the college at Princeton might have surprised Madison's relatives and neighbors: up-and-coming Virginians usually went to the in-state college, William and Mary, as Thomas Jefferson had done just a few years earlier.[47] But the climate in Williamsburg was thought to be unhealthy, and William and Mary had a reputation for rowdiness and impiety.[48] The college at Princeton, by contrast, had recently been presided over by the formidable clergyman and thinker Jonathan Edwards, who was anything but impious — a few people today may still recall with a shudder Edwards's "Sinners in the Hands of an Angry God" — and was now headed by the imposing Witherspoon, another immigrant from Scotland, a Presbyterian clergyman, and a formidable thinker in his own right with (as one historian puts it) "a driving mentality and a flare for aggressive leadership in both religion and public affairs."[49] Under Witherspoon's administration, Princeton was at the time a more advanced and cosmopolitan center of learning than either Yale or Harvard.[50] And so, after carefully weighing the pros and cons,[51] James's family sent him off to Princeton, accompanied by his slave Sawney.[52]

There Madison mingled with young men from throughout the colonies—north, middle, and south[53]—and he made friends with classmates who would become prominent in the new republic. William Bradford, who would later be attorney general of the United States. Philip Freneau, who would become America's foremost poet of the day. Samuel Stanhope Smith, who would later serve as Princeton's president.[54]

"Jemmy" was a dedicated student. He did, to be sure, join in some of the usual undergraduate pranks and escapades, and he found the time to write some bawdy doggerel for the amusement of classmates.[55] Brookhiser reports of this period that "Madison's squibs are filled with talk about whoring, pimping, chamber pots, and other sophomoric paraphernalia."[56] Mainly, though, he studied. He completed the regular program in just two years, studying so obsessively—he slept only four to five hours a night—as to undermine his already fragile health.[57]

Witherspoon's curriculum consisted of the usual languages and classics, and also religion: although not quite the Spartan spiritual ordeal that Thomas More had experienced with the Charterhouse monks, James's daily routine at Princeton included morning prayer, scripture recitation, and evening prayer and psalm singing.[58] But Witherspoon also emphasized more modern thinkers, including Locke and other authors in the civic republican and liberal traditions:[59] these would make their mark on Madison's thinking. Witherspoon himself was an ardent patriot—he later served in the Continental Congress and signed the Declaration of Independence—and he strove to instill in his students "the spirit of liberty," including a commitment to the right of private judgment or freedom of conscience.[60] Indeed, under Witherspoon's leadership, Princeton acquired the reputation of being a "seedbed of sedition and nursery of rebels,"[61] as historian Ralph Ketcham puts it. Madison fully absorbed these patriotic and libertarian commitments.

Returning home after graduation at the age of twenty-one, Madison was still undecided on a career. He seems to have given some thought to the ministry.[62] He considered law, and studied for it, but never actually qualified for the practice.[63] His choice of vocation was constrained by his precarious health and his lugubrious premonitions of an imminent demise. "I am too dull and infirm now to look out for any extraordinary things in this world," he wrote to his college friend William Bradford ("my dear Billey"), adding that he had "little spirit and alacrity to set about anything that is difficult in acquiring and useless in possessing after one has exchanged time for eternity."[64] (In fact, Madison lived to age eighty-five, and of course he had an extraordinary political career.) While trying to settle on something, he continued his avid reading, devouring whatever good books he could get hold of.

Eventually, events made his choice of vocation for him. As the Revolution became a reality, at the age of twenty-four Madison was selected (along with his father and nine neighbors) for the local "Committee of Safety"[65] — a pro-independence "quasi-formal body," as Noah Feldman explains, that was "something more than an ad hoc mob and less than a sovereign government."[66] He was also commissioned a colonel in the county militia and participated in a few drills and a march, though he never actually served in the field: again, tenuous health was an impediment.[67] The young patriot was zealous for independence and unsparing toward anyone who did not share his zeal. At one point he sharply criticized the politically astute Benjamin Franklin for caginess that Madison perceived as waffling. "The heart of man is deceitful above all things," he wrote, quoting Jeremiah but in reference to Franklin, "and desperately wicked."[68] When an Anglican pastor invoked conscience in declining to join in a day of fasting for the anti-British cause, Madison, the soon-to-be champion of conscience, applauded the local committee for shutting down the dissenting cleric's church and stopping his salary, but he protested that these measures were too lenient: the unhappy clergyman should also have been tarred and feathered for his "insolence."[69]

And then the feeble firebrand was elected to represent his county in the Williamsburg convention, with the purpose of framing a government for the newly independent commonwealth — independent in aspiration, at least. Which brings us back to the point where we began.

MADISON'S RETICENT RELIGIOSITY

But one other feature needs to be considered—namely, Madison's religion, such as it was, or whatever it was. Through much of his life, Madison was almost as unforthcoming about his religious convictions as Thomas More had been about his reasons for refusing to take King Henry's oath. Or at least so historians report.[70] Much is accordingly left to inference and conjecture.

Then again, the historians may be mistaken. They may have been looking at the matter from the wrong angle, or looking at the wrong indicia. We will return to the question.

A few facts are solid enough. James's father, James senior, was a vestryman for the local Church of England, and hence was responsible for seeing to the church's affairs—and for collecting the taxes from which the church's clergy were paid.[71] James's mother Nelly was a devout Anglican/Episcopalian throughout her long life. James himself was baptized when he was two weeks old,[72] and as a boy he attended weekly Sunday services with his family and community at the Brick Church, a two-hour ride from his home.[73] Church services in Virginia were hardly the dauntingly pious affairs of Puritan New England, however: the sermon rarely lasted longer than twenty minutes,[74] and there was good deal of conviviality, banter, flirtation, and inspecting and comparing of horses.[75]

At Princeton, Madison studied under John Witherspoon, who, as noted, was a learned and earnest clergyman. But Witherspoon was hardly Madison's only pious mentor: from his early school days through graduation from college, every one of his teachers was, as biographer Ralph Ketcham reports, "either a clergyman or a devoutly orthodox Christian layman,"[76] and these instructors inculcated religion seamlessly along with other subjects. Thus, Madison's schoolboy notebooks recorded that in a lesson on logic, master Donald Robertson explained what a syllogism is with the following example:

1. No sinners are happy.
2. Angels are happy; therefore
3. Angels are not sinners.[77]

This upbringing left its mark, at least for a time. Thus, when Madison returned home from Princeton, he conducted family worship in his home—"a mark (then as now) of orthodoxy," as one historian comments.[78] He wrote to his friend and classmate William Bradford to urge the aspiring lawyer to "season [your studies] with a little divinity now and then." After all, "a watchful eye must be kept on ourselves lest while we are building ideal monuments of Renown and Bliss here we neglect to have our names enrolled in the Annals of Heaven."[79]

But was the Christian fervor that Madison acquired from this devout upbringing more than a youthful phase? Maybe not. It seems that Madison during this period enjoyed reading Voltaire, Diderot, and other irreverent French iconoclasts—although he also criticized them as "loose in their principles" and "enemies of true religion."[80] Biographer Irving Brant notes "the jeering glee with which he seized upon and exaggerated the frailties of preachers."[81] Madison's later claim in the "Memorial and Remonstrance" that religious establishment produces "pride and indolence in the clergy, ignorance and servility in the laity, in both, superstition, bigotry and persecution"[82] hardly conveys a favorable view of the religion that he had grown up in and that his father had helped to administer. Then again, in the same document Madison also reverently declared that "[t]he first wish of those who enjoy this precious gift [of Christianity] ought to be that it may be imparted to the whole race of mankind."[83] The "Memorial and Remonstrance" was a political and rhetorical document, of course, promulgated anonymously, and both in criticizing the clergy and in extolling Christianity, Madison might have merely been appealing to beliefs or prejudices that he took to be widespread among his fellow Virginians.[84]

Later, Madison attended church occasionally with his wife Dolley. But unlike Dolley and his mother Nelly, he was never confirmed in a church.[85] As a mature politician and as president, Madison enjoyed talking with visitors about religion—but not so much to learn or debate theological truth, it seems, as to try to understand what the various beliefs on offer were.[86] It was a time of intense religious ferment and fragmentation, and Madison seems to have been intrigued by the flowering of evangelical opinion and rationalist opposition. His occasional hints from those years suggest a tentative inclination toward unitarianism or deism.

Biographer Ralph Ketcham sums up what he takes from the inconclusive evidence: Madison "neither embraced fervently nor rejected utterly the Christian base of his education. He accepted its tenets generally and formed his outlook on life within its world view."[87] Other interpreters ascribe a more earnest piety to their reticent subject.[88] Once again, Madison's public silence on the subject leaves him susceptible to diverse interpretations.

Perhaps the uncertainty in the interpretations faithfully reflects the uncertainty of their subject? He was a careful and thoughtful man, and given the cacophony of boisterous opinions that surrounded him throughout his life—some pious, others rationalist and skeptical—it would be understandable if he found himself unable to join unreservedly in the confident dogmas of either the devout or the doubters.

And yet there was one exception to Madison's reticence. Throughout his long life, he was steadfastly and vocally enthusiastic about one religious tenet—namely, the imperative of conscience. For Madison, as for Thomas More, conscience was authoritative, and it also was in its essence a religious faculty. Conscience referred to a person's sincere convictions concerning, as Madison put it in the "Memorial and Remonstrance," "the duty which we owe to our Creator, and the manner of discharging it."

MADISON AND THE FREEDOM OF RELIGION

His commitment to conscience made Madison an ardent supporter of religious freedom, which in turn entailed religious disestablishment. Or so he believed and contended.

The subject was one that was very much on the minds of Virginians during the period in which Madison's views and vocation were forming. From the colony's early years, the Church of England had been legally established in Virginia. Two central features of that establishment were that Anglican minsters received a salary from a special tax that was imposed on each household, and that the clergy of dissenting religions were required to obtain a license from the state in order to preach or lead congregations. These features chafed, with some Virginians at least.

The tax for support of ministers could provoke controversy even among faithful Anglicans. Virginia law originally exacted a set sum to be paid in the form of a prescribed quantity of tobacco. But when the price of tobacco rose, the legislature amended the law to permit payment in cash instead, thus effectively reducing the financial burden on citizens but also the clergy's compensation. Clergy complained; the English Privy Council nullified the amendment; Virginians in turn inveighed against what some perceived as the clergy's greed. The fiercely independent Patrick Henry, although no proponent of disestablishment (as we have already seen), nonetheless denounced the clergy as "enemies of the community" and seized on the English interference in Virginia affairs to complain of the tyranny of King George. One clergyman who sued for his salary on sound legal grounds was duly rewarded by the local jury—with a judgment of one penny.[89]

Presbyterians and Baptists had an additional ground of grievance, of course: they had to pay the tax, thus subsidizing a church they did not belong to or support, and they also had to fund their own ministries out of their own pockets. Then as now, such exactions were the source of seething resentments.[90]

In addition, the licensing requirement for dissenting ministers could cause difficulties. A troublesome dissenting pastor might be denied a license; a feisty clergyman—typically a Baptist of the more aggressive "Separatist" variety—might not deign even to apply, confident in the conviction that he already enjoyed the approval of the only Authority who mattered. The result could be that a recalcitrant evangelist might find himself behind bars (where he might continue preaching anyway, through his cell window, to a congregation gathered outside the jail). After returning home from college, Madison wrote to his friend William Bradford about some Baptists in a neighboring county who had been jailed for preaching without a license. "That diabolical Hell conceived principle of persecution," he fumed, "rages among some and to their eternal Infamy the Clergy can furnish their Quota

of Imps for such business. This vexes me the most of any thing whatever." Madison concluded by urging his friend to "pray for liberty of
conscience to revive among us."[91]

By the 1770s, there was a growing sentiment, especially among
younger Virginians attuned to newer Enlightened ideas, of opposition
to the religious establishment. The first James Madison to speak out
stridently against the establishment was not the future president but
rather his cousin, the future bishop. In 1772, as a student at William
and Mary, cousin James gave a fiery oration arguing for a Lockean
theory of government, the ideal of the autonomous individual, and
religious liberty. The future Episcopal leader denounced supporters
of the established church as "Enemies to Truth . . . [who] hold the prepared Fetters, and declare their Resolution to enslave." The oration
ended with a plea: "Fellow Students, . . . [w]e were born to be
free. . . . Crouch not to the Sons of Bigot-Rage."[92]

The Princetonian Madison shared in these sentiments. But his opposition went beyond youthful rebellion against a stodgy institution.
In his early twenties, back from college but still reading diligently
while trying to decide what to do with his life, Madison also pondered
the deeper question: was the model of Christendom—and of little,
local Christendoms in Virginia and New England and elsewhere—
necessary to the maintenance of political and social order? In a letter
to Bradford, he posed "the following Queries."

> Is an Ecclesiastical Establishment absolutely necessary to support
> civil society in a supreme Government? and how far it is hurtful to a
> dependent State? I do not ask for an immediate answer but mention
> them as worth attending to in the course of your reading and con-
> sulting experienced Lawyers and Politicians upon. When you have
> satisfied yourself in these points I should listen with pleasure to the
> Result of your researches.[93]

Is an ecclesiastical establishment necessary to hold civil society together? That was the question. Thomas More would likely have answered yes. So would the Virginians among whom Madison had grown
up.[94] Madison himself would ultimately give the opposite answer.

Had he already reached that position at the time he pressed the question with Bradford? John Noonan, an eminent legal scholar and jurist, thought so: "At twenty-two [Madison] had seen what government and religion required—seen it in the transparent clarity with which a brilliant mathematician perceives a new relationship of numbers."[95] Noonan's effusive interpretation goes beyond what the evidence itself confirms. But whether or not Madison had reached his conclusion by age twenty-two, he got there eventually. The "Memorial and Remonstrance," possibly the most renowned statement by an American on these matters, would make the position abundantly clear: a church establishment is *not* necessary to support the social order, and indeed is subversive of that order. And even if Madison was the only one who knew it at the time, that position had been foreshadowed in—perhaps even subtly entailed by—the terse language of Madison's amendment to article 16.

Or at least he himself seems to have thought so,[96] even if his fellow delegates did not.

But then if society no longer had an ecclesiastical establishment to hold it together, what would replace that institution in supplying the ties that bind? What was the prospect quietly waiting to emerge from the pregnant words that Madison managed to insert into article 16? What exactly was young Jemmy up to?

III

An Elusive Achievement

Attempting to discern Madison's purpose and achievement, we should start once again with the question that we began with, and that will be surprisingly difficult to put behind us. What exactly was so momentous about the change in article 16's language—a change that Madison quietly but determinedly insisted on? What major transformation did Madison manage to slip past the seasoned Virginia delegates without their being quite aware of what they had done?

For convenience of reference, let us recite again the relevant provisions (highlighting the phrases that later scholars have deemed to be especially important). The original provision as written by George Mason had been worded in this way:

> [R]eligion, or the duty which we owe to our divine and omnipotent Creator, and the Manner of discharging it, can be governed only by reason and conviction, not by force or violence; and therefore . . . all men should enjoy *the fullest toleration in the exercise of religion, according to the dictates of conscience*, unpunished and unrestrained by the Magistrate, unless, under colour of religion, any man disturb the peace, the happiness, or safety of society, or of individuals. And . . . it is the mutual duty of all, to practice Christian forbearance, love and charity towards each other.[97]

Madison's first proposed amendment would have altered this language to read this way:

> That Religion or the duty which we owe to our divine and omnipotent Creator, and the manner of discharging it, being under the direction of reason and conviction only, not of violence or compulsion, *all men are equally entitled to the full and free exercise of it according to the dictates of conscience*; and therefore that no man or class of men ought, on account of religion to be invested with peculiar emoluments or privileges; nor subjected to any penalties or disabilities unless under color of religion, any man disturb the peace, the happiness, or safety of Society. And that it is the mutual duty of all to practice Christian forbearance, love, and charity towards each other.[98]

As noted, this amendment with its prohibition of "emoluments or privileges" would effectively have ended Virginia's religious establishment, and it was voted down. So Madison's second amendment—the one that actually passed—changed this language to read as follows:

> That religion, or the duty which we owe to our Creator, and the manner of discharging it, can be directed only by reason and conviction,

not by force or violence; and therefore *all men are equally entitled to the free exercise of religion, according to the dictates of conscience*; and that it is the mutual duty of all to practice Christian forbearance, love, and charity toward each other.

We might begin by noting several small alterations that seem more stylistic than substantive. For instance, Mason's version had declared that religion could not be directed by "force or violence," but Madison's initial proposal would have changed the phrase to "violence or compulsion." Biographer Irving Brant, seeking to magnify Madison's revisions as "drastic," claimed that the replacement of "force or violence" with "violence or compulsion" represented a significant substantive change.[99] But Brant's claim perhaps tells us more about the determination of later admirers to credit Madison with something momentous than it does about the actual meaning of the amendment. Both versions condemned "violence"; Madison's version merely reversed the order of the terms and substituted "compulsion" for "force." It is hard to conceive how this amounted to a major change in substance. Moreover, Brant's claim is undermined by the fact that Madison's second amendment—the one that actually got adopted—reverted to Mason's language of "force or violence."[100]

Here is another merely stylistic adjustment: Madison's version did not contain the honorific adjectives ("divine" and "omnipotent") that had attached to the "Creator" in the original Mason version. But these words were likely deleted as pious superfluities—wouldn't it be understood by everyone that the Creator is divine and omnipotent?—and in any case, it appears that the adjectives had already been taken out in committee even before Madison proposed his amendments.[101]

Madison's second amendment also eliminated the explicit qualification providing that the exercise of religion did not include the right to "disturb the Peace, the Happiness, or Safety of Society, or of Individuals." But this qualification was also presumably taken to be implicit even if not spelled out explicitly, and it was thus superfluous. No one would have supposed, under either version, that in the name of religion anyone could claim a legal right to disturb the peace or threaten his neighbor's or society's safety; nor is it likely that the delegates would have adopted anything so radical. Indeed, Madison's first amendment had included Mason's qualifying language, and his second amendment was plainly intended to be *less* controversial or objectionable, not more so. One eminent scholar and jurist, John Noonan, thought otherwise: Noonan suggested that Madison may have intended to make the right of religious exercise absolute, subject to no restrictions whatsoever.[102] But, to invoke a common example, it seems highly unlikely that anyone in the convention, including Madison, would have supposed that if a religion teaches the necessity of human sacrifice, article 16 meant that the government has to allow the practice.

So then again, what exactly was the crucial substantive change about which Madison was so quietly insistent? Whereas the original provision had endorsed *"the fullest Toleration* in the Exercise of Religion, according to the Dictates of Conscience," Madison's revised version got rid of the "Toleration" and instead provided that "all men are *equally entitled* to the free exercise of religion, according to the dictates of conscience." Was this the nub of the matter?

Maybe so; at least, a consensus of later historians has so concluded.[103] Jack Rakove expresses that consensus in arguing that Madison's achievement was to take religious freedom beyond the realm of toleration.[104] In a similar vein, John Noonan tersely summed up (what he saw as) the dramatic change: "Tolerance, out; free exercise, in—a decisive move."[105]

But however venerable, this seems a questionable characterization for at least two reasons. First, Noonan's description seems at best only half true. In fact, *both* versions—Mason's original version and Madison's revision—purported to protect "the exercise of religion" in accordance with "the dictates of conscience." To be sure, Madison added the adjective "free" to "exercise of religion." But surely the "free" was implied in the Mason provision as well. If the law affirmatively requires government to permit you to exercise your religion, "unpunished and unrestrained by the Magistrate," as Mason had put it, then the law leaves you free to exercise your religion, doesn't it? So it is misleading to say that Madison's amendment brought "free exercise, in." Free exercise was already in. Explicitly in.

Which points to a second problem with Noonan's characterization: Noonan posits a dichotomy between religious "toleration," on the one hand, and the "free exercise" of religion, on the other. Other historians have embraced the same dichotomy;[106] indeed, they have sometimes written as if the distinction reflects some sort of essentialist or Platonic truth.[107] And yet it seems that this is not a dichotomy that Mason—or many others[108]—contemplated or recognized. Thus, the Mason version explicitly mandated *both* "the fullest toleration" *and* freedom for—or a prohibition of government interference in—the "exercise of religion" according to "the dictates of conscience." For Mason and like-minded delegates, it seems, toleration was not an alternative to legal protection for the free exercise of religion; it was a *description* of such protection.

Still, the fact that Mason and his brethren did not recognize a distinction does not necessarily mean that the distinction was unreal or unimportant. Mason and most of his fellow delegates seem to have believed that "the fullest toleration of the exercise of religion" and "the free exercise of religion" were essentially the same thing, which was why they could adopt Madison's revised wording with little or no discussion. But Madison and later observers have supposed that these are in some important sense different. So, who was—or who is—right? How exactly is "the free exercise of religion" different from mere "toleration"?

The standard answers to that question turn out upon examination to be disappointing. Perhaps the most common suggestion is that the term "toleration" implies that religious freedom is not a "right" but rather a mere "privilege," or maybe a "dispensation," granted by government as a kind of indulgence. Under the Mason version, on this understanding, Virginians would have enjoyed the freedom of religion only as a matter of governmental grace. By contrast, Madison's version elevated religious freedom into a "right."[109] In this vein, Rakove asserts that, for Madison, "[f]reedom of religion was no longer a legal privilege extended by the state, but a right that all its citizens possessed."[110]

Rakove, Noonan, and company are correct in observing that the term "toleration" *could* be taken to imply a mere "indulgence" rather than a "right."[111] Presented with this characterization, though, George Mason would likely have protested—and would have urged the commentators to go back and actually read the language. Hadn't he made it perfectly plain—in the very first article of what was after all a "Declaration of *Rights*," not a "Declaration of Rights and Indulgences"—that "all men are *by nature* equally free and independent and have certain *inherent rights*"? His article 16 was surely meant as a specification of one of those "inherent rights" equally enjoyed by "all men." True, Mason's wording in article 16 itself did not use the *word* "right." But then Madison's version did not use that word either. Nor, for that matter, would the Free Exercise Clause in the First Amendment to the United States Constitution use the word "right." What was important, it seems, was not the word but the substance, and in substance all three provisions did affirm a legally protected freedom of individuals to practice their religion. Or, if you like, a right.

In a similar vein, a common comment suggests that toleration and free exercise grow out of, and thus in substance reflect, fundamentally different rationales. Toleration is a policy of prudence or expediency, some scholars suggest, or perhaps of exhaustion; it amounts to a concession that although in principle religious dissenters have no actual right to practice their religion, suppressing such dissent has become too costly or burdensome.[112] On this interpretation, the significance of Madison's revision was that it elevated religious freedom from a matter of mere expediency or prudence to a matter of principle.

The obvious problem with this suggestion, though, is that it simply does not fit the substance of the Mason and Madison versions. To be sure, toleration might sometimes be the product of prudential considerations, but so might a "right" to religious freedom. And, indeed, in his "Memorial and Remonstrance" Madison himself offered an array of such prudential considerations in support of religious freedom. But this was plainly not the case with "the fullest toleration" that Mason's article 16 would have mandated. On the contrary, both Mason's version and Madison's amendment were based on exactly *the same rationale* or premise, worded in almost exactly the same way. Both derived the freedom of religion from the claim that "religion, or the duty which we owe to our Creator, and the manner of discharging it, can be directed only by reason and conviction, not by force or violence." From this premise, both versions immediately and confidently deduced that government is presumptively forbidden from interfering in the subjects' exercise of religion.

The deduction was a hasty and contestable one, as we will see. But the important point for now is that both Mason and Madison relied on the same deduction from the same premise.

The inaptness of the "prudence vs. principle" interpretation also reveals the mistake in another familiar suggestion—namely, that in contrast to "free exercise," toleration was insecure or unstable because a government might in the future choose to revoke a policy of toleration.[113] Pressing this point, Rakove emphasizes that just such a revocation had occurred in France in 1685 when Louis XIV had rescinded the Edict of Nantes, which had granted toleration to the Protestant Huguenots.[114] The observation is correct, but also puzzling—because although it is surely true that just as a matter of power a government might revoke a policy of toleration, exactly the same is true of a commitment to free exercise as well. Mason's article 16 might have been repealed by some future legislature, yes, but so might Madison's article 16—or Jefferson's "Virginia Statute for Religious Freedom" (as indeed the statute itself expressly acknowledged).[115] And if the suggestion is that a policy of toleration is more susceptible to such revocation because it is based merely on contingent considerations of prudence, we have already seen the flaw in this suggestion. Mason's "fullest toleration" was *not* based merely on considerations of prudence; on the contrary, Mason's provision recited exactly the same justification that Madison's did.

Or perhaps the crucial difference is that Madison's version expressed—as Mason's "fullest Toleration" did not—a commitment to religious equality.[116] In this vein, some scholars have emphasized the "equally" in Madison's statement that "all men are *equally* entitled to the free exercise of religion, according to the dictates of conscience."[117] This is a possibility that will call for more extended consideration. But an initial response would be that the "equally" in "equally entitled," like the "free" in "free exercise," merely made explicit what was obviously implicit and entailed anyway. If you say simply and without qualification that *everyone* has, say, the right to vote for mayor, doesn't it automatically follow that everyone *equally* has that right, whether or not you utter the word "equally"? Similarly, if "all men" are afforded legal protection for the exercise of their religion—if they are afforded *the same* legal protection for the exercise of their religion[118]—doesn't it automatically follow that they *equally* enjoy that protection?

In that respect, Mason's version might easily have said—or might be interpreted as saying—that all men are equally entitled to the "fullest toleration" for the exercise of their religion. And once again, that provision was one specific implementation of article 1's declaration that "all men are by nature *equally* free and independent and have certain inherent *rights.*"

While lauding Madison for his commitment to equality, Martha Nussbaum makes much the same point with respect to Jefferson's "Virginia Statute for Religious Freedom." Although that statute does not explicitly use the language of equality, Nussbaum says, the statute nonetheless "rests . . . on an account of equal natural rights. Words such as 'no man shall' and 'all men shall' make it very clear that the rights in question are given to all without exception, on a basis of equality."[119] Nussbaum's point is sound enough, but it equally applies to Mason's version of article 16.

But maybe the key word here was not the "equally" in "equally entitled" but rather the term "toleration" itself, which perhaps just inherently implies or entails an absence of equality. Doesn't "toleration" imply putting up with something you disapprove of, which in turn implies an inequality between your own position and the one that you disapprovingly tolerate?[120]

Perhaps. In response, it might be argued that Mason's article 16 was not using the term "the fullest toleration" in this way. Still, an impressive array of scholars has understood toleration in this sense, and they have accordingly inferred that in eliminating the term "toleration," Madison was embracing a new and transformative commitment to religious equality. This seems a potentially plausible interpretation, but it also presents complications that the more laudatory interpretations typically pass over. So we need to consider this interpretation more closely.

THREE STAGES: FROM ORTHODOXY TO TOLERATION TO EQUALITY?

In modern liberal democratic societies, "toleration" is a term that is used generically or sometimes more specifically and that can have both positive and negative connotations. In a general sense, "tolerance," or "toleration," is typically regarded as a virtue, just as "intolerance" is usually a vice. (Except with respect to particular matters or issues—racism, sexual harassment, sexual exploitation—for which the currently prescribed attitude is one of "zero tolerance.") If you say "Joseph is a tolerant man," your comment will typically be taken as a compliment. Today, anyway: it was not always so.[121] But the term is also sometimes understood in a more specific sense in which toleration is a sort of halfway measure situated somewhere in between outright intolerance, on the one hand, and full and equal acceptance, on the other. On this understanding, if our ideal is full and equal acceptance (or, as the currently canonical phrase puts it, "equal concern and respect"), toleration gets us only halfway there.

From this perspective, the historical development culminating in modern liberalism and religious freedom can be seen as occurring in three (rough and no doubt overlapping) stages. Stage one is the phase of an *imposed official orthodoxy*. The rulers determine (probably in consultation with the church) what the truth is in matters of religion and then impose that truth, punishing deviations from the official orthodoxy. Heresy, blasphemy, and sacrilege are prohibited. The medieval inquisitions would be a classic manifestation of this position. This would also be the position embraced, and implemented, by Thomas More—and also, somewhat later following the Peace of Westphalia, of the regimes of *cuius regio eius religio* (the religion of the prince shall be the religion of the realm).

Toleration enters at stage two. Now the government continues to embrace and support an official religious orthodoxy—Catholicism, or Anglicanism, or Lutheranism, or whatever. But at least some dissent is allowed—or "tolerated." Virginia before 1776 would have been in this stage: the Church of England was the established religion of the commonwealth, but Baptists and Presbyterians and Quakers were allowed to worship according to their own beliefs so long as they obtained a license.

Toleration thus makes more space for the exercise of conscience and religion than the stricter regime of imposed orthodoxy did. And yet the dissenting religionists are still just that—dissenters. To borrow a contemporary formulation, they are "outsiders in the political community."[122] This state of affairs, in which one religion is still preferred and state-supported, might naturally produce resentment on the part of the "outsiders," even if they are left free to practice their religions. Such resentment is apparent in Thomas Paine's characteristically unsubtle protest that "[t]oleration is not the opposite of intoleration, but is the *counterfeit* of it. Both are despotisms."[123] Or, as Goethe put it, "To tolerate is to insult."[124]

And so there would be an understandable desire or impetus, in some quarters anyway, to remove that outsider status—to go beyond toleration by insisting that all citizens be treated as full and equal members of the society, regardless of their religious beliefs (or lack thereof). The achievement of that equality would reflect the completion of the progression from imposed orthodoxy to equal liberty. In this third stage, government would maintain a stance of religious detachment or neutrality; it would eschew announcing or approving any religious creed or doctrine, so that regardless of their particular faith or lack thereof all citizens can stand as equals before the state and the law.[125] No more "insiders"; no more "outsiders."

Something like this three-stage schema is reflected in familiar modern interpretations and expressions. Michael Walzer expresses a common notion when he comments that "[t]o tolerate someone else is an act of power; to be tolerated is an acceptance of weakness. We should aim at something better than this combination, something beyond toleration, something like mutual respect."[126] And one of the most celebrated of Supreme Court decisions appears to regard[127] the eschewal of any official orthodoxy as the core of American constitutionalism. "If there is any fixed star in our constitutional constellation," the Court said in *West Virginia State Board of Education v. Barnette*,[128] "it is that no official, high or petty, can prescribe what shall be orthodox in politics, nationalism, religion, or other matters of opinion or force citizens to confess by word or act their faith therein."

The three-stage schema might help us understand why Madison's amendment to article 16 has come to seem so momentous. With the best of intentions, George Mason's version may have sought to offer the most ample protection for the free exercise of religion according to conscience. Even so, his measure was explicitly situated in stage two; it lodged protection for religion and conscience in the halfway house of "the fullest toleration." Conversely, by ushering religious freedom out from under the roof of toleration and specifying that the right to religious exercise was one to which everyone is "equally entitled," Madison moved his state and later his nation into stage three.

This interpretation would thus vindicate Madison's judgment, and that of later historians, that the change from Mason's wording to Madison's signified some sort of enlightened transformation in the government's relation to religion and religious freedom—a transformation that was consolidated with the enactment of Jefferson's "Virginia Statute for Religious Freedom."

So far, so good. And yet a serious problem immediately appears. If Madison and Jefferson aimed to move from a position of toleration to one in which government ensured religious equality by eschewing any official support for or endorsement of any religion, then it seems that they dramatically failed to accomplish what they set out to achieve, or to practice the ideal to which they were ostensibly committed.

MADISON'S INCOHERENCE?

Much as we might wish to overlook the fact, Madison's and Jefferson's position itself was firmly and explicitly grounded in religious premises that were overtly theistic and implicitly but unmistakably Christian. Moreover, these theistic premises were put forward with the purpose and expectation that they would be both acted on and officially endorsed by government. Far from eschewing any officially approved religious doctrines, Madison and Jefferson presupposed, affirmed, and acted on such doctrines.

Take the language of Madison's article 16. The proposition that we owe a "duty . . . to our Creator" that "can be directed only by reason and conviction" was an overtly theistic premise. And a contestable one: not everyone would agree that there is a Creator, or that we owe this ostensible Creator any duty, or that any such duty can be directed only by reason and conviction. To mention just some obvious instances: an atheist (like Diderot, whom Madison apparently had read) would disagree with the first of these clauses; a certain kind of deist of the standard description[129] would presumably disagree with the second; and an ancient pagan—or, probably, a medieval inquisitor— would likely disagree with the third. Moreover, at a time when there were Jews living in Virginia,[130] article 16 ended by declaring that "it is the mutual duty of all to practice *Christian* forbearance, love, and charity toward each other."

Later, in the "Memorial and Remonstrance," Madison repeated and expanded upon article 16's contestable theological propositions— and urged the state legislature to embrace and act upon the propositions. He also added, almost gratuitously, that "[t]he first wish of those who enjoy this precious gift [of Christianity] ought to be that it may be imparted to the whole race of mankind." And the "Memorial and Remonstrance" concluded, on behalf of its subscribers, by "earnestly praying, as we are in duty bound, that the Supreme Lawgiver of the Universe, by illuminating those to whom it is addressed, may . . . turn their Councils from every act which would affront his holy prerogative . . . and . . . guide them into every measure which may be worthy of his blessing."[131]

John Noonan summarizes the point by explaining that Madison's position explicitly rested on a discernible theology:

> Mr. Madison's theology assumes . . . there is a God living and distinct from every human creature; this God is the Creator and the Lawgiver and the Governor of the world; he is a 'he'; he takes an interest in, and satisfaction from, the homage humans render him and he will condignly punish humans who neglect to observe the commands that he communicates through conscience.[132]

The "Memorial and Remonstrance" was of course not itself a governmental document. But the law that Madison and the "Memorial and Remonstrance" helped to secure—the "Virginia Statute for Religious Freedom"—*was* an official statement and enactment. And recall the reverberating language of that statute. "Almighty God hath created the mind free." How is that assertion not religious? To be sure, the theistic reference was more generic than it might have been: Madison managed to defeat a proposal to substitute "Jesus Christ" for "Almighty God."[133] But even so . . . And in eighteenth-century Virginia, who could the statute possibly have been referring to if not to the Christian God, or at least to the God of the Bible, when it reverently invoked "the plan of the Holy Author of our religion, who being Lord both of body and mind, yet chose not to propagate it by coercions on either, as was in his Almighty power to do"? How could an atheist, or a Native American, or a Muslim, have read that language without perceiving that this was still—officially and unapologetically—a Christian or at least a biblical commonwealth, and that he or she was, in that respect at least, a tolerated "outsider"?

Indeed, much later, in a convention that met in 1901 to amend the state constitution (primarily with the goal of denying the franchise to blacks), a Richmond lawyer named John Garland Pollard made exactly this point. Pollard moved to delete the word "Christian" from article 16, arguing that it was unjust and "sectarian" to "enjoin upon the Jewish citizen . . . Christian forbearance, love and charity." Although Pollard's proposal was not adopted, it prompted some strongly supportive letters from people, including a Richmond rabbi, who evidently agreed that the Christian character of article 16 treated non-Christians as less than equal citizens.[134]

In short, religion was explicitly and inextricably built into Madison's and Jefferson's very rationale for religious freedom, and this overtly religious premise was openly asserted in both the official and unofficial statements of that position. So if the transition from stage two to stage three—from toleration to religious equality—is supposed to have been a change away from a government that tolerates diverse faiths under an official religious orthodoxy to a religiously detached

or neutral government that eschews official reliance on religious doctrines, it would seem that Madison and Jefferson pretty clearly failed
to make any such transition.

Martha Nussbaum, celebrating Madison's ostensible commitment
to equality, contends that "Madison takes up the radical position of
Roger Williams: the very fact that the state endorses one religion,
Christianity, above another is itself a violation of the equality of citi-
zens."[135] That might indeed be the "radical position" that Nussbaum
wishes Madison had taken, and therefore strains to attribute to him.
But Madison's actual language flatly contradicts Nussbaum's claim.[136]
[I]n a similar vein, Jack Rakove contends that "[b]oth [Madison and
Jefferson] imagined a republic where religion was wholly privatized."[137]
If that is what they imagined, however, they studiously concealed any
such imaginings in their public statements surrounding their celebrated
achievement in Virginia.[138]

So, what to conclude? That Madison was trying to move Virginia,
and later the nation, from the halfway house of toleration into a world
of religious equality, but that he utterly failed to make that transition?
Failed even to grasp how utterly he had failed—to grasp how even his
own carefully meditated and classic manifesto arguing for the change
was itself, beginning with its very first and celebrated paragraph, a bla-
tant violation of the very principle he was seeking to secure?

And of course Madison's and Jefferson's behavior in this particular
matter was hardly aberrational. As Daniel Boorstin has demonstrated
with copious examples, Jefferson invoked theistic religion over and
over again as a justification for nearly every political idea or proposition for which he is celebrated.[139] "The word 'right' was always a sign-
post pointing back to the divine plan of the Creation," Boorstin shows,
and "no claims could be validated except by the Creator's plan."[140]

Other Americans thought and acted similarly. Throughout the
eighteenth and nineteenth centuries, and well into the twentieth—and
still, for that matter, under George W. Bush and Barack Obama
and Donald Trump and now Joe Biden[141]—American governments
and political leaders have openly and repeatedly and unapologetically
invoked and endorsed and praised religion. They have sponsored official prayers and days of thanksgiving, have insisted that Christianity

is part of the common law[142]—on this particular point, Jefferson did *not* concur[143]—and have included overtly religious language in the Pledge of Allegiance and the national anthem and the national motto ("In God We Trust"). The Supreme Court declared in the late-nineteenth century that this is "a Christian nation"[144] and, in the mid-twentieth, that "we are a religious people whose institutions presuppose a Supreme Being."[145] Presidential inauguration ceremonies have reeked of religious observance.[146]

So the notion that with Madison and Jefferson, Virginia and then the nation somehow moved beyond any officially supported or endorsed religion into a condition in which all religious faiths or lack thereof are equally esteemed seems just massively and manifestly false. Just ask Michael Newdow, the lawyer-doctor-atheist who on a premise of religious equality has brought numerous lawsuits attempting to eliminate such religious practices and references—and whose efforts have been repeatedly rebuffed in the courts.[147]

In recent decades this situation has become, for some, an embarrassment. And so scholars and jurists and commentators have looked back with reproach on a nation that supposedly embraced the separation of church and state and the principle of religious equality and yet continued to practice and openly promote a "de facto establishment," as Mark DeWolfe Howe put it,[148] or a "civil religion," as Robert Bellah and others have described.[149] This longstanding tradition has come to be viewed by critics as inconsistent and hypocritical—a counterpart in the area of religion to the inconsistency and hypocrisy of a nation that solemnly declared "all men are created equal" to be a self-evident truth and yet continued to practice slavery and then Jim Crow segregation for almost two centuries.[150]

But the incoherence and hypocrisy (if that is what it is) began, we might say, with Madison and with Jefferson. Historians have tended to spare these men in their critical judgments. Why? Perhaps because Madison and Jefferson at least recognized the egalitarian ideal and attempted to move the nation in the direction of that ideal, even if they themselves failed to fully understand and conform to it? Or, conversely, should the fact that Madison and Jefferson embraced the ideal of religious equality and yet openly and repeatedly betrayed it make them even more culpable than their less Enlightened contemporaries who probably did not grasp the newer stage-three ideal in the first place and who likely would have rejected the ideal if it had been clearly presented to them?

Then again, it might be that this whole indictment—of Madison and Jefferson and, by extension, of America—is misconceived from the start. Perhaps, in crediting Madison with attempting to move the state and the nation from stage two (toleration) to stage three (equality under a religiously neutral government) and then criticizing him for failing to conform to his own ostensible commitment, we have fundamentally misunderstood the man. Perhaps this is not what he was trying to do at all.

But then we are back to square one and the seemingly unshakeable question. What *was* Madison trying to do? And what was the significance of his amendment to article 16?

The *Institutional* Transformation: Ending *Eecclesiastical* Establishment

We might make some progress in answering this question if we attempt to bracket some of our standard modern assumptions and distinctions, refrain from supposing that Madison must have been doing something that would lead ineluctably *to us*, and consider how the world would have looked *to him*. In this spirit, we might acknowledge that the three-stage schema—from 1) imposed religious orthodoxy to 2) toleration to 3) religious equality—that has come to frame our thinking on these subjects was not a common notion in Madison's day. Nor were other associated ideals that are by now almost axiomatic—the ideals of "secular" or of religiously "neutral" government—embraced or perhaps even comprehensible at that time.[151] Conversely, most residents of England, or of European nations generally, or of the American states, would have been intimately familiar with (or would even have taken for granted) something that for Americans is by now a distant memory. Namely, a state-established *church*.

So to the young James Madison, it would scarcely have been comprehensible that citizens when acting in public matters, and governments in their own decision-making, would somehow eschew reliance on what most citizens and officials believed and regarded as the pertinent governing truths. Even if, or especially if, those beliefs and truths were "religious." What sense could such a suggestion even have made? "Most of you embrace body of beliefs X, and you also think these beliefs are fundamental and directly pertinent not only to your personal lives but also to some of the most important political decisions that you as a commonwealth must make: but you must refrain for political purposes from invoking or relying on body of beliefs X. Instead, you should make important political decisions *without* referring to or relying on the beliefs that seem to you most pertinent to those decisions." Such a prescription would seem almost lunatic, wouldn't it? (At least in a world in which people have not been rendered receptive to such contortions and compartmentalizations by the example of jurists like William Brennan, whom we will meet in the next chapter, and the theorizing of influential thinkers like John Rawls.)

Conversely, the prospect of eliminating the government's support for and preferment of a *church*, or a religious *institution*, would have seemed daring—a bold "experiment," as Jefferson put it[152]—but at least imaginable, and not without some precedent. For example, Pennsylvania, although it officially and explicitly embraced some Christian commitments and language,[153] had not designated any particular church for governmental support. Madison had expressed his admiration for Pennsylvania as a model for Virginia to emulate.[154] The Netherlands, he thought, provided another instructive example of a Republic without an established church.[155]

And indeed, the evidence suggests that it was this *institutional* transformation that Madison, and also Jefferson, had in mind. Thus, Madison had asked his friend William Bradford to consider whether "civil societies" can do without "Ecclesiastical Establishments." Madison himself concluded that the answer to that question was "yes, they can," and his efforts in the 1776 Virginia convention and again after the Revolution appear to have been calculated to implement that answer—in other words, to end Virginia's "ecclesiastical establishment." In this sense, toleration—even "the fullest Toleration"—was suspect because even if a provision embraced a right to toleration and extended that right equally to "all men" (as Mason's version did), the term "toleration" was still associated with an official state-favored church. Madison's goal was to end that institutional arrangement—a goal that was achieved with the enactment of Jefferson's statute in 1786.

Three years later, sponsoring and securing the adoption of the First Amendment to the United States Constitution, Madison seems to have had a similar aim at the national level—namely, the prevention of any ecclesiastical establishment or national church. To be sure, modern interpretations have read into that amendment's establishment clause much more expansive purposes that are more in line with the three-step schema familiar today: courts and scholars have supposed that the amendment must have mandated something like secular or religiously neutral government. But the historical evidence is unsupportive. One researcher, Donald Drakeman, summarizes the conclusion of his investigations:

> [I]t is important to appreciate that [the First Amendment establishment clause] was not the statement of a principle of secularism, separation, disestablishment, or anything else. It was the answer to a very specific question: Would the new national government countenance a move by the larger Protestant denominations to join together and form a national church? The answer was no.
>
> At the time it was adopted, the establishment clause addressed one simple noncontroversial issue, and the list of those who supported it demonstrates that it cannot reasonably be seen as encompassing a philosophy about church and state.[156]

And in defending this interpretation against competitors, Drakeman relies primarily upon the straightforward explanation of the provision given in Congress by—who else?—James Madison.[157]

Probably the most celebrated (and also denounced) explanation of the amendment, of course, was not the one offered by Madison in Congress, but rather that given a few years later by Madison's friend and ally, Thomas Jefferson, in a letter to a Baptist congregation in Connecticut. The First Amendment religion clauses served, Jefferson famously opined, to create "a wall of separation between church and state."[158] Like the non-establishment clause itself, Jefferson's "wall" metaphor would be repeatedly interpreted in the twentieth century against the backdrop of the three-stage schema to mean that government must be secular, or religiously neutral, or detached from any religious orthodoxy or belief.[159] But Jefferson himself said no such thing. *His* "wall" was not between government and "religion," or between "religion" and political discourse and decision-making, but rather between *church*—a religious institution or "ecclesiastical establishment"—and *state*.

If we suppose that Madison and Jefferson were intent not on instituting religiously neutral or detached government but rather on the more *institutional* goal of ending "ecclesiastical establishments," then their supposed inconsistencies and hypocrisies largely disappear. Or at least so it seems on first inspection. Madison could assume and declare the authority of "the Creator" in article 16 and in the "Memorial and Remonstrance"; he could invoke Providence in the *Federalist Papers*;[160] he could in a presidential inaugural address appeal openly and eloquently to the "guardianship and guidance of that Almighty Being whose power regulates the destiny of nations, whose blessings have been so conspicuously dispensed to this rising Republic, and to whom we are bound to address our devout gratitude for the past, as well as our fervent supplications and best hopes for the future."[161] These are hardly the actions or utterances of a statesman who has resolved, as Jack Rakove contends, that religion should be "wholly privatized." And yet Madison could oppose governmental involvement in the business of *churches*.

Thus, Madison could at least privately harbor serious reservations about the propriety of appointing legislative chaplains.[162] Wasn't that practice reminiscent of a government-appointed ministry? And as president he vetoed a bill granting corporate status to the Episcopal Church in Alexandria. The church needed no authorization from the government to carry out its Christian ministry, Madison said—in that respect the legislation was "altogether superfluous"—and, even more seriously, the law impermissibly intruded government into "the organization and polity of *the Church*."[163]

As president, similarly, Jefferson would with characteristic eloquence invoke deity and plead with his fellow citizens to pray for him and for the nation.[164] Conversely, the designation of particular days of worship and praise had historically been a matter that churches had performed (and often disagreed about, and sometimes even fractured over). So Jefferson conscientiously refrained from attempting to take over that churchly function.[165]

In interpreting Madison and his ally Jefferson as seeking not to institute secular or religiously neutral government but merely to end the institutional alliance of church and state, we exonerate them (along with their fellow Americans who embraced a similar position) from charges of incoherence or hypocrisy. Or do we?

On first look, it seems that Madison is in the clear. He did for the most part oppose religious establishment as an *institutional* arrangement; if he and even more so Jefferson also publicly invoked and relied on religious *beliefs*, they had never indicated any objection to that practice in the first place. Even so, might they perhaps be faulted for failing to trace out or acknowledge the implications of their own premises? Might their dedication to religious disestablishment and religious equality have entailed a commitment to a government that is religiously neutral—a commitment that they failed or refused to recognize and hence violated (along with most of their fellow Americans over the next century or two)?

Disestablishment without Neutrality?

As noted, historians have sometimes described post-Jeffersonian America as having maintained a "de facto establishment" of religion—a description that hints at hypocrisy in a nation that had officially repudiated religious establishments. Or they have suggested that the formal or official disestablishment achieved under Madison and Jefferson was merely the initial stage in a greater transformation that needed to be completed by a "second disestablishment,"[166] and perhaps a third and even a fourth[167]—a transformation in the direction of an ideal of secular or religiously neutral government, thus realizing the commitment to religious freedom and equality that was implicit but imperfectly achieved in the "first disestablishment."

But these descriptions beg important questions, and they fail to recognize the integrity and potential attractiveness of the position urged by Madison and Jefferson—namely, official or institutional disestablishment that is *not* taken to entail religiously detached or neutral or secular government. Suppose we suspend for the moment any assumption that the ultimate goal or ideal must necessarily be secular or religiously neutral government. We can now appreciate how institutional disestablishment was a major achievement in its own right. (Which is not to say that everyone would agree that this was a *desirable* achievement: Thomas More, for one, presumably would not.)

Thus, in a government with an established church, the fundamental official truths will be determined by an institution that not all of the citizens belong to or support, but that citizens generally will be required to subsidize. Suppose the official church is the Church of England, as it had been in the mother country and also in Virginia. Now it will be a state-sponsored belief that "[t]here is but one living and true God, everlasting, without body, parts, or passions; of infinite power, wisdom, and goodness; the Maker, and Preserver of all things both visible and invisible." And that "in every person born into this world, it deserveth God's wrath and damnation." Also that "[w]orks done before the grace of Christ, and the Inspiration of his Spirit, are not pleasant to God, forasmuch as they spring not of faith in Jesus Christ, neither do they make men meet to receive grace."[168] These are the official truths of the realm not because citizens or a majority of them believe as much—the citizens *may* believe these things, or they may *not* believe them, or they may have no clue what some of these propositions even mean—but rather because the officially preferred church says so. And everyone's tax dollars will be used to pay that church's clergy to teach these ostensible truths.

Compare this with a situation in which there is no official or established church, but in which the state constitution explicitly enjoins everyone to practice "Christian forbearance and charity," and in which a landmark statute declares that "Almighty God hath created the mind free" and that religious coercion is contrary to "the plan of the Holy Author of our religion." If we are mostly interested in a principle under

which government is not supposed to endorse or act on religious beliefs, this second situation will look very much like the first one: both
situations will present obvious violations of the ostensible commitment to religious neutrality. But that observation would fail to notice
the massive differences. In the second situation, the proposition that
"Almighty God hath created the mind free" becomes a governmentally
endorsed truth not because any church said so but rather because—
and only to the extent that—the proposition gains the support of the
citizens through whatever majoritarian processes they have adopted
to express their will. And all of the enfranchised citizens will be permitted to participate in those processes, regardless of which church (if
any) they belong to.

   True, we might if we choose still say that there is an officially supported religious "orthodoxy." But now it will be not only a relatively
minimalist orthodoxy but also a sort of free-floating one that can find
its content and equilibrium in accordance with the (probably shifting)
beliefs of the citizens. If the citizens are religious, religious beliefs will
likely be part of the political discourse that influences—and sometimes
achieves expression by—government. As John Marshall wrote during
a public debate in the 1830s, "[t]he American population is entirely
Christian. . . . It would be strange, indeed, if with such a people, our
institutions did not presuppose Christianity, & did not often refer to
it, & exhibit relations with it."[169] Conversely, if the citizens are resolutely secular—"secular" in the contemporary sense of not religious—
the orthodoxy will likewise be secular. And if beliefs among the
citizens are an eclectic mixture of religious and secular, the orthodoxy
will be mixed as well.

   To be sure, insofar as citizens happen to adhere to religious beliefs, you could characterize a government that acts on and sometimes
officially and explicitly expresses those beliefs as creating a "*de facto*
establishment*" of religion. But that would be a tendentious and arguably misleading description. Confronted with this description, someone like Madison might vigorously object. He might say that an
"establishment of religion," or an "ecclesiastical establishment," is by
definition legal and official, so that the very idea of a "*de facto* estab-

lishment" is subtly oxymoronic—like, say, the idea of an unwritten text, or a silent scream. He might say that it is more instructive to describe this political arrangement not as a *de facto* establishment but rather as a . . . democracy. As a government of the people, by the people, and for the people, and thus as a government that expresses and acts on what the people believe.

Suppose, by contrast, that some institution—a Supreme Court, say, purporting to "interpret" a constitutional provision that when originally enacted had no such meaning or purpose—were to say that government is forbidden to declare or act on religious beliefs, even if those beliefs are widely held and regarded as pertinent by the citizens themselves. This imposed prohibition would not be in any sense a fulfillment of some commitment supposedly implicit in the original decision to eschew an official or established church. On the contrary, it would be a *pro tanto* reversion to the earlier situation in which some particular institution—one to which many citizens do not belong or contribute, and which they may not support—dictates what beliefs shall (or, in this case, shall *not*) be included in the political discourse that shapes and is expressed by government.

But what about the commitment to religious equality to which Madison and Jefferson seem to have been committed? They might explain that disestablishment does indeed bring about religious equality in a crucial sense. Before, when the Church of England was the official church of the commonwealth, members of that church were in a real sense "insiders," while Baptists and Presbyterians—and Quakers, and Jews, and atheists—were "outsiders." The lines indicating who was an "insider" and who was an "outsider" were officially and legally drawn. And everyone's tax dollars were spent to proclaim and promote the beliefs of the "insiders." Now, with disestablishment, all citizens stand as equals before the government and the law regardless of their religion or lack thereof. Is this not the achievement of "religious equality" in an essential sense?

"Maybe so," the modern egalitarian responds, "and yet the merely institutional and formal disestablishment leaves untouched the problem we have noticed already: if government announces and acts upon religious beliefs, citizens who disagree with those beliefs will be made to *feel like* 'outsiders.' And in that respect, the government will fall short of showing them 'equal concern and respect.'"

But if they could have anticipated this more modern criticism, Madison and Jefferson would likely have responded—incredulously, perhaps—that this sort of psychic equality surely is nothing more than a chimera. In making decisions, or in acting to promote one policy rather than a competing policy, governments will inevitably accept and act on some beliefs while rejecting other beliefs. How else could a government make decisions on contested matters? Moreover, governments do not just rule by fiat; they naturally do—and, most would agree, *should*—attempt to explain and justify their decisions and policies by presenting the premises or rationales that support those decisions and policies. In a pluralistic society, some citizens will inevitably disagree with those premises or rationales.

These citizens may thus *feel* like "outsiders." Indeed, in a certain practical or sociological sense they *are* outsiders (just as Republicans in California or Democrats in Utah or socialists in Texas are outsiders today). But that sort of phenomenon can hardly be deemed a violation of equality in any practically viable sense; on the contrary, this side of the Millennium—or, in other words, so long as not everyone agrees on the relevant beliefs and policies—that sort of *de facto* outsiderness is simply inevitable. And it would not be Madison and Jefferson but rather any government or court that purported to embrace such an utterly unrealistic and unachievable egalitarianism that would inevitably be guilty of inconsistency and hypocrisy.[170]

Even if this conclusion is correct, though, and even if it serves to exonerate Madison against charges of inconsistency, the conclusion may nonetheless be disappointing. As noted, Madison's amendments to article 16 and Jefferson's "Virginia Statute for Religious Freedom" have been described as transformative—as the beginning of the liberal project and "the birth of the modern self." And they have been taken as reflecting Madison's status as "one of the most inventive and constructive thinkers of his age," as one historian puts it.[171] Now it is turning out, it seems, that those measures were more in the nature of a rearrangement of the institutional furniture. An institutional rearrangement, in fact, that was not even novel but rather calculated to imitate patterns already existing in other places, such as Pennsylvania and the Netherlands.

Institutions are important, no doubt, but still . . . So, have we been wrong in supposing that these revered luminaries were aiming for something more dramatic and fundamental than this? Something more—what?—more principled, maybe, or more philosophical in nature?

And indeed it may be that describing Madison's achievement as mere institutional disestablishment does understate—and even partially misstate—his contribution and his vision. To see how, though, it will help to return to and consider his essential argument from a different perspective, and to consider a different kind of criticism of that argument.

III

THE CONTESTABLE "[T]HEREFORE"

In defending Madison against the charge of inconsistency and hypocrisy, we have had to attribute to him arguments that seem consistent with his position but that he did not actually make—and that he had no reason to make. He had no reason to make them because he was arguing not against modern critics far advanced (or far gone?) in their egalitarianism but rather against the traditional position which held that a religious establishment—a state-recognized and supported church—was necessary for the maintenance of civil society. That is the position that he was seeking to overthrow.

And so we can ask: how successful was Madison in his argument not against future or imaginary egalitarian critics but rather against the traditionalist establishmentarians he was in fact trying to address and refute? In considering that question, we may be able to gain a clearer idea of how Madison subtly transformed the relations of government and religion, and also the fundamental meaning and function of conscience.

In the "Memorial and Remonstrance," Madison offered a variety of arguments for religious disestablishment. Some were prudential in nature—and local, with little application beyond his immediate context.[172] Others were still prudential but of broader potential application.[173] But Madison's primary argument—and the argument made both in article 16 and in the "Memorial and Remonstrance"—was not merely prudential in character; rather it advanced what Madison seems to have regarded as a sort of logically compulsory truth that transcended any particular historical context. This is the supposed logical truth that, according to John Noonan, the young James Madison saw "in the transparent clarity with which a brilliant mathematician perceives a new relationship of numbers."[174]

Here is the argument, once again. "Religion, or the duty which we owe to our Creator, and the manner of discharging it, can be directed only by reason and conviction, not by force or violence": that is the premise. Now the conclusion: "and *therefore* all men are equally entitled to the free exercise of religion, according to the dictates of conscience."

So, how solid is the logic attached to Madison's "therefore"?

We might begin by simply stipulating to the correctness of the premise—the claim, that is, that religion in order to be efficacious must be based on sincere conviction, not on force or violence. By now, this premise will seem to most of us almost axiomatic, as it evidently did to Madison himself and most of his contemporaries. God cares, surely, about what we sincerely believe, and about what we do with actual sincerity or conviction. So it does no good for me to recite under compulsion a religious creed with my lips if I do not actually hold or believe that creed in my heart and mind—not even if the creed to which I pay lip service happens to be correct. God looketh on the heart, as the Bible teaches,[175] and mine is still the heart of a heretic.

Does anyone today disagree with these propositions? Even a contemporary atheist would likely concur that if there *were* a God, that God would care about what people sincerely believe, not about what they are forced to intone.

To be sure, in some historical contexts, lots of people would have disagreed: Madison's premise would have seemed mistaken, or maybe close to incomprehensible. Consider, for instance, the environment in which Christianity arose—namely, the pre-Constantinian Roman

Empire. The Romans proudly described themselves as "the most religious people in the world": they faithfully and dutifully sacrificed to the gods, consulted the auguries before making political or military decisions, and paid obeisance to the divine emperors.[176] But their religion was a matter not so much of private or personal belief and worship, with the object of gaining individual salvation, as of communal rites calculated to enlist the favor of the gods in support of the city. What any particular individual *believed*, or whether he or she was sincere in this belief: these things were pretty much beside the point. For a Roman to have said, "It would be hypocritical and wrong for me to join in this sacrifice to Jove because I'm not sure I actually believe in him" would have been approximately as cogent as for a modern American to tell the IRS, "It would be hypocritical and wrong for me to pay my taxes because I'm not sure that I fully support this government's policies."

Madison, though, was living not in pagan Rome but rather in a society shaped by generations of Christian tradition. And in that tradition, his basic claim—that only a sincere faith has spiritual efficacy—had been recited for centuries, beginning with apologists like Tertullian and Lactantius (or, it might be argued, Jesus himself) and continuing through more recent thinkers like John Locke and Roger Williams.[177] So the claim had come to have a truistic quality, which was why Madison could confidently assert the claim without qualification or support.

But if Madison's premise would have provoked no dissent in a Christian context, the same could not be said of his "therefore"—namely, that compulsion in matters of religion can serve no useful purpose and that people should accordingly have a right to religious freedom. On the contrary: over the centuries, Christians who could hardly be deemed unintelligent or unreflective—Augustine, for example, or Thomas Aquinas, . . . or Thomas More—had in essence shared Madison's premise but rejected his conclusion.

Here, it seems, we are in the presence of some important historical divide. For Madison and many others (including most Americans, and most Westerners since his time), the traditional and medieval position has seemed not only oppressive but illogical, even incomprehensible. If you concede that only a sincere religious profession can be acceptable to God, and also that forcing people to profess or practice a religion will not make them sincerely believe it, then why *doesn't* it irresistibly follow that compulsion in matters of religion can do no good, and hence that people should be left free in such matters? Religious freedom just seems like the obviously true and correct position—even if most people and most civilizations throughout history have somehow failed to comprehend that obvious truth. In this spirit, even an erudite scholar and man of faith like John Noonan could casually dismiss the views of earlier Christians like Augustine or Aquinas as the product of unreflective acquiescence in benighted convention.[178]

But can the considered position of these earlier thinkers be so easily brushed aside? Attempting to do justice to the traditional position, we might consider two different kinds of objections to Madison's "therefore."

The Traditional Objections

While accepting that a coerced profession of faith had no spiritual efficacy, pre-modern Christians like Thomas More had nonetheless offered carefully thought-out reasons justifying the use of government and law to support an established religion and to suppress heresy.[179] The arguments were lengthy and complex, but we might distill the most common arguments into three basic rationales. We might call these the *pedagogical* and *contagion* rationales—we will focus on those here—and the *social order* rationale, which we will mostly defer for a few pages.

The pedagogical argument suggested that although ultimately only a sincere faith was efficacious, compelled conformity to the true faith might nonetheless lead a person to come to understand the truth of propositions that he or she had initially opposed in ignorance or without proper understanding. An early formulation of this rationale came from Augustine, who was converted to the rationale by hard historical experience. Augustine initially "had believed that no one should be forced into the unity of Christ," Perez Zagorin explains, "[b]ut then proven facts caused him to give up this opinion when he saw Donatists in his own city 'converted to Catholicism by the fear of imperial laws[.]'. ... Reclaimed Donatists, he contended, were now grateful that 'fear of the laws promulgated by temporal rulers who serve the Lord in fear has been so beneficial' to them."[180] As Benjamin Kaplan observes: "For Augustine, persecution was a form of tough love. ... [T]he church persecuted the wayward for their own good."[181]

The argument should not be so hard for us to understand; after all, we often act on the same rationale ourselves. We compel children to attend school, for example, and to study and demonstrate mastery of prescribed bodies of knowledge, such as math and sciences. And in testing these students, we do not ask—or care—what the children personally believe; rather, we mark down their grades and potentially fail them if they do not give the correct answers. In this way, we think, the children will come to understand and accept what we know to be the truth.

But it is not just children, and not just precise or "hard" subjects like science and math. Where I work, for example (as in many workplaces), every employee must be certified and recertified by completing an annual online tutorial, said to be mandatory, teaching the approved attitudes and norms governing gender and sexual interactions and the correct responses to deviations from these established proprieties. The tutorial accepts only the officially pre-approved answers to its multitude of questions; if through carelessness or perversity or even—heaven forbid!—misguided conviction you give an incorrect answer, you will not be permitted to proceed with the mandatory course. Your only option, in the end, is to recite the officially preferred dogma. In this way, it is evidently supposed, the employees will be cured of deviant beliefs or assumptions that they may have acquired.[182]

To be sure, compelled conformity did not and does not always succeed in liberating the perverse from their supposed errors. In the traditional establishmentarian view, though, even if such compulsion failed in its pedagogical function, the contagion rationale provided an alternative justification for religious coercion. Although an obstinate heretic might not be brought to understand and confess the truth of the orthodox faith, silencing the heretic would nonetheless protect the faith of more innocent others who were presently orthodox in their beliefs but whose sound faith might be disturbed and subverted by exposure to heresy[183]—just as quarantining someone who is sick can curb the spread of disease even if it does not cure the sick person. Commenting that "it is a great pity to see many good, simple souls deceived by and led out of the right way by the authority of men they regard as both good and knowledgeable," Thomas More had contended that "rulers are . . . obligated not to allow their people to be seduced and corrupted by heretics."[184]

Once again, this rationale shouldn't be so hard for us to grasp, living as we do in a period in which expression of an unacceptable opinion on an array of sensitive matters involving race, sex, sexual orientation, or personal identity can get a person promptly "cancelled," or banished from social media, or removed from his or her position in the media, in government, in the academy, or in other kinds of activities—thereby presumably preventing the spread of the noxious attitudes or opinions.

The pedagogical and contagion rationales were directed to the saving of souls, and what could be more important than that? But even setting aside for the moment matters of eternity, preventing the spread of heresy was vitally important on the purely mundane level. That is because, as we saw in our chapter on Thomas More, it was Christianity that provided the "ties that bind"—the ties that held together both the individual life and the social order, consecrated them, and prevented them from fragmenting into two or three or a hundred pieces. As W. E. Garrison explained, with perhaps a touch of overstatement:

> For more than fourteen hundred years . . . it was a universal assumption that the stability of the social order and the safety of the state demanded the religious solidarity of all the people in one church. Every responsible thinker, every ecclesiastic, every ruler and statesman who gave the matter any attention, held to this as an axiom. There was no political or social philosopher which did not build upon this assumption . . . all, with no exceptions other than certain disreputable and "subversive" heretics, believed firmly that religious solidarity in the one recognized church was essential to social and political stability.[185]

So, how did Madison respond to these centuries-old arguments in favor of religious establishment that had been propounded by some of the leading intellectual lights in Western history?

With respect to the first two of these venerable arguments, the answer is that . . . he didn't. Thus, in article 16 itself, the conclusion favoring religious freedom was presented as just following automatically and inexorably from the premise that only a sincere religion is efficacious. Only sincere faith counts; *therefore*, a right of religious freedom. *Q.E.D.*

In the "Memorial and Remonstrance," Madison expanded slightly on article 16's "therefore." But what exactly did his elaborations add? The argument began with a more fulsome statement of the basic and uncontroversial premise. It is "a fundamental and undeniable truth"— now the quote from article 16—"'that Religion or the duty which we owe to our Creator and the Manner of discharging it, can be directed only by reason and conviction, not by force or violence.'" Next came the familiar conclusion, this time connected to the premise with a "then" instead of a "therefore": "The Religion *then* of every man must be left to the conviction and conscience of every man; and it is the right of every man to exercise it as these may dictate." Nothing new so far.

After declaring this right to be "unalienable," however, Madison went on to give some ostensible reasons why the conclusion follows from the premise. Except that the reasons consisted merely of restating what had already been asserted in the premise. *Why*, from the proposition that faith must be sincere, does it follow that everyone has a complete and unalienable right to religious freedom? It follows, Madison explained, first, "because the opinions of men, depending only on the evidence contemplated by their own minds, cannot follow the dictates of other men." But that assertion (which tacitly bypassed the classic pedagogical rationale without actually noticing it) was merely a repetition of the claim that coercion cannot get anyone to believe something they do not actually believe. That is and already was the argument's premise, but the conclusion itself still stands in need of some justification.

Madison then gave a second "because": there is an unalienable right to religious freedom "because . . . [i]t is the duty of every man to render to the Creator such homage, and such only, as he believes to be acceptable to him." But again, at least on first inspection (we will take a second look shortly), this assertion seems to be not so much a "because" or a reason as yet another restatement of the basic premise, in which religion is declared to be a duty to God that can be directed only by sincere belief.

One can imagine one of the illustrious Thomases — Aquinas or More — rising up to challenge Madison at this point. "Please, James," our Thomas might object, "you keep repeating yourself, but you never actually get around to justifying your conclusion. We all agree that only a sincere faith is ultimately acceptable to God; you don't need to keep telling us that. Even so, might not religious compulsion serve a pedagogical function in helping wayward believers come to an under-standing of the truth? Our predecessor Augustine thought so; indeed, he was compelled to that conclusion by concrete experience. Or, alter-natively, might not such compulsion at least prevent the heretically in-clined from corrupting others with their errors and perversities?"

Madison appears not to notice these possibilities. Perhaps he never considered them. Given the historical prevalence of the rationales, and considering Madison's erudition, this may seem unlikely. And yet we have already seen how easy it is even for capable or award-winning contemporary historians and observers, imbued with our modern as-sumptions and distinctions, to look at but nonetheless largely miss what Madison himself was doing and saying; so perhaps in the same way he simply missed what the proponents of established religion had said, over and over again, for centuries. In any case, viewed against the backdrop of the centuries-old debate on the subject, Madison comes across as embarrassingly naive: he starts in innocent fashion by reciting something that everybody already knows and has known for centuries and then, seemingly oblivious to all of the complications and counter-arguments, simply leaps directly and confidently to his contested and problematic conclusion as if he had discovered some self-evident truth.

Indeed, his naivete might seem to extend not merely to the reason-ing but also to the humans who were doing (or not doing) that reason-ing. The picture Madison consistently presents is one in which "every man" in a sober and detached way takes up the central questions about

God and religion and, unaffected by the views of those who surround him, arrives at answers to those questions based "only on the evidence contemplated by [his] own mind[]." But our doubting Thomases might reply that, precisely contrary to Madison's depiction, it is "a fundamental and undeniable truth" (to borrow Madison's own phrase) that the vast majority of human beings do *not* come by their religious opinions in this detached and purely rational fashion.

Madison's picture badly distorts the reality in at least two ways, our critic might suggest. First, most people's religious (and other) opinions are powerfully influenced by the opinions of other people—their parents, their friends, their teachers, their colleagues. Is it merely a peculiar accident that most philosophers in the thirteenth and seventeenth and even eighteenth centuries were theists whereas most philosophers today are atheists or agnostics? Second, as Thomas More emphasized in his treatment of religious belief and heresy,[186] most people's religious beliefs (like other beliefs) are significantly shaped by what we might describe as personal but nonrational features—qualities such as trustingness or cynicism, pride or humility, tendencies to independence or to conformity, desires of various kinds—including the desire to rationalize or justify one's own life and conduct, or to appear to others or oneself to be a bold or independent thinker, or to suppose that the world has some kind of sense and purpose, or that the world is as we believe it should be.[187]

This is not to deny that thinking, logic, and evidence enter into the formation of opinions: if they had not believed that, our Thomases would not have devoted much of their lives to writing summas, treatises, and dialogues. But the thinking takes place by and within humans who are far from being merely free-floating reasoners. The traditional pedagogical and contagion rationales operate on this sort of complex view of human beings and human beliefs. By contrast, Madison's presentation of religious belief as the product of detached and almost disembodied thinkers—disembodied both culturally and historically—seems quite fantastic as a depiction of how human opinions are actually formed.

Then again, perhaps we are once again being unfair to the man. After all, Madison might remind us, he never set out or pretended to engage in some debate for the ages with the likes of Thomas Aquinas or Thomas More. He was, on the contrary, engaged in political advocacy with his own contemporaries, seeking to dislodge Virginia's established church that so many of them had supported. In the High Middle Ages, or perhaps even in seventeenth-century Massachusetts, the pedagogical and contagion arguments might have seemed familiar and cogent enough—and thus in need of being addressed or refuted. But in the by now irrevocably pluralistic environment of late-eighteenth century America, it was unlikely in the extreme that forcing an unwilling dissenter to subsidize the established church would somehow bring him or her around to the orthodox creed. And the contagion of heretical ideas, if that is what it was, had already passed any point of containment.[188] So whatever their merits in other historical contexts, the hoary rationales had already lost their force. And in omitting to address those rationales, Madison was not irresponsibly begging the important questions; he was, rather, sensibly and mercifully declining to waste words beating up on straw men.

This interpretation may mean that for all the praise it has garnered, Madison's "Memorial and Remonstrance" does *not* have the force of a mathematical demonstration, as John Noonan suggested; it does not establish any timeless truths; nor does it qualify as a major or notably thoughtful contribution to the centuries-old philosophical debate on the abstract question of the possible efficacy of religious coercion. But then again, Madison was not writing a philosophical treatise on an abstract question. He was acting as a politician and statesman, attempting to fend off a present and very specific proposal—namely, the assessments bill supported by Patrick Henry—that he viewed as an unwise and oppressive.

As a politician and statesman, however, Madison could not afford to ignore the third of the traditional arguments—what we have called the social order argument. This was the belief that he had asked about years earlier with "my dear Billey"—the belief that an ecclesiastical establishment is necessary to the maintenance of civil society. Madison understood that many of his fellow Virginians shared this belief. He came to disagree, and he aimed to end the establishment of religion. But then what *would* take its place in supplying the ties that bind society together?

To that still very live question Madison *did* at least suggest an answer. More than one answer, actually. Before considering Madison's answers to the social order rationale, however, we should consider a different kind of challenge to Madison's "therefore."

THE NON SEQUITUR OBJECTION

This second kind of challenge does not invoke the traditional "pedagogical" and "contagion" rationales, or even the "social order" rationale, for a government-supported church and religious orthodoxy. Rather, it asserts that, just in purely logical or analytical terms, Madison's "therefore" amounts to a non sequitur. Contrary to Madison's assumption (and that of most Americans and indeed most residents of liberal democracies since then), the conclusion simply does not follow from the uncontroversial premise. Granted, a coerced and insincere profession of faith has no spiritual efficacy, but it does not follow that there is any right to religious freedom or that government has any obligation to leave us free to practice our various religions.

To see why not, let us imagine that we are orthodox Christians who wield plenary political authority in our community. And it comes to our attention that a smallish group of our fellow citizens has organized a dissenting church, grounded in what we are confident is a demonstrable heresy. For convenience, let us label this the neo-Manichean heresy. But the problem is not just that this dissenting church's neo-Manichean doctrines are false and heretical. In addition, on the basis of these heretical doctrines, the church engages in worship practices and prescribes behaviors that violate community norms.

Perhaps, like seventeenth-century Quakers, the dissenters refuse to honor the customary modes of showing respect to fellow citizens and government officials, and they thereby undermine community solidarity.[189] Perhaps, like nineteenth-century Mormons, the heretical church teaches that a man should marry more than one wife.[190] Perhaps, like Jehovah's Witnesses, the church refuses to comply with minimal mandatory requirements of civic allegiance, such as recitation in public schools of the Pledge of Allegiance[191] or willingness to serve in the military. Maybe the church's members believe in faith healing and hence refuse to get necessary medical attention when their children are sick.[192]

Maybe the church's worship practices involve the use of a harmful substance that is prohibited by law[193] — or maybe even the sacrifice of animals in a way that constitutes cruelty under the community's laws and that is psychologically damaging to children.[194]

And so we resolve to do the sensible thing — namely, to enforce the applicable laws and norms against the transgressing church and its members. Before we can act, though, James Madison or some like-minded citizen appears before us and objects, arguing that it would be wrong to suppress or to enforce the law against the religious dissenters. Rather, we should respect their right to practice their religion, at least up to the point that the practices violate some truly compelling governmental interest.

"Why on earth should we do that?," we ask. And the objector says he will be happy to explain.

"First of all," he suggests, "we can all agree — can't we? — that 'it is the duty of every man to render homage to the Creator.'" "Yes, of course," we respond; we are, after all, devoutly orthodox Christians. "And can't we also agree," our Madisonian continues, "that 'religion, or the duty which we owe to our Creator, and the manner of discharging it, can be directed only by reason and conviction, not by force or violence'? Can we agree, in other words, that it does no good, or provides no acceptable or efficacious 'homage to the Creator,' to force a person to recite articles of faith that he does not believe, or to participate in religious exercises against his will and his belief?" Again, we assent.

At this point, our Madisonian exclaims triumphantly that his conclusion naturally and inevitably follows: "*therefore*, all men are equally entitled to the free exercise of religion, according to the dictates of conscience." To which we in turn respond uncomprehendingly that nothing of the sort follows. Our objector's "therefore" seems to us to signify an indefensible and even inexplicable leap of illogic.

But let us try to be more precise. The Madisonian propositions, to which we have happily assented, *do* seem to show that if our goal were to cause the dissenters to render an acceptable homage to God, perhaps with an eye to their salvation, forcing them to practice our orthodox religion against their will would not achieve that goal. (Bracket for now the traditional pedagogical and contagion arguments, which we have waived for purposes of this second, non sequitur objection.) We quickly add that allowing the dissenters to freely practice their heretical religion will likewise do nothing to bring about any acceptable homage to God, or to achieve anyone's salvation. People will honor God or get to heaven, we agree, by sincerely professing and practicing the true faith: from this it follows that they will not honor God or get to heaven *either* by professing under compulsion the true faith without actually believing it *or* by practicing a religion that is contrary to God's truth.[195] So it seems that the goods of honoring God or attaining salvation, however superlative those goods may be, are neither here nor there; these goods provide no reason either to restrict or to accommodate the dissenters' heretical religion.

"Most importantly, though," we continue, "all of this talk of homage and salvation is merely an irrelevant distraction. *Not* because those are illusory or unimportant goods: heaven forbid! But because in proposing to enforce our laws against the dissenting church, we never said or supposed that our purpose was to secure the dissenters' salvation or to coerce them into an acceptable homage to God. We were motivated, rather, by the more mundane purpose of maintaining and protecting community norms—norms embodied in our customs of respect or civic allegiance, or in our laws regulating dangerous substances or marriage or protecting children or animals." So our Madisonian has basically come forward and advanced an argument that at best negates a possible reason for suppression that we had not thought to act on in the first place. "You are right," we might respond, "that it would do no good to suppress the dissenters' church for *that* reason, but that was not our reason for enforcing our law against the dissenters anyway. So your argument is simply irrelevant to our decision, and to our policy."

And so Madison's "therefore" amounts to a stark non sequitur.[196] Or at least so it seems.

But that conclusion might provoke suspicion. Although Madison was a mortal who could make no claim to inerrancy, he has usually been credited, both by his contemporaries and his descendants, with being a careful thinker. And the argument we have been considering is not one that he offered casually or off-handedly; on the contrary, it is an argument that he pressed consistently over a period of years. *Maybe* he somehow overlooked a gross fallacy in his position. Or maybe we have not yet sufficiently appreciated what his argument actually was.

Let us return and take another look. Just in case. Another look may help us to appreciate the force of Madison's logic; more generally, it may help us appreciate what his innovative and distinctive historical contribution actually was.

THE NEW (OLD) GOSPEL OF CONSCIENCE

Here, once again, is Madison's core contention: "It is the duty of every man to render to the Creator such homage, and such only, as he believes to be acceptable to him." It is easy to read that sentence, utter a quick "of course," and then quickly move on to examine the conclusion—which is basically what we have been doing up to this point. But if we pause and pay close attention to what Madison's contention says, and also to what it *does not* say, what might easily pass as a platitudinous premise becomes a daring but potentially cogent claim.

Look again. "It is the duty of every man to render to the Creator such homage, and such only, as he believes to be acceptable to him." On that premise, taken literally, if the disciples of our heretical neo-Manichean church believe their worship practices and their behaviors to be a form of homage that is acceptable to the Creator, then it *is* their duty to render such homage. It does not matter that the neo-Manicheans are mistaken and that their doctrines are actually false. The only thing that matters, rather, is that *the neo-Manicheans believe* their religion is acceptable to God. If that is their sincere conviction, then they have a duty to act on that conviction.

So says Madison. But we have not yet come to the audacious part.

What we have seen so far might amount to little more than a manifestation of what we called in the previous chapter the practical tautology at the heart of conscience. Ideally, we would do what *is* right—that is just what it means for something to be right—but given our fallibility, in practice this tautology can only mean that we should do what *we believe* to be right. The tautology tells us what we should do, given our beliefs, but without more it has no necessary implications for those who must monitor or regulate what we do—our parents, our teachers, the government. A student insists that she wrote down on the test what she believed to be the correct answers. The teacher responds, "Excellent; that is what you, as a student, are supposed to do. Of course, as a teacher, what *I* am supposed to do is to mark down your grade for wrong answers—even though you believed those answers to be correct."

In a similar vein, the non sequitur objection suggested that although Madison's premise is correct, nothing follows in the way of "rights" or limitations on government. In effect, the government says to the neo-Manicheans, "We accept that you are attempting to worship God in the way you believe to be right: we commend you for that. And of course we would not interfere if we agreed with you that God requires this sort of worship, 'lest haply [we] be found even to fight against God.'[197] But, alas, we don't believe that God actually commands or approves of your worship practices. In fact, we are quite sure that He doesn't. And, as it happens, those practices violate our laws. And so your sincere but (in our opinion) mistaken beliefs about what God wants give us no reason to refrain from enforcing our laws against you."

But Madison is not finished; his proposition is susceptible of a more ambitious interpretation. When he declares that "[i]t is the duty of every man to render to the Creator such homage, and such only, as he believes to be acceptable to him," Madison might intend more than the practical tautology; he might mean that the duty imposed by *the Creator* is just that—namely, to render such homage as people believe to be acceptable to him. So if you believe that God wants you to worship Him by lighting a candle at midnight, then God *does* want you to light a candle at midnight. He wants you to do that even though He never independently issued any such directive; indeed, and paradoxically, He wants you to do it even if He also thinks that lighting candles at midnight is a silly or superstitious practice. *You believe* God wants you to do this; God knows you believe this; and therefore God *does* want you to do this[198] (even though, again paradoxically, in a different sense God might not want people, presumably including you, to do it).

Now, if you fail to light the candle, you will of course be violating what *you believe* to be your obligation to God, thereby contravening the practical tautology, but, more importantly, you will be violating what *is* your obligation to God. An obligation that God expects you to comply with. And anyone who steps in to prevent you from lighting the candle—your parents, your neighbor, ... the government—will thereby be placing themselves in opposition to God.

If Madison's proposition is interpreted in this way, then the non sequitur objection is deflected, and if the proposition is actually accepted, then the argument would seem to offer a powerful reason for respecting the subjects' rights of conscience. To refer to our earlier case: it may be true that in acting to enforce our laws against the neo-Manicheans we were never thinking to secure their salvation anyway, and it may also be true that (as we orthodox Christians feel certain) the neo-Manicheans' doctrines are demonstrably false and their modes of worship are offensive to God. Even so, if they sincerely believe they should render homage to God in this way, then in a different sense God *does* require such homage from them.[199] And so if we interfere with their religious practice, we will be placing ourselves in opposition to God. Which is something that, as orthodox Christians, we presumably would very much want not to do.

The whole argument turns on the intriguing and contestable claim that God does in fact want us to do what we believe He wants us to do—even if that is contrary to God's will.

That is an audacious claim. Think about it: Madison's bold understanding of the authority and efficacy of conscience implies that all of the theological reflections and disputations of Christians and others over the centuries—all of the treatises and tracts and summas and sermons devoted to discovering or demonstrating the truth about God and God's providential order—have been ... what? Not exactly a waste of time and effort—because presumably it is still good to understand God correctly rather than incorrectly. And yet the energy and effort poured into this theological enterprise—the blood, sweat, and tears; the searching reflections and agonizing examinations and introspections and inquisitions—have been far less urgent than millions of Christians over the ages have supposed. Because the ultimate, overarching objective of such efforts has been ... salvation. The goal has been to enable Christians to believe and live in a way that is acceptable to God. And it turns out, at least according to Madison, that as long as a person is sincere in his or her belief, it doesn't matter in this respect whether that belief is true or false: either way, the person is rendering an acceptable homage to God.

As noted, this claim is at least paradoxical: it means that the same conduct might be both contrary to God's will and yet also required or commanded by God. Is the claim also absurd? Perhaps. Is it plausible to suppose that God wants us to do what we believe He wants us to do—sacrifice our first-born child, perhaps—even if He solemnly prohibits the thing we (mistakenly) believe He wants us to do? Can our religious duty be so exclusively grounded in the sincerity of our convictions without regard for the actual truth of those convictions?

Moreover, Madison's audacious claim raises all sorts of conundrums. What if Margaret sincerely believes that God wants her to erect and maintain a shrine on Mt. Nebo, while Calvin sincerely believes that God wants him to tear down and destroy all shrines? And so forth.

And yet for all of its audacity, Madison's claim is not exactly radical, or at least it is not radically novel. Didn't the medieval Church teach something very similar—that a person is obligated to do what he or she believes to be right even if that runs contrary to what the Church itself teaches?[200] And of course the medieval Church purported to be teaching God's truth. So the medieval doctrine implies—doesn't it?— that God wants a person to do what he or she believes to be right even if that is contrary to what God actually wants.

And didn't Thomas More in effect acknowledge the power of conscience to consecrate error, as we saw in the previous chapter? Wasn't it on something like that premise that More permitted his own family, even his beloved Meg, to take the oath that he understood to be wrong and pernicious, steadfastly declining to instruct them in the errors of that oath? More thought that *for him* to take that pernicious oath would entail eternal damnation. But he also thought that as long as his family believed the oath to be acceptable, it would be proper *for them* to take it.

In short, Madison's conception was like More's. In this respect, anyway.

His conception was also very different from More's. We will try in a moment to be more precise about how Madison's notions about conscience were and were not the same as More's: for now it is enough to say that there was distinguished precedent for Madison's interpretation of conscience.

Moreover, there are understandable reasons why someone like Madison in particular might find this theological position especially compelling. Throughout his life, as we have seen, he was engulfed by sincere and often impassioned theological diversity, maintained and embraced by people he loved and respected. His father and mother and his wife professed the Anglican creed. His esteemed mentors Donald Robertson and John Witherspoon adhered to Presbyterianism. The Baptists with whom he sympathized as a young man, and who later were important allies in Virginia politics (among other things securing his election to Congress) embraced still a different creed, and a fundamentally different kind of piety. (And if we today might dismiss these differences as negligible, they certainly did not appear inconsequential to the Baptists who were being thrown in jail for refusing to conform to the Anglican orthodoxy—or to the Anglicans who were putting those Baptists in jail.)[201] The French iconoclasts whom Madison avidly read as a young man—Voltaire and Diderot and company—were caustically hostile to Christianity itself. His friend and ally Thomas Jefferson, as well as Thomas Paine and many others among the "Enlightened" of his generation, were proponents of an ostensibly more "rational" religion that was likewise contemptuous of orthodox Christianity. And yet there were also highly intelligent orthodox Christians among the enlightened—people, again, like Madison's mentor John Witherspoon.

Situated in the midst of this diversity of religious opinion, a careful, reflective person like Madison might naturally conclude that there was no way for anyone—or at least for him—to be certain which if any of the competing creeds and anti-creeds were right and which were wrong. After all, when so many different teachers were propounding so many different and contradictory religious doctrines, how could a reflective person sensible of his own finitude and fallibility be confident that one of those doctrines was the true one? Better, perhaps, just to suspend judgment—to attend church with one's wife from time to time, but not to commit oneself to any particular sect or faith. He might thus come to embrace a sort of generic, least-common-denominator theism, affirming the existence of a Creator or Providence but withholding judgment on the doctrinal specifics that Christians had wrangled over for centuries. Which, it seems, is very likely the minimalist creed that Madison actually did embrace.

But now an urgent practical and even existential question would present itself — one that modern secular scholars working in a secular environment may fail to appreciate. Over the centuries, Christians had placed great emphasis on precisely defined theological truth, not just from finickiness but from a concern for their immortal souls. A person who holds erroneous or heretical notions about God loses out on the possibility of salvation — or of having his name "enrolled in the Annals of Heaven," as Madison had put it in a letter to William Bradford.[202] But on that premise, it seems that whole congregations of faithful, good-hearted souls who were worshiping God according to their sincere convictions — maybe the Anglicans (including Madison's wife and parents), maybe the Baptists, maybe the Unitarians, maybe all of them? — would end up missing out on salvation because, in a world in which warranted certainty is not available to finite and fallible mortals, they had the misfortune of having put their money and their trust on the wrong theological horse.

Was this a tenable conclusion? Could an infinitely benevolent God place his beloved children in such a terrifying predicament — in a position in which everyone was basically playing a kind of theological Russian roulette, with eternal damnation as the consequence of getting it wrong?

On the contrary, the axiom that God is good — that God *is* Love — prohibits any such monstrous conclusion. Doesn't it? But then what *does* God expect of us? What else but that we render him homage in accordance with our good faith convictions, whatever those happen to be? If we believe and live as we sincerely think God wants us to, we will be doing all that a just and loving God could reasonably ask of us. And so we will be doing what God *does* ask of us.

Is any other conclusion consistent with the transcendent goodness of God?

Reasoning along these lines, a person like Madison might come to embrace as his most central theological conviction not the Apostles Creed or the Nicean Creed — or, for that matter, the dogmas of the

Gnostics or the Manicheans or even of the French philosophes like Voltaire—but rather the doctrine of conscience. At the core of the theology would be not the Trinity nor the Incarnation nor the divine unity but rather . . . the imperative of Conscience.

Was this the theology that Madison ended up embracing? The Gospel of Conscience? Again, his reticence makes it difficult to be sure. But the interpretation seems consistent with all that he did and all that he said.

Indeed, we might even conclude that he was not after all as reticent about his religious convictions as historians have supposed. True, he said little to indicate what he thought about competing Christian positions and doctrines—Trinitarianism or Socinianism or Unitarianism; Arminianism or Calvinist predestination. But the reason was—or may have been—that these matters were simply not any essential part of his faith. What *was* central to that faith was . . . conscience. And on that subject, as we have seen, he was not reticent in the least. On the contrary, from his young manhood to the end of his life he was passionate—publicly passionate—in support of the sanctity of conscience.

The basic creed would be this: Our first obligation, and an obligation that precedes and takes priority over any obligation to government or society, is to render homage to God as our conscience dictates. That is what we should do; that is what God demands of us. Anyone, and any government, that prevents us from doing this will be acting in opposition to what God requires.

Which is pretty much what Madison said in the "Memorial and Remonstrance." If Madison's understanding of our duties to God is correct, it seems a powerful argument. And the entire argument rests upon a particular paradoxical and yet compelling understanding of conscience. "Man's conscience is more sacred than his castle," Madison wrote in an essay entitled "Property"; it is "the most sacred of all property."[203]

Understood in this way, Madison's position escapes the non sequitur objection. And it provides an implicit response to the pedagogical and contagion objections as well. The "Memorial and Remonstrance" is not as naive as we were suggesting a moment ago. Rather, it is an intriguing contribution, after all, to the perennial debate about the efficacy of coercion in matters of religion—and a powerful argument for freedom of conscience.

THE TIES THAT BIND, ONCE MORE

We have thus far deferred consideration of Madison's response to what had been perhaps the most common rationale for established religion, or what we have called the "social order" rationale. The idea, once again, was that a common religion is necessary to hold the society or the community together.

We saw in the last chapter how in the world of Thomas More, Christianity and the Church-administered Christian sacraments provided the ties that bound human beings to one another (including to those human beings who have died and those not yet born) and that consecrated the community and the government. Virginians were less theologically ambitious and less religiously demanding; even so, they had typically believed that the established church served this necessary function of supporting social unity.[204] Madison came to think otherwise; indeed, he argued that an established church was a source of contention that undermined the social order. And yet the question remained: If a society abandoned its established church, what would keep the community intact? What *would* supply "the ties that bind"?

In order to appreciate Madison's response to that question, though, we should first note one respect in which our description of religion's social function in this chapter and the last one has been a significant oversimplification. In Thomas More's England, and also in pre-Revolutionary Virginia, religion may have served a supportive function; even so, religion was never the sole or perhaps even the primary basis of social order.

We noted in the last chapter that a community is, as an important modern book has it, an "imagined" entity: people constitute a community if they conceive of themselves, or *imagine* themselves, as a community.[205] And religion is one—but only one—of the possible sources of such imaginings. What causes the people of England—or Virginia, or the United States of America—to think of themselves as a community? A common religion, perhaps. But many other things as well. For

Thomas More's England, for example, there was a common history, composed of remembered events like the Norman Conquest and the battle of Agincourt. A common language and literature (Beowulf, the Venerable Bede, Chaucer) and legends (Vortigern, King Arthur). Common political traditions and ideals, expressed in revered documents such as the Magna Carta and in the common law tradition and in the customs of royalty and hereditary succession. And common interests, involving matters like security against foreign invasion and internal violence, and of course commerce.

Religion and the established church, we might say, was merely one among these factors that bound the people together into a community. But religion was also a distinctive factor, because as we saw in the previous chapter, it was religion that in a sense *consecrated* the various communal events and connections. Religion took what might otherwise be a merely mundane and contingent collection of traditions, institutions, and interests and endowed them with a kind of sacredness. It grounded these commonalities in eternity.

In Madison's time, likewise, a sensible answer to the question of what holds Virginians (and, eventually, Americans) together and elevates this uncouth and contentious collection of human beings into a community might be: lots of things. Again, a common heritage and history, solidified by the mutual struggle of the Revolution. Common political ideals, as expressed in, for example, the Declaration of Rights that the young Madison had helped to draft, and the Declaration of Independence written by his friend Jefferson, and, eventually, the Constitution and the Bill of Rights which Madison would also help to write and enact. And common interests in commerce and continental expansion.

In his "Memorial and Remonstrance," Madison allusively invoked various of these uniting factors. His argument that an established church would discourage people from emigrating to the state drew upon the common interests in commerce and expansion. His argument that an ecclesiastical establishment produced contention and division invoked the common interest in peace and stability. In the spirit of and with at least implicit reference to the Declaration of Independence and the Declaration of Rights, the "Memorial and Remonstrance" repeatedly invoked the unifying political ideals of equality, natural rights, and the social contract. These things, and not an established church, were what he was primarily counting on to hold the commonwealth together.

And yet if the "Memorial and Remonstrance" proposed to dispense with the *established church*, it also pervasively recognized the centrality of *religion* in constituting the commonwealth. Its arguments explicitly drew upon what it took to be commonly held religious convictions. The central arguments, as we have seen, were based on religious premises that were taken to be shared by his fellow citizens. Thus, the "Memorial and Remonstrance" assumed a general commitment to Christianity—"this precious gift" that Madison's fellow citizens were presumed to wish "imparted to the whole race of mankind." As noted, the document ended by inviting its audience to join in "earnestly praying" to "the Supreme Lawgiver of the Universe," asking that transcendent authority to guide the citizens "into every measure which may be worthy of his blessing."

Religion was thus an important factor in the network of community; it was also a distinctive factor that, as in More's England, served in a sense to ground and consecrate other unifying factors. In the Declaration of Independence, Jefferson had assumed and articulated this consecrating function. The purpose of government was to protect "unalienable rights," yes; but where did those rights come from? They were the rights with which we are "endowed by the Creator." As Jefferson elsewhere put the point: "Can the liberties of a nation be secure when we have removed a conviction that these liberties are the gift of God?"[206] Equality is another of the essential unifying ideals, but what is the basis of that equality? It is, as the Declaration proclaims, that "all men are *created* equal"; as George Fletcher has observed, "Behind those created equal stands a Creator, who is the source of our inalienable rights 'to life, liberty, and the pursuit of happiness.'"[207]

In the "Memorial and Remonstrance," similarly, Madison began by deriving the right to conscience and religious freedom from our duties to the Creator, and he went on to argue that all of our other rights are "held by the same tenure." Which was why, he argued, if we do not respect the right to religious freedom, all of our other rights will be in jeopardy as well.[208]

In sum, Madison had concluded that an "*ecclesiastical establishment*" was not necessary to the preservation of civil society. But he evidently assumed that *religion* would continue to be one of the ties that bind and thereby help to constitute a disparate people into a community, and that religion would also be the necessary foundation for some of the other essential common commitments as well.

IV

The Establishment — and Transformation? — of Conscience

But this project of at the same time disestablishing religion and yet counting on religion to help hold the community together is madness, or so we might imagine Thomas More objecting. Left to their own devices and their own exquisitely fallible reasoning, people will inevitably diverge in their religious opinions, and these divergences will splinter the community, pulling it in a hundred different directions. Without an officially established religion, therefore, faith will inevitably fragment into a sort of religious war of all against all.

More could already perceive this fragmentation gaining momentum in his own time. The next two centuries would provide bloody confirmation of his fears. And the process of fragmentation and proliferation seemed sure to continue. In America, within Madison's lifetime, religions were already beginning to multiply like amoebae in a petri dish. So then, how could religion provide a common bond holding the community together?

And yet, as we have seen, it is not quite correct to say that Madison aimed to disestablish religion. True, he insisted on *eccelesiastical* disestablishment. There would be no official *church*. But there would in an important sense be a common *religion* — and indeed a governmentally established religion.

And what would that religion be? Christianity? Not quite. It is true that most Virginians of his time were Christians, and that Madison's own arguments assumed as much. Even so, it was not exactly Christianity that Madison strove to establish by law. Rather, and unsurprisingly, he moved to establish ... *his own* religion. Namely, the Gospel of Conscience. That was the religious tenet that was legally established in article 16, and in the "Virginia Statute for Religious Freedom" (and that would have been explicitly and legally protected in the Constitution itself if Madison's own proposal had been adopted).[209]

As John Noonan aptly put the point, with the passage of Jefferson's "Virginia Statute for Religious Freedom," "Conscience, not church, became by law established."[210] Indeed, the distinction was not even as sharp as it may seem because, as has been argued elsewhere, in Protestant thought conscience had in an important sense already *become* the church—a sort of "inner church." Thus, whereas in the medieval and early modern thought of Thomas More's era the institutional church was deemed to be a necessary mediator between God and human beings—through the priests and the sacraments that we considered in the chapter on Thomas More—Protestant thought had transferred these essential functions to the individual conscience.[211] John Witte explains that in Protestant thinking, "[e]ach individual stands directly before God, seeks God's gracious forgiveness of sin, and conducts life in accordance with the Bible and Christian conscience."[212] So we might almost say that Madison not only did not disestablish *religion*; he did not even disestablish *the church*. Rather, he acted to establish, in and by law, not the outward institutional trappings of the church but rather the real church—namely, the conscience.

But insisting on the terminology of "church" would be provocative, and unnecessary. The important point is that for Madison, conscience was a religious faculty with a religious function. And it was that religion—the religion of conscience—that would be established by law, and would thereby serve to hold the state and later the nation together.

So Christianity might divide into dozens and then scores and then hundreds of different sects and denominations. These various sects and denominations might teach incompatible doctrines, so that on one level it would seem that, logically, many (and perhaps all) of their teachings must be in error. And indeed, many of the sects and denominations themselves would insist on the point: all of their rivals *were* in error.[213] And yet within the encompassing religion of conscience, with its capacity to consecrate error, all of the different sects and denominations were also doing God's will and living as God wanted them to live—so long, that is, as their practitioners were sincere in their convictions. Much in the way that Franciscans and Dominicans and Jesuits were sometimes rivalrous groups united under the broad canopy of Catholicism, so Methodists and Episcopalians and Baptists and Catholics—and later Mormons and Adventists, and possibly Jews and Muslims, and maybe even secular humanists?—were all rival subfaiths, sometimes in bitter contention with each other, and yet joined together and validated under the common cover of the religion of conscience.

With respect to church and state, we think of Thomas More and James Madison as diametrically opposed figures: More was a fierce proponent of an established church, while Madison was fervently opposed to that institution. More, as we saw in the last chapter, lived in a world that was passing out of existence; Madison lived in and helped to build the world that was emerging out of that lost world. And yet, in another sense, the two men may be seen not so much as antagonists but rather as proponents of a common political conviction. Of two common convictions, really. Most obviously, both men were devoutly committed to the sanctity of conscience. Less obviously (because of Madison's commitment to *institutional* disestablishment), both men accepted that a legally established *religion* was a core part of what held a society together.

They disagreed, to be sure, about what that religion should be. For More, it was institutional Catholicism; for Madison it was the Gospel of Conscience. This was no small divide. Madison took what for More was a sort of peripheral corollary of the Christian faith and made it the centerpiece of his credo. For More, it was Christianity that consecrated conscience. For Madison, it was conscience that consecrated Christianity—and that consecrated other sincerely held faiths as well.

In making conscience the central article of his faith, was Madison also transforming the meaning of conscience? Perhaps. Both More and Madison could affirm: "I must do what (I believe) God wants me to do." But the emphasis is subtly shifting, from an accent on "God" to an accent on the "I." "I must do what (I believe) *God* wants me to do" is becoming "*I* must do what *I believe* (God wants me to do)."

Might someone complete the transformation by just lopping off the final clause—so that conscience means something like "I must do as I believe"? Get rid of the "God," in other words, and save only the "I believe"?

Madison himself did not go that far. Probably he would have opposed any such alteration. He was, after all, a logical man: what would be the sense or authority of conscience, he would likely have objected, if it is detached from God?

But if Madison did not make this change, his successors would. As we shall see.

The Gospel of Conscience: Religion for a Pluralistic World?

As a candidate for state-established religion, Madison's religion of conscience was better adapted than More's Catholicism to the conditions of eighteenth-century America—and nineteenth-century America, and twentieth-century America. There was by Madison's time no realistic possibility of holding Americans together within a single denomination under an officially established church. The beauty of Madison's religion was that it could countenance a whole host of disparate and clashing faiths, and yet unite them under a common encompassing uber-faith. *E pluribus unum.* Each faith could regard itself as true and the others as false, and, paradoxically but powerfully, the overarching religion of conscience could pronounce all of them approved and justified in these beliefs. We have already seen how the religion of conscience was perfectly suited to a reflectively detached person like Madison; it was also well suited to a pluralistic country like America.

Well suited—but also vulnerable. We might close this chapter by quickly noticing three points of vulnerability.

First, we have already noted the conundrums to which the religion of conscience would inevitably give rise. One church teaches that a man must marry more than one wife. Another church teaches that it is a grave sin to marry more than one wife. A dominant faction in Congress agrees with this second church and also believes that God will not bestow His favor upon a nation that permits such abominations. The religion of conscience indicates that each of these groups must do as it sincerely believes that God ordains—indeed, that *God wants* each of the groups to do as it believes He ordains. How to resolve such conflicts? The community does not want to place itself in opposition to God, but how is that lamentable condition to be avoided?

Second, the religion of conscience both does and doesn't tend to distance religion—and the community, and life—from commitments to truth. On the one hand, the religion teaches that you must live in accordance with what you sincerely believe, and to say that you sincerely believe a thing is surely to say that you believe that thing to be true. That is just what it means to believe. Would it make sense to say, "I sincerely believe X, although I take no position on whether X is *true*"? But, on the other hand, the religion of conscience implies that for the existentially crucial purposes of this life and the next, it doesn't really matter much whether what you believe actually *is* true, so long as *you believe* it is true. Just as Thomas More seems to have thought that his family was permitted to take the oath so long as they did not understand its profound errors, you will be fine in holding to your present beliefs, even if they are in mistaken, so long as you don't understand that they are mistaken.

Surely this instruction might induce a kind of complacency with respect to truth—even a deliberately cultivated and insulated complacency. A complacency that would not exist if you thought that your salvation depended not merely on sincerity but on actually getting the theology right. If what matters is sincerity, not truth, why risk compromising your sincerity by reflecting or investigating, and perhaps thereby digging up complications and stirring up doubts? Better just to leave well enough alone: that is the safe course. Ignorance is bliss—as it was for Thomas More's family. As long as they didn't understand the errors of the oath, they could safely take it. As long as you don't know what the truth is (and how could you know, seriously?), you can't be guilty of acting against it.

And yet a faith that induces a complacency toward truth is likely vulnerable over the long run. Isn't it? Isn't there something self-defeating in the stance that says, "I sincerely believe *X*—and I don't want to hear about anything that might contradict my belief"? Can such a stance even constitute genuine sincerity of the kind that Madison commends in article 16 and in the "Memorial and Remonstrance"? Does the Gospel of Conscience—the view that makes conscience rather than theological truth the central consecrating tenet of its creed—have the effect of eroding the very possibility of genuine conscience?

But, third, despite its theological minimalism, Madison's religion of conscience does depend on the truth of one theological proposition—namely, the existence of God. The imperative of conscience was inextricably grounded in our "duties to our Creator," and the power of conscience to consecrate error (which was precisely the power that made the religion of conscience so suitable to a pluralistic community like America) rested on the premise that a benevolent God surely would not condemn—rather, He would lovingly accept—his children who sincerely worshiped Him in the ways they thought right, even if they happened to be mistaken. Take away God, though, and the whole edifice would seem to collapse. Error now is simply error.

This may not have seemed like an urgent danger to Madison. The overwhelming weight of thinking and of eminent thinkers over the previous centuries had taught that there is a God. Despite their differences, his Anglican parents and wife, his Presbyterian mentors Robertson and Witherspoon, his Baptist political allies, his rationalist friend Jefferson, and his Masonic brothers all maintained the same thing: the world is the product of a supreme and benevolent Creator. A writer taking the name of "Elihu" observed during the debate on the Constitution that "[i]t is almost the only thing that all universally are agreed in; everybody believes there is a God; not a man of common sense in the United States denies or disbelieves it."[214] Darwin and Feuerbach and the Higher Criticism were all waiting till the next century to make their disruptive appearances.

True, there were a handful of atheists in Europe, like Diderot and probably Hume, and possibly even an atheist or two in America—Joel

Barlow, for instance.[215] Even so, atheism was an exotic and marginal opinion that hardly seemed threatening.[216] Observing that "the infinity of time and space forces itself on our conception," the elderly Madison explained in an 1825 letter to a friend that "the mind . . . finds more facility in assenting to the self-existence of an invisible cause possessing infinite power, wisdom and goodness, than to the self-existence of the universe."[217]

A century later the situation would be different. Two centuries later it would be different still. By then it would be belief in the Christian or Western or biblical God that would be closer to seeming exotic and marginal, at least among the Enlightened—the philosophers and scientists and academicians.[218]

And once confidence in a superintending Providence and in our duties to the Creator waned, what would become of the Gospel of Conscience? Would a prevailing, nontheistic secularism mean the liberation of conscience? Or its demise? Or perhaps its transformation into something almost the opposite of what it had been for Thomas More and for James Madison?

CHAPTER THREE

Conscience and Compartmentalization

The Disintegration of William Brennan and of America

I

Not that almost anyone would have objected anyway, but the Senate was confronted with a fait accompli. It was February 1957, and the Senate was considering whether to confirm as a Supreme Court justice President Dwight D. Eisenhower's nominee—a diminutive, unpretentious, until just recently relatively unknown New Jersey judge named William J. Brennan Jr. (The "Jr." will turn out to be significant.) But in fact Brennan had already been serving as a justice, for months, and how likely was it that he would be turned out of office at this point? Brennan had been hastily placed on the Court the previous year, while Congress was in recess, because he was—and yet in a limited but crucial sense was willing *not to be*—a Roman Catholic.

Or at least his Catholicism, together with his commitment to set aside or bracket that Catholicism *while acting as a judge,*[1] had been a prerequisite for his hurried appointment. Had Brennan not been a Catholic, Eisenhower would not have nominated him. Had he not been willing to suspend his Catholicism for official purposes, he probably would not have been selected or confirmed.

Brennan ascended to the Court, we might say, because he was a fragmented man—a willingly, willfully fragmented man. And his personal fragmentation portended a similar fragmentation for his fellow citizens. And for the nation that over the next three-and-a-half decades he would help to shape.

An Almost Accidental Appointment

It had happened in this way.[2] In September 1956, a vacancy on the Court had suddenly opened up when Justice Sherman Minton announced his retirement, effective October 15. Eisenhower was in the midst of a reelection campaign, and although he would go on in November to defeat Adlai Stevenson by a hefty margin, two months earlier victory had seemed far from certain. How would voters feel about Eisenhower's precarious health? He had after all recently suffered a heart attack, and then had spent a month laid up in the hospital with an intestinal blockage. And a charismatic young Senator named John Kennedy, a Catholic, was campaigning vigorously and effectively for Stevenson in the Northeast.

The inside wisdom was that Eisenhower, a Republican, could demonstrate his statesmanship and enhance his electability by appointing a Democrat and a Catholic to fill Minton's spot. And so the president had instructed his aides to make this happen—and quickly.

But whom to select? There were plenty of Catholics in the country, of course, and plenty of Democrats, but the nominee also needed to be professionally qualified and not too far advanced in age. Candidates known to the president's team who met all of these criteria had been scarce.

And then Attorney General Herbert Brownell had remembered a state court judge with an Irish name—Brennan, it was—whom he had met at a recent Justice Department conference on court reform. Brennan's appearance at the conference had been accidental: his widely respected and better-known boss, Arthur Vanderbilt, chief justice of the New Jersey Supreme Court, had been scheduled to address the conference, but Vanderbilt had fallen ill and so had sent Brennan to deliver his speech. Or at least so Vanderbilt would later claim, although Brennan's own recollection was otherwise.[3] In any case, Brennan had spoken at the conference, and Brownell had been impressed.

In an odd fortuity, it turned out that one of Eisenhower's aides had grown up in Newark and had actually known the young Bill Brennan and his family. Like his locally powerful city councilman father, now deceased, Brennan was a Democrat. And a quick call to Brennan's parish priest confirmed that the judge was indeed a professing Catholic. Perhaps not a particularly pious Catholic—Brennan's sons would later recall their father often dropping them off for Sunday mass on his way to the golf course[4]—but then piety was not what the president was looking for.

True, Brennan did not have the glittery resume that many Supreme Court justices could claim. He had not been a governor, like Earl Warren, or a senator, like Hugo Black, or the chair of an important federal agency, like William Douglas, or even a Rhodes scholar, like John Marshall Harlan. (Or someone with an eminent pedigree and name—like *John Marshall* Harlan, grandson of an eminent justice.) Though he had graduated from Harvard Law School, he had not exactly distinguished himself there. He hadn't made law review, and in response to an inquiry from their mutual teacher Justice Felix Frankfurter, Paul Freund, a star student in the same class and now a Harvard law professor, reported that he had no recollection of Brennan but that he had checked and found that his inconspicuous classmate's grades had been unimpressive.[5] In fact, the practically minded Brennan had not even taken the law school's course in constitutional law.[6]

Still, his career in New Jersey as a successful lawyer and then judge and associate state supreme court justice seemed solid enough. The aforementioned Arthur Vanderbilt, though perhaps disappointed that he himself had been passed over for an honor many thought he deserved in favor of a relative anonymity, nonetheless gave Brennan a thumbs up.

And thus, improbably, on a Friday evening in late September, Brennan received a surprise call informing him that the president would like to meet with him the next day. Without a clue as to the purpose of this meeting (or so he pretended),[7] Brennan caught a red-eye train and arrived at Union Station early on Saturday morning. There he was

met by Brownell, who escorted him to Eisenhower, who chatted with
the candidate for twenty minutes—no legal topics were discussed—
and pronounced himself satisfied. The announcement was hurriedly
made the same day; by the time Brennan returned home that evening,
his house was already the hectic scene of inquisitive reporters. It was
still September—more than a month before the election. Using his authority to make recess appointments, the president immediately named
Brennan to the Court, to begin serving the same day that Minton's retirement became effective.

But if Brennan's Catholicism had been a prerequisite for the appointment, it was also a cause for concern with some Americans—and
in particular for a group calling itself the National Liberal League. The
fear, ostensibly anyway, was that a Catholic justice would be basically
just a minion of the pope. Several Catholics had already served on the
Court, actually, one of them (Roger Taney) as chief justice, but the
country's periodic waves of anti-Catholic suspicion had recently been
stirred up by Paul Blanshard's bestselling *American Freedom and
Catholic Power*. Blanshard's attack on Catholicism as a threat to democracy had been endorsed by luminaries such as John Dewey, Al-
bert Einstein, and Bertrand Russell.[8]

When they met in February to ratify the appointment, the Senators considered how to address this concern. Their initial thought was
that it would be inappropriate to make an issue of the nominee's religion, and Brennan was led to expect that the subject would not come
up. But as critical letters poured in, a different approach was considered: perhaps it would be better to let Brennan clear the air and allay
suspicions.

In the hearings before the Judiciary Committee, the question was
posed by Senator Joseph O'Mahoney of Wyoming, himself a Catholic.
"You are bound by your religion to follow the pronouncements of the
Pope on all matters of faith and morals," the Senator observed to Brennan. Did this obligation pose a potential conflict? Senator Estes Ke-
fauver of Tennessee objected that the justice's religion was his own
business; other committee members agreed.[9] But Brennan answered
the question anyway. He reassured the senator, and the nation, that he
had taken the oath of office without reservation, and that "there isn't

any obligation of our faith superior to that [oath]." Just to make sure his position was clear, the justice went on to emphasize:

> And my answer to the question is categorically that in everything I have ever done, in every office I have held in my life and that I shall ever do in the future, what shall control me is the oath that I took to support the Constitution and laws of the United States and so act upon the cases that come before me for decision that it is that oath and that alone which governs.[10]

Four centuries earlier, an eminent Catholic jurist, Thomas More, had resigned from the office of lord chancellor and had refused to take a mandatory oath, suffering execution as a consequence, out of *faithfulness* to his church. Now the situation was flipped: William Brennan emphasized his fidelity to the judicial oath as a way of demonstrating his *independence* from his church, and thus his suitability for high office. Both figures presented themselves as men of integrity and conscience. But More's conscience had impelled him to give his highest loyalty to God—he was, as he said, the king's loyal servant but God's first—and hence to the church, and as a result he could not take the oath. Brennan's conscience, conversely, bound him to the oath, and to the office; consequently, in the case of any conflict, he would not follow the church.

Although Catholics in the mold of More might (and did) find Brennan's stance troublesome,[11] the senators were satisfied. After all, they had not wanted to bring up the subject of religion at all. And they went on to approve Brennan for the Court, overwhelmingly, with only a fading Joseph McCarthy in opposition. (McCarthy, who took umbrage at a comment some years earlier in which Brennan had described the senator's anticommunism campaign as a "witch hunt," would die just three months later.)[12]

And so it turned out that Brennan's suspect Catholicism, which necessitated his solemn declaration that his religion would not influence his judicial performance, was scarcely a bump on his path to confirmation. Or on his path, following confirmation, to becoming one of the longest serving and most influential justices in history—

controversial, and yet loved and admired by both jurisprudential friends and foes for his personal warmth and unassuming modesty.[13] And arguably as quietly powerful a force as any of his contemporaries in any branch of government in shaping the America that would emerge over the last decades of the twentieth century.[14] Legal historian Bernard Schwartz asserts that "[i]f we look at justices in terms of their role in the decision process, William J. Brennan Jr. was actually the most influential associate justice in Supreme Court history." He "play[ed] a crucial role in the Court that transformed America."[15]

Although Brennan's constitutional jurisprudence has had its vigorous critics, in general his contribution to that America has been widely admired as well. Which is hardly surprising. In retrospect, and notwithstanding the inevitable ups and downs, the century's last four decades seem to have been a time of growing prosperity accompanied by notable gains in civil rights and in respect for the dignity of the person. And William Brennan is closely associated with these developments. Indeed, the "essential dignity of man," as he put it, was for him the central unifying and motivating ideal throughout his career on a transformative Court.[16]

By contrast, in the decades since Brennan's retirement in 1990, the nation has become increasingly and alarmingly polarized. Political scientists report that "[d]islike, even at times hatred, of the opposing party and its leaders reflects a growing divide between Democrats and Republicans over a wide range of economic and social issues. But it also reflects a growing divide over race, religion and values—a chasm that could become dangerous as partisans come to see each other not just as political adversaries, but as enemies who want to harm the nation."[17] Lee Drutman observes that the "level of hatred—which political scientists call 'negative partisanship'—has reached levels that are not just bad for democracy, but are potentially destructive." It was not always this way, Drutman explains: four decades ago (in the midst of Brennan's tenure on the Court), opposing parties maintained relatively congenial relations. Since that time, however, politics has experienced an "escalating cycle of dislike and distrust." Such mutual hatred is "a prelude to democratic collapse."[18]

Talk of potential civil war, insurrection, or secession, once confined to a minuscule lunatic fringe, has become increasingly familiar.[19]

Stridently accusatory rhetoric pervades public discourse on all sides of the political aisle. British journalist and long-time observer of America Nick Bryant notes that "[o]ften it feels as if the only thing that unites the nation is mutual loathing. America seems to be engaged in a forever war with itself."[20] And the polarization and rhetoric often carry over into the appointment and confirmation of justices: the bitterly acrimonious conflicts surrounding the failed nomination of Robert Bork and, a generation later, the trench warfare and straight party-line appointment of Justice Brett Kavanaugh are conspicuous instances. The very notion of a president appointing a candidate of the opposition party after a twenty-minute chat and with virtually unanimous bipartisan support seems today like a quixotic story out of some Camelotish romance.

In these circumstances, many might wish for such days, and for someone with the personal charm and quiet gravitas of a William Brennan—or, if only it were possible, for Brennan himself—to restore a measure of stability and civility to our public discourse.

And yet it will turn out upon reflection that the frightening polarization and fragmentation on display today are at least in part a legacy of the jurisprudence advanced and exemplified by William J. Brennan Jr.—not so much of particular decisions he made, exactly, as of the overall reconception of the American Republic reflected and forcibly implemented in those decisions. That reconception has been accompanied by a parallel and disintegrating revision of the meaning of conscience, and indeed of the person, or the self.

And those revisions—and the fragmentation they would come to entail—were themselves already subtly foreshadowed in the scarcely noticed but quietly portentous declaration of religious independence that Brennan made before the Senate Judiciary Committee. As we will see in this chapter.

An Obvious and Necessary Compartmentalization?

Like many a public official before and after him, Brennan resolved to deal with questions about the relation of his religion to his public duties by compartmentalizing. Religion would be for his private or personal life, and it would be confined to that domain—sealed off from his public office and duties. So he declared to the Senate. As he later explained, "I had settled in my mind that I had an obligation under the Constitution which *could not be influenced by any of my religious principles.* As a Roman Catholic I might do *as a private citizen* what a Roman Catholic does, and that is one thing, but to the extent that that conflicts with what I think the Constitution means or requires, then my religious beliefs have to give way."[21]

This was a tactically convenient position for Brennan to take, of course—it neatly deflected a potential objection to his confirmation—but it also must have seemed like the obviously correct position anyway. He had in effect been practicing such compartmentalization throughout his life. Thus, he had attended public high school, and later the University of Pennsylvania and the Wharton School, and then Harvard Law School—all non-Catholic environments. In college, he had hung out at the Delta Tau Delta fraternity, not at the Newman Center.[22] Later, he became a successful lawyer at a prominent New Jersey law firm of Waspish character—with the position came membership in an exclusive country club and summer vacations in Cape Cod—and then a labor lawyer for the government during World War II.[23] In all of these roles, Brennan would naturally have needed to regard his Catholicism as something essentially extraneous to his various associations and activities.

Which was likely easy enough for him to do, since he had never been especially devout in any case. Through his growing-up years, although his mother required attendance at mass, young Bill regarded the exercise as "an agony we went through every Sunday whether you liked it or not."[24] As an adult his church attendance had been sporadic (although he seems to have become somewhat more regular after his appointment to the high court).[25]

But compartmentalizing his religion into a "private" sphere was not only convenient for Brennan himself: it surely seemed to him to be the right and necessary strategy for America generally. And understandably so. By the 1940s and 50s, after all, a country that had once been overwhelmingly Protestant now included large populations of Catholics; Jews had become an important minority; and the future would bring growing numbers of Mormons and Muslims, even Hindus, Buddhists, and Sikhs. Not to mention people with no religious beliefs or commitments at all—both the professing and the *de facto* atheists and agnostics. Nonbelievers may have been scarce in James Madison's day—almost invisible[26]—but in Brennan's time they were common enough and conspicuous enough. In his judicial opinions, Brennan would emphasize this expansive religious diversity.[27]

So then, how were all of these diverse believers and nonbelievers supposed to get along in mutually respectful fashion? Brennan instinctively hit upon the answer that so many others have given in one form or another, an answer that by now seems foreordained. Namely, compartmentalization. But compartmentalization of a particular kind, separating things that had once seemed, and by their intrinsic nature might seem to be, inseparable. More specifically, everybody's religion should be treated with respect so long as it is confined to the private domain, but it should not enter into anyone's more public interactions. As history amply demonstrates, "religion" is *not* an inherently private matter—quite the contrary, actually—but Brennan resolved to treat it as such.

Nor was he either original or alone in this resolve. Al Smith, a Catholic and the unsuccessful Democratic candidate for president back in 1928, had taken a similar position; so would John Kennedy, who three years after Brennan's confirmation would successfully run for the office.[28] The senators who thought it was inappropriate even to ask Brennan about his religion demonstrated that they already took some such compartmentalization pretty much for granted. By now the position is so familiar that it has become almost axiomatic, and normative—for Catholics and non-Catholics alike. Perhaps most conspicuously, it is a common (but not necessary) premise upon which hosts of pro-choice politicians have been able to claim—to the public and, presumably, to themselves—to be serious Catholics while taking political positions directly at odds with the teachings of their church: the Governors Cuomo, Nancy Pelosi, and Joe Biden are recent and prominent instances.[29] Supreme Court nominees—Catholic or not—routinely invoke a similar compartmentalization in explaining why their religion or other philosophical or political beliefs are not a disqualification.

Catholic officials in particular have been motivated to embrace this compartmentalization: that is because, much like Jews in the modern world, they have been forced as adherents of a minority and suspect faith—the faith that Paul Blanshard among many others had attacked as un-American—to struggle with the challenge of achieving acceptance and respect in a religiously alien culture.[30] But it is not just Catholics: in modern America and many other advanced nations, conditions of pluralism ensure that everyone's faith (or lack thereof, or opposition thereto) will be a minority position. Compartmentalization may thus be attractive to adherents of any faith, creed, or philosophy. And so the basic proposition is by now almost a truism in American public life[31] and in other liberal democracies as well. *Of course* a public official should not allow his or her religious beliefs—and perhaps other philosophical or personal beliefs—to influence the performance of the office. Peter Berger reports that

> [d]uring the time when Tony Blair was prime minister of the United Kingdom, one of his spokesmen was asked why Blair, who was known to be a very religious person, never spoke about religion in public. The spokesman gave a marvelous reply: "We don't do God here!" This pronouncement describes the behavior of most politicians in Western and Central Europe today.[32]

The same pressing question that underlies this intuitive compartmentalization—how can a people live together peacefully and respectfully under conditions of religious and philosophical and cultural diversity?—has been a central topic of reflection and debate among modern political philosophers and legal theorists, and the most influential answers adopt basically the same compartmentalization strategy embraced by Brennan and Kennedy and Blair and so many others. The hugely influential theorizing of John Rawls and his numerous philosophical fellow travelers becomes complex and sophisticated—subject to all manner of refinements and "provisos"—but the central idea is that in their public deliberations and decision-making, officials and even citizens should try to bracket their "comprehensive doctrines" (of which religion is surely the quintessential instance) and should instead debate and decide on the basis of a shared or "overlapping consensus" of considerations described as "public reason."[33]

For William Brennan—and for Al Smith before him and John Kennedy shortly after him—a compartmentalization in which religion is relegated to the private realm seems to have come naturally, without tension or serious reflection. For these men, their religious affiliation may have been sincere enough, and it may have figured in their sense of who they were,[34] but none of them gave indications of making religious doctrine, worship, or practice a vital object of attention or reflection in a way that might alert them to the possible conflicts that someone like Thomas More had experienced so acutely.

Thus, when Al Smith ran for president as the Democratic candidate in 1928, he seemed genuinely baffled when a long article in the *Atlantic Monthly*, quoting numerous statements from popes and other Catholic authorities, argued that Smith's Catholic faith imposed obligations that might conflict with his duties to the nation. Smith commented ingenuously, "I never heard of these bulls and encyclicals and books."[35] Asked by a journalist what he thought about a particular papal encyclical, Smith replied, "What the hell is an encyclical?"[36]

Brennan's leading biographers likewise observe that given his "ignorance of Catholic theology,"[37] he was like John Kennedy: both men "found it necessary to pledge to compartmentalize their private faith, when it was not likely to guide them anyway."[38] When shortly after his confirmation he was asked to give a talk to the St. Thomas More Society in Washington, Brennan began by duly noting that More had been revered for his integrity and for his "towering intellect, devotion to learning, and steadfast pursuit of justice," and also that More "chose God, and with Him, death, when forced to choose between conscience and life." These preliminary acknowledgments out of the way, Brennan proceeded to devote his talk to what evidently interested him most—More's success as lord chancellor in expediting litigation and reducing judicial backlog.[39]

And indeed, one wonders how many politicians have solemnly pledged not to let their religion influence their public performance when the truth is that religious faith and doctrine have little influence over their lives at all in any domain, public or private.

For more earnest believers, though, such compartmentalization may be more difficult, or impossible. Axiomatic though the compartmentalization position has become, it also harbors potential problems. Problems of fragmentation—first of the person, and then of the political and social order.

II

Disintegrating the Person

Let us start by noticing how compartmentalization creates a prospect of fragmentation on the individual level — fragmentation that may affect the individual on both the public and private sides of life.

Public Embarrassments

As a *person*, we say, or as a private individual, a judge or legislator or president is free to be a Catholic — or a Muslim, or a Socialist, or a disciple of Ayn Rand, or some combination thereof. But as a *public official*, he or she should bracket these personal convictions and act on the basis of . . . what?

The law? Well, yes, of course, but that answer hardly helps with, say, a legislator who is tasked with *making* the laws. The public interest? Yes again, but of course the very nature of politics and government is to disagree about what the public interest is or requires. Most people might naturally reflect on or debate what the law should be, or what the public interest is, by consulting their fundamental convictions about what is true and good and just — convictions that for the devout are likely to be grounded in their religious beliefs. So then if a public official is not supposed to be influenced by those beliefs, what *is* she supposed to refer to in carrying out her public responsibilities? What principles or criteria *should* guide the compartmentalizing official in her public duties?

Think of it this way: suppose you are, say, a faithful Catholic, and, unlike William Brennan, you have diligently attended mass and studied the church's teachings and have earnestly tried to live your life in accordance with those teachings. When questions have arisen or decisions have needed to be made — decisions about family or vocation or morals or sex — you have conscientiously tried to act as church teachings direct. Now, though, you find yourself in some important public office, and you have been made to understand that although you are free to live a Catholic life "as a private citizen," as Brennan put it, your religion should not influence your public decision-making. It is your first week on the job, and an important, fraught decision looms. How, or in accordance with what criteria, are you supposed to make that decision?

It is as if you had been speaking English your whole life, and then you take on a new job and your supervisor tells you, "By the way, in this workplace English isn't spoken. Don't speak any English here." So then, how are you supposed to talk? What are you supposed to say? If English is something that you and maybe some family and close friends have spoken only at home or in rarified contexts—in select Sunday gatherings, maybe—your supervisor's instruction should pose no problem. You are already comfortable enough—*more* comfortable, probably—doing without English. But if English is the medium in which you think and communicate, then what are you supposed to do?

Sometimes there might be an obvious and satisfactory answer to this question. In our analogy, maybe your job has placed you in, say, a Spanish consulate or classroom or football team, and then it may be clear enough that you need to speak Spanish, not English. (If you *can* speak Spanish, that is; if you can't, you had better not take the job.) Approaching more closely to our main question, maybe you find yourself in a position that brings with it its own governing principles or criteria. If you became employed as an accountant, for example, it would make sense for your boss to tell you, "Although you may be a Catholic (or a Libertarian, or a Socialist), and that's perfectly okay, when performing *this* job that won't be relevant: just apply the rules of accounting." Or maybe you have been hired as a baseball umpire. You should accordingly discharge your umpireal duties in accordance with the rules of baseball. Just call balls and strikes (as recent judicial nominees like to say).[40]

Indeed, even if you have convictions that conflict with some of the understood rules of the job—you believe that batters really ought to get five strikes, maybe, or that the designated hitter rule is a travesty and the betrayal of a sacred tradition—it would still be at least intelligible to say that when performing your job as an umpire you should bracket those private convictions and operate under the official rules. This instruction might conceivably provoke qualms of conscience—how can you in good faith enforce an abomination like the three strikes rule?—but, still, you would know what is expected of you. If the conflicts between your convictions and the rules and requirements of the job are severe enough, you should probably just decline or resign from the job (as Thomas More did).

Unfortunately, these observations do not answer our question regarding how you should act in a public office such as president, or legislator, or Supreme Court justice. That is because those offices do *not* come with determinate criteria or rules of decision dictating how officials should act. Or rather there are some rules, or guidelines, but they leave much to the discretion of particular officials. These offices are not the kind of "ministerial" jobs, as lawyers say, in which functionaries merely follow definite rules or carry out specific orders. Rather, these offices confer authority or discretion or judgment on the people who hold them: that is the essence of such jobs.

This is most obviously true, perhaps, of legislators and presidents. No rule can tell these officials whether to raise or lower taxes, whether to permit or shut down immigration on the Southern border, whether to declare war or instead engage in diplomatic negotiations. With judges it is sometimes pretended otherwise: the judge simply "follows the law" (or "calls balls and strikes"). But if this description was ever plausible, it is utterly implausible today, especially for the Supreme Court, especially on fiercely disputed constitutional questions. As Alexander Bickel observed, if the job of a Supreme Court justice were like that, having nine justices on salary would be a stark case of featherbedding.[41] Justice Brennan in particular emphatically disavowed the idea that constitutional decisions can be dictated by some formula or method such as merely finding and mechanically following the "original meaning."

So then, if there are no rules that dictate how to make the looming decision, and if you are not supposed to rely on convictions that have guided you in all of the important and sometimes unimportant matters of your own life, then how or on what criteria *are* you supposed to act?

The Rawlsian "public reason" project speaks to this difficulty. Or maybe it speaks past and around the difficulty. As noted, broadly speaking and subject to a variety of refinements and qualifications, public reason instructs officials and even citizens that when making political decisions they should not rely on "comprehensive doctrines" such as their religious convictions. In this respect, though more complex or sophisticated, Rawlsian public reason is very much in the spirit of the compartmentalization strategy employed by Justice Brennan and so many others. But if public reason purports to say how or on what criteria public decisions should *not* be made, it cannot offer determinative criteria dictating how those decisions *should* be made: it cannot and does not pretend to provide some sort of formula or algorithm that generates answers to particular political questions. (And if it did so provide, judgment-wielding public officials like legislators would seemingly become obsolete: it would be enough to retain some detached CIC—calculator in chief—who would simply feed problems into the "public reason" machine and then announce the answers.)

Even if and after "comprehensive doctrines" are screened out, in short, judgment or discretion are still required. And so, once again, as a judgment-wielding public official, how are you supposed to make such judgments if you are forbidden to rely on the normative criteria that you believe in and that otherwise guide you in your life?[42]

Private Predicaments

If the compartmentalization advocated in different versions by Brennan, Rawls, and many others creates difficulties on the public side—or for officials who must make public decisions and judgments without relying on the normative criteria that they most fully embrace and live by—it can create problems on the private side as well.

Here the difficulties are more subtle: that is because it seems that compartmentalization is more permissive in the private sphere, allowing people to act on whatever criteria or beliefs they take to be true and pertinent. If you are a Catholic, like Brennan or Kennedy, you are free in the private domain to act on your full set of Catholic beliefs. Same for socialists, and Randian libertarians, and proponents of other faiths or philosophies.

Except that . . . the compartmentalization permits you to act on these beliefs on a condition—namely, on the understanding that these beliefs must be confined in their operations to the private domain. The truths affirmed by such beliefs are, in a sense, private or personal truths. But that very condition subtly undermines the quality of truth-fulness in those beliefs, even for the person acting in private.

If a proposition is true after all, then it is . . . true. Despite modern relativizing tendencies to talk about ideas as being "true for me" or "true for you" but not necessarily true in general, these qualifications make an incoherent hash of the very idea of truth. If "2 plus 2 makes 4" or "e=mc²" or "humankind is the product of a long evolutionary process of natural selection" are true propositions, then they are true for me, for you, for everyone, in public or in private. Conversely, if we say that a proposition is *not* true for everyone or in general, then it will seem to follow that the proposition is not really, not quite, *true* at all.

Take again the pointed instance of abortion. If you sincerely be-lieve that abortion is the taking of an innocent human life, and hence is tantamount to murder, then you should believe that proposition to be true whether you are speaking as a private person or in a public role (such as legislator, president, or Supreme Court justice). What would it even mean—what sense would it make?—to say that the proposi-tion "abortion is equivalent to murder" is "true for me" but not true for others? Or "true for me as a *person* but not as an *official*"? It does not necessarily follow, of course, that you must favor a legal prohibi-tion: for all sorts of reasons (respect for women's freedom, difficulty of enforcement, reflection on the famous violinist argument of Judith Jarvis Thomson,[43] or whatever), you might think there should be a legal right to abortion even though abortion is equivalent to murder. What will be more difficult, though, will be to say something like: "As a pri-vate person, I believe the proposition 'abortion is equivalent to mur-der' to be true. But as a public official, I do not accept or act on that proposition; and *therefore* I favor a legal right to abortion."

To be sure, some propositions may be true but limited in their scope; they might thus seem to be true in one place or context but not in another. But this appearance is misleading. If I say "it almost never rains in September," my statement may be true for where I live, in San Diego, but not true for Miami or Manila. But it hardly follows that my statement is true for me but not for people in Manila. The sensible interpretation, rather, is that I am actually asserting that "it almost never rains in September *in San Diego*," and that statement will be true (or false) whether uttered in San Diego, Florida, or the Philippines. Or, if I do *not* mean my statement to be geographically limited in this way, then the statement is not "true for me"; it is simply false—for me and everyone else. Because in some places—Miami or Manila—September sees plenty of rain.

Indeed, even the classic instances of purely subjective statements— statements about "matters of taste"—provide no exception. The statement "strawberries are delicious" might seem to be one that can be true for me but not for you. But a clearer rendering—"strawberries taste good to *[fill in name—e.g. Barry Jones]*"—if true at all, will be true for everyone. If Barry Jones does in fact love the taste of strawberries, then anyone who says otherwise is simply wrong.

In short, forcing yourself to think of some ideas or notions as "true for you," or "true only for personal or private purposes" depends upon conceptual contortions that will likely tend to undermine your confidence in or commitment to these ideas as true—actually *true*—at all. "True" will degrade down into something like "convenient" or "gratifying" or "fulfilling to me personally." In that way, compartmentalization about basic beliefs will affect not only a person's public performance; it will affect, and potentially erode, his or her private beliefs and commitments as well. And indeed, as we will see, there is reason to believe that this sort of erosion of commitments to truth is rampant today.[44]

Are You Really You?

But let us set these difficulties aside for the moment. Let us suppose that some species of public reason *can* enable you to make official decisions without appealing to your religious or other personal convictions, and let us also suppose that some clever thinker has devised a coherent way of explaining how a belief can be true for you, or true in the private domain, but not true for others or in the public domain. Now a different difficulty arises.

Suppose again that you are a public official, and that in performing your office you dutifully bracket the convictions that guide you in your personal life; you instead make decisions based on some prescribed set of approved public criteria. Criteria that, but for the imposed

compartmentalization, are not the main or only criteria you would consult with respect to such decisions. Now we have to ask: is it really *you*
who is making the decisions? Or are you instead just role-playing, as
we say—discharging your duties by acting *as if* you were somebody
else working and living under different rules or normative criteria?

Or we might put the question in this way: what is it that makes
the "private citizen" and the public official—Bill Brennan kneeling or
receiving communion at mass, and the Honorable William J. Brennan
Jr. dressed in robes and sitting at the bench—the same person, or the
same character, at all?

We commonly say in some contexts that a person is "playing a
role" and therefore is "not being herself." The observation can apply
in various settings—going out on a first date, for example, or meeting
your partner's parents for the first time—but take the pure case: an
actor plays Hamlet one evening and Hannibal Lecter a month later.
We understand that Hamlet is not the same character as Hannibal
Lecter—even though each was played by the same actor—and that
neither Hamlet nor Hannibal Lecter is the same character as the actor
himself. We can even imagine the actor defending himself in some
public place against accusations of depravity made by an outraged
viewer who recently watched a Hannibal Lecter film. "That character
you saw in the movie wasn't *me*. I was just playing a role, acting out
a script. Hannibal Lecter and I are two completely different characters.
He *is* a monster—I agree with you there—but if you got to know me,
you'd see that I'm actually a really nice guy. Just ask my mother: she'll
tell you."

But wouldn't a similar description apply to an official who for
public purposes acts and speaks and decides under normative criteria
different from those that she herself most fundamentally believes in
and lives by? Suppose once again that you are a devout Catholic who
gets elected to the legislature, say, and you are again led to understand
that when acting as a legislator your Catholic beliefs should not influence your decisions. You should compartmentalize in the way that
William Brennan and John Kennedy did. So you try diligently to honor
that imposed compartmentalization. Now what is the unifying con-

nection between, on the one hand, the *you* who as a private individual prays the rosary, attends mass, and embraces and tries to live in accordance with Catholic teachings and, on the other hand, the *you* who as a public official ignores those teachings and operates under a different set of normative criteria?

Suppose again, to take the familiar and vivid instance, that the legislature is considering whether to impose a restriction on abortion. As a Catholic, and in accordance with your church's teachings, you believe that abortion is an egregious evil: it constitutes the unwarranted taking of an innocent and precious human life. Nor does the church teach that this is a doctrine limited in its application to some private or personal realm. On the contrary, the church quite explicitly teaches that this doctrine is *not* confined to the private sphere[45]—abortion is no more a matter for purely private judgment than homicide in general is—and *as a faithful Catholic*, you agree. *As a legislator*, nonetheless, you have been led to believe that you are not supposed to be influenced by church teachings in making public decisions. So, following the example of Biden, Pelosi, the Cuomos, . . . William Brennan, you vote against the restriction—publicly, cheerfully, proudly. You earn stellar ratings from Planned Parenthood. But in what sense is the Catholic you who deplores abortion as a moral enormity the same character as the legislative you who without compunction votes to authorize and perhaps even subsidize abortions? Insofar as you carry out your public duties by bracketing your actual convictions and normative criteria and acting on some other criteria, aren't you basically in the same position as the actor who is not being himself but rather is playing a role or acting out a script?

The bottom line is that the kind of compartmentalization endorsed by Brennan and Kennedy and countless others, like any strategy or position that directs people to make decisions while bracketing or suspending their actual normative beliefs or criteria, has the effect of dividing the public person from the private person. Of fragmenting, or disintegrating, the people subject to such restrictions. And indeed, the very terms—"compartmentalization," "fragmentation," "disintegration"—if not exactly synonymous, seem to designate

overlapping concepts.[46] There is the private person, and then there
is the public actor or official, and these seem to be two quite different
characters.

UNIFIED BY CONSCIENCE?

Unless . . .

Unless, that is, there is some unifying feature that somehow holds
the private and public persons together. But this would need to be the
right kind of unifying feature. Thus, we could of course say that there
is a unity in the sense that the private and public characters share a
common physical body and also a common brain or mind. But then
so does the actor who plays Hamlet one day and Hannibal Lecter the
next, and those continuities do not negate the fact that the vacillating
prince and the depraved cannibal are two utterly different characters
and that neither is the same as the actor himself. The problem of fragmentation results from the fact that the private and public characters
are operating under different normative criteria, or under different
normative scripts. So what we would need, it seems, is some overarching normative criterion or authority that would operate for and
on, and would thus serve to unite, the private and public persons.

So, is there such an overarching normative authority?

Maybe there is. And the most promising candidate, it seems, would
be a by now familiar acquaintance. Namely, . . . conscience.

So suppose we could confront nominee William Brennan (as the
reticent Senate Judiciary Committee did not) with the questions we
have just been discussing. "You say, Justice Brennan, that you will follow Catholic teachings in your personal life, but that you will not allow
these teachings to influence your performance as a judge. Instead, in
your judicial role, you will act by other criteria—presumably some kind
of legalish criteria (which we will not ask you to specify at the moment). So then, if you as a private person and as a judge operate under
different criteria—under different scripts, so to speak—is there any
connecting or unifying normative feature that explains how we can
meaningfully say that you are still the same person whether you are

kneeling in church or sitting at the bench?" And we can imagine that Brennan might answer that, yes, of course he is the same person. Because in each domain he follows the dictates of his conscience.

He lives by religious teachings in the personal realm because that is what his conscience directs him to do. And he is guided by different, legal-type criteria when acting as a judge because, again, that is what his conscience (informed by his judicial oath) directs him to do. So there is no risk of different normative criteria slicing him into two different people, or two different characters. There is a common and continuous element uniting the private person and the public official. Conscience.

Although Brennan's emphasis on his obligations under the judicial oath alluded to the controlling authority of his conscience, he was not pushed by the senators to spell out his compartmentalization strategy in this way. The Senate, having acknowledged citizens' expressed concerns by raising the question of conflicting loyalties, was anxious to move on to other matters, and so Brennan was not called upon to articulate his position more clearly, or to defend it. By contrast, John Kennedy, as a candidate for president, *was* pushed, and in response he made explicit this appeal to the overarching supremacy of conscience.

Thus, in a famous speech to a convention of Baptist ministers,[47] Kennedy like Brennan insisted on the priority of his oath of office over any religious duties. Also like Brennan, Kennedy took the position that his obligations to his church did not apply to him as a public official.[48] Pressed in the ensuing question-and-answer session to say what he would do if a conflict between his religious commitments and his public duties should arise, Kennedy stressed that his highest duty was to his conscience. Rather than violate conscience, he said, he would resign the office. And he made it clear that such a contingency would involve a potential conflict with his conscience, not with his church. Thus, when a questioner referred back to "your statement that if you found by some remote possibility a real conflict between your oath of office as President, that you would resign that office if it were in real conflict with *your church*," Kennedy immediately corrected the questioner: "No, I said with *my conscience*."[49]

So perhaps the overarching authority of conscience provides the remedy for the potential fragmentation created by the compartmentalization strategy. Just as for James Madison the establishment of conscience was a central device for holding a religiously pluralistic nation together, so on a more personal level the authority of conscience may be what holds together those individuals who as public officials would otherwise be threatened, by compartmentalization, with personal fragmentation.

And yet difficulties will arise. So this answer to the problem of fragmentation will require closer examination. First, though, we need to notice how the compartmentalization that Brennan (along with Kennedy and many others) adopted for himself became more than merely a personal strategy. How it came to be imposed on the nation as a whole.

III

DISINTEGRATING THE NATION

For William Brennan, as we have noted, the compartmentalization strategy, with its relegation of religion to the private domain, likely seemed attractive and even necessary not only for himself but for the nation as a whole, religiously pluralistic as it had become. And as a Supreme Court justice, he had power to import this compartmentalization into the nation's fundamental law. Which is exactly what he did. As a justice, Brennan read the compartmentalization that he had adopted *for himself* into constitutional law, so that it became normative for *everyone*.

This was a portentous development, even if for someone like Brennan and most of his judicial colleagues it was also a natural and necessary and thus almost unnoticed one. So we need to consider how this development occurred and how it represented a major and now officially imposed reconceptualization of the American republic.

The transformation did not happen all at once, of course, or in one blockbuster judicial decision; it occurred over time, and at different times with different people. As a matter of constitutional law, though, the crucial turning point was in the early 1960s with the school prayer decisions, *Engel v. Vitale*[50] and *Abington School District v. Schempp*,[51] which invalidated the traditional and widespread practice of school-sponsored prayer and Bible reading in the public schools. Although critics of modern religion clause jurisprudence have often singled out the 1947 case of *Everson v. Board of Education*[52] as the seminal—and in the critics' view misguided—decision, in fact the school prayer cases better deserve the description of being pivotal or transformative.[53] And the guiding voice in those cases and thereafter was that of William Brennan.

Thus, although earlier decisions and dissenting opinions in *Everson* had hinted at the prospect, it was in the school prayer decisions—and particularly in the second decision, *Schempp*—that the Court officially decreed that government and governance in America must be confined to the realm of the secular—a decree that amounted to a radical break with the American past. In *Schempp*, the Court articulated the main elements of what became and for more than half-a-century remained the controlling constitutional doctrine. Government must be "neutral" in matters of religion[54]—must maintain a neutrality that is "strict," the Court sometimes says, or even "absolute"[55]—and this neutrality entailed that 1) governments must act only for "secular purpose[s]" and 2) governments must not act in ways that have a primary effect of advancing or inhibiting religion.[56] To these two requirements—the secular purpose and effect requirements—the Court later added a third component—a prohibition against "excessive entanglement" between government and religion. These three elements were codified in a case called *Lemon v. Kurtzman*,[57] thus creating the so-called "*Lemon* test," which remained constitutional doctrine up until the final draft of this book.[58]

Somewhat later, in the mid-1980s, the Court announced a corollary to the *Lemon* test: government is constitutionally forbidden to do or say anything that would send a message *endorsing* religion. This corollary—the so-called "no endorsement" doctrine—was articulated in a concurring opinion by Justice Sandra Day O'Connor in a case called *Lynch v. Donnelly*.[59] But Justice Brennan's dissent in the case suggests that he had assumed that such a prohibition was already entailed by the *Lemon* test itself.

The upshot of these decisions was that in their purposes, actions, and expressions, American governments, state and federal, would henceforth be confined to the realm of the secular. Religion, conversely, would be respected and protected in its designated sphere — namely, the private domain. That at least has been the official constitutional doctrine, although implementation has been notoriously irregular. Justice Brennan's personal compartmentalization thus became that of the nation as a whole, projected now onto the nation's fundamental law.

And Brennan's influence was crucial in this development. Although the majority opinion in the pivotal prayer decision, *Schempp*, was written by Justice Tom Clark, the indispensable opinion in the case was Justice Brennan's lengthy, compendious concurrence. Indeed, if one were to select the leading opposing opinions in the school prayer cases for their care and seriousness, the honors would go on one side to trial judge Bernard Meyer's opinion in the first case, *Engel v. Vitale*,[60] and on the other side to Brennan's concurrence in the second, *Schempp*.

Judge Meyer, a young Democratic appointee who would go on to have a distinguished judicial career in New York, was not a supporter of school prayer. In a case challenging the practice, Meyer initially declared the practice invalid, but then took the case under advisement, carefully studied the issue for six months, and then wrote a careful, exhaustive opinion explaining why his initial and preferred conclusion — namely, that school prayer is unconstitutional — simply could not be squared with the relevant history, precedent, or tradition.[61]

Although on appeal the Supreme Court reached the opposite conclusion, looked at alongside Meyer's careful and scholarly opinion, the majority opinion in *Engel* by Justice Hugo Black seems a paltry production. Black's conclusory opinion cited not a single precedent, considered the history in only the most simplified and generalized terms, and addressed none of the complexities or counterarguments. Justice Douglas, although enthusiastically agreeing with Black's conclusion, complained in a private note to Black that "I still do not see how most of the opinion is relevant to the problem."[62] Constitutional scholar Paul Kauper described Black's opinion as "short and bland and noteworthy as much for what it did not say as for what it did say."[63]

A year later, in the second case, Justice Tom Clark's majority opinion in *Schempp* was considerably longer — but almost as unimpressive.

Clark mostly limited himself to quoting recent opinions—primarily those of the dissenters in *Everson*.[64] *Why* must government be confined to the secular domain? Because, Clark responded, we the justices (or at least some of us) have said so.

Thus, the only opinion in the cases that seriously engaged the contrary arguments made by Meyer and others was Brennan's concurrence in *Schempp*. Like Meyer, Brennan carefully and systematically analyzed all of the relevant precedents and examined the various complications. He also addressed founding era history—the kind of history we considered in the previous chapter—and indeed purported to base his conclusion on historical understandings of religious freedom and the establishment clause. The rulings invalidating school prayer, he insisted, "accord[ ] with history and faithfully reflect[ ] the understanding of the Founding Fathers."[65] But in behalf of this almost Orwellian claim, Brennan made a sharp distinction—one that would become central not only to his own thinking but to later debates about "original meaning"—between the general principles and purposes adopted by the founders and their specific answers to particular concrete questions.[66] Modern constitutional law should be shaped by the former, Brennan argued, not the latter—in part because the nation had changed dramatically, and had increased in its religious diversity, since the founding period. Under contemporary conditions, Brennan argued, a school-sponsored prayer violates the framers' principles and purposes even if the framers would have drawn the opposite conclusion in their own time.

To be sure, this emphasis on principles and purposes over specific understandings was neither a novel position[67] nor an uncontroversial one.[68] But it represented the best and perhaps the only way of reaching the conclusions that Brennnan and the Court preferred while attempting to maintain the appearance of continuity with the founders.

While contributing a substantial concurring opinion, Brennan also declared that he fully joined in everything in Clark's majority opinion. And, like the majority, he stressed that government must maintain "strict neutrality" in matters of religion.[69] Even so, the relation between Brennan's concurrence and the majority opinion was complicated. Instead of the two-part "secular purpose and effect" doctrine announced by the majority, Brennan proposed an alternative three-part doctrine.[70]

Under his proposal, school prayer was unconstitutional because it was, he thought, an essentially religious activity. But government would not necessarily be required to refrain from all interactions with religion, and Brennan's opinion concluded with a detailed catalogue of matters in which some such involvement might be permissible.[71]

And yet Brennan's comprehensive opinion turned out to be important not for its specific prescriptions but rather because it provided the intellectual support for the doctrinal change wrought by the Court. Thus, it was the majority's "secular neutrality" position and its "secular purpose and effect" requirements—not Brennan's own three-part test—that were destined to prevail in constitutional doctrine. And Brennan himself enthusiastically acquiesced in this development; indeed, he became perhaps the most aggressive champion of the *Lemon* doctrine.

So, for instance, Brennan opined in his *Schempp* concurrence that legislative prayer was different from school prayer; though religious in nature, legislative prayer did not seem to transgress any of his three proposed prohibitions, and thus might well be constitutionally permissible.[72] But when the issue was squarely presented two decades later, Brennan did not repeat this analysis or stand by his previous conclusion. Rather, confessing that "after much reflection, I have come to the conclusion that I was wrong,"[73] he invoked the *Lemon* test with its secular purpose and effect requirements to argue strenuously that the practice was unconstitutional. Reasserting the compartmentalization that he had long adopted for himself, Brennan declared that "in our society, religion 'must be a private matter for the individual, the family, and the institutions of private choice.'"[74]

Similarly, Brennan became the most vociferous advocate of public secularism in other establishment clause cases that the Court would confront over the next two-and-a-half decades, including cases involving public aid to religious schools and governmental expressions or displays endorsing religion. He took the "no endorsement" prohibition more seriously than did its putative sponsor, Justice O'Connor, and hence would have invalidated arguably religious expressions that she voted to uphold.[75] In another pair of cases,[76] Brennan wrote the majority opinions in decisions striking down what were by consensus valuable and effective state and federal remedial education programs in which public school teachers were sent into private schools, including religious schools, to teach classes on subjects like remedial reading and math. Although these teachers were strictly instructed not to teach religion, and although (as Justice O'Connor argued in an impassioned dissent) there was no evidence that any of them had done so over the nineteen-year life of the federal program,[77] for Brennan this was not enough: the bare possibility that some teachers might be influenced by the religious setting to mix some religion into their instruction was warrant enough to invalidate the programs.

Establishment clause jurisprudence during Justice Brennan's tenure on the Court became basically a project in implementing the "secular republic" conception first articulated and imposed in the school prayer decisions. And Brennan, the man who was sincerely Catholic "as a private citizen," was the Court's most aggressive enforcer of secularism upon the public domain. Which is hardly surprising. Because the "secular republic" conception amounted, as we have seen, to the projection onto the nation of Brennan's personal compartmentalization relegating religion to the private sphere.

RECONCEIVING THE REPUBLIC

The radical change represented by the "secular republic" conception was perceived more clearly by the public than by Brennan or his colleagues. Thus, the prayer decisions set off an avalanche of public outrage[78] which evidently took the justices—and the nation's more educated elite—by surprise.[79] To them, the decisions seemed unproblematic and also (except to Justice Douglas, who approved, and to Justice Stewart, who did not) narrow in their implications.[80] So the outpouring of public wrath seemed almost inexplicable, except perhaps as an indication of yokelism or bigotry.[81] And yet in perceiving the decisions as transformative, it was the public, not the justices or the elites, who were more farsighted. With benefit of hindsight, we can see how the prayer decisions amounted to nothing less than a fundamental reconception of the American republic.

Through most of the nation's history, religious ideas and vocabu-lary had been central to how many and probably most Americans had conceived of their country.[82] As Berkeley sociologist Robert Bellah ex-plained, Americans from the outset "saw themselves as being a 'people' in the classical and biblical sense of the word."[83] Bellah described this conception as a form of "civil religion"—by which, he explained, "I refer to that religious dimension, found I think in the life of every people, through which it interprets its historical experience in the light of tran-scendent reality."[84] Citing the appeals to deity in the Declaration of Independence, Bellah argued that

> [i]t is significant that the reference to a suprapolitical sovereignty, to a God who stands above the nation and whose ends are standards by which to judge the nation and indeed only in terms of which the na-tion's existence is justified, becomes a permanent feature of American political life ever after.[85]

This situation continued into the 1960s, when Bellah began writing on the subject. "Biblical imagery provided the basic framework for imagi-native thought in America up until quite recent times and unconsciously, its control is still formidable."[86]

Not *all* Americans had conceived of the nation in these terms, of course; from the beginning there had also been Americans who in-terpreted the nation in more secular ways.[87] And of course Americans had opposed any sort of established church—largely for religious rea-sons. Moreover, they had repeatedly affirmed a commitment to reli-gious freedom—again, as we saw in the previous chapter, mostly for religious reasons. But not only had they—not all, but many of them, including many of the most prominent voices and leaders—understood their country in religious terms and categories; they had regularly in-voked religion in reflecting on or debating public issues, including the most momentous matters, such as slavery, equality, emancipation of women, war, and of course religious freedom.

Probably the supreme manifestation of this propensity for under-standing fundamental and existential issues in religious terms was Abraham Lincoln's majestic Second Inaugural Address, interpreting

the Civil War and imploring Americans to end the division "with mal-
ice toward none, with charity for all, with firmness in the right as God
gives us to see the right." The speech, now engraved on the Lincoln
Memorial, was as eloquent and profound, and as magnanimous, a statement as any American political leader—or perhaps *any* political leader—
had ever issued. And the address was, as one historian observed, a
"theological classic, containing within its twenty-five sentences fourteen references to God, many scriptural allusions, and four direct quota-
tions from the Bible."[88]

   But the open use of unapologetically religious concepts and vocabulary in public discourse had hardly ended with Lincoln. Franklin
Roosevelt, as one historian reports, "frequently asserted that God directed history, labeled himself God's agent, and insisted that the United
States would prosper only if its citizens sought divine guidance and
followed biblical principles."[89] The man who appointed Brennan to
the bench, Dwight D. Eisenhower, had famously declared that "our
form of government has no sense unless it is founded in a deeply felt
religious faith."[90] Just four years before Brennan's appointment, the
Supreme Court itself had declared that "[w]e are a religious people
whose institutions presuppose a Supreme Being."[91] And indeed, even
as the Supreme Court in *Schempp* was signaling that religion is a personal matter that belongs in the private domain, a visionary and powerfully charismatic African-American pastor was leading one of the
most important liberating movements in American history, understood
and promoted in unapologetically religious terms,[92] including the revered and profoundly theological "Letter from a Birmingham Jail."[93]

   The traditional practice of prayer and Bible reading in public schools
both reflected and helped to sustain this religious conception of the republic. The prayers were typically brief, lasting in most instances for
only a few seconds, and theologically innocuous. Probably they did
little to instill genuine piety.[94] The Regents' Prayer struck down in *Engel*
was typical; the product of a diverse advisory committee composed of
Catholic, Protestant, and Jewish clergy, the prayer tersely provided:
"Almighty God, we acknowledge our dependence on Thee, and we beg
Thy blessings upon us, our parents, our teachers, and our Country."[95]
Even so, the symbolism of such prayers was powerful. Through such

exercises, the formative institutions that had long been regarded, as Noah Feldman explains, as "sites for the creation of American identity"[96] conveyed to young people—and to Americans generally—the conception of a nation "under God," as the Pledge of Allegiance (borrowing from Lincoln's Gettysburg Address) put it.

Conversely, the Court's elimination of such traditional exercises—and its ruling that the exercises were forbidden by the nation's fundamental law—conveyed a very different conception. It conveyed the idea of a "secular" nation in which religion, though permitted and even protected, would henceforth be a purely private matter—a proposition that the Court would repeat over and over again during Brennan's tenure.[97] In that respect, the decision's symbolism matched and reenforced its legal doctrine in defining government and the public sphere as secular.

So then, were the justices actually as oblivious as they seemed to the transformation they were ratifying and imposing? Perhaps. This area, like many others, has been subject to verbal and conceptual slippage—to what a classic study by Harvard historian Mark DeWolfe Howe described as "the unnoted change in the meaning of familiar words and the consequent transformation of controlling concepts."[98] Thus, it was easy enough, as we saw in the last chapter, to read Jefferson's metaphor as declaring a "wall of separation between government and *religion*" without noticing that this was not what the sage had actually said.[99] "Church" . . . "religion" . . . "God" . . . whatever: for those carelessly or perhaps carefully inattentive to distinctions, these all mush together into a sort of undifferentiated lump of piety. Don't they?

Moreover, the term "secular" has been slippery in its shadings. In one sense, the idea that government should be "secular" is utterly uncontroversial; the idea would have been perfectly acceptable to—indeed, insisted on—by the likes of Thomas More and Thomas Aquinas. But "secular" for them did not mean "not religious"; rather, it carried the same meaning—basically something like "concerned with matters of this world"[100]—that it did when priests who worked in the world, in a parish, were described as the "secular clergy," in contrast to the "regular clergy" who retreated from the world to a monastery. Brennan and his brethren, by contrast, could recite old truisms while now meaning something quite different by them—namely, that government in its purposes and rationales and expressions and actions must stay clear of religion.[101]

Whether or not the justices noticed the change, however, the doctrine and symbolism of *Schempp* suggested a conception of the country and a compartmentalization that departed drastically from earlier (and, for many, ongoing) understandings. And the Americans who reacted with outrage seem to have perceived this.[102]

A Dis-integrating Reconception

This new conception of the "secular republic" had the effect of imposing a kind of double dis-integration on the nation. First, as we have just been noticing, the new orthodoxy created a historical division that worked to distance and alienate the nation as currently conceived from many of its most central and cherished expressions, traditions, and self-conceptions. Borrowing a metaphor, we might say that the new understanding as it took hold operated to erect a different sort of "wall of separation"—a wall separating Americans from their past.[103] Second, the new doctrine, insofar as it was effective, imposed on the life of the American people the same kind of potential fragmentation that Brennan's compartmentalization had imposed on himself and on other (perhaps more earnestly devout, and thus more seriously conflicted) officials who adopted it.

Over the next generations, justices, lawyers, and scholars would struggle to address and contain these disintegrating tendencies—with limited success.

The Wall of (Historical) Separation

With respect to the historical division, the challenge has been how to interpret and relate to the pervasive and typically unapologetic religious rhetoric and reasoning employed by earlier Americans, including founders and luminaries like Washington, Jefferson, Madison, and Lincoln. Consider again one notable instance: just on the face of things, it appears that Lincoln's Second Inaugural Address—that profound and revered but also pervasively theological statement—ought now to be condemned as a violation of the principle that government should be confined to the secular domain and should avoid making statements that "endorse" religion. A strict enforcement of the modern doctrine might require that the speech be sandblasted off the wall of the Lincoln Memorial.[104]

For judges, a question has been how to deal with legal challenges — challenges that seem well-founded on the modern "secular republic" orthodoxy — to the manifold public and official religious expressions from the past: the words "under God" in the Pledge of Allegiance (taken from the Gettysburg Address), the national motto ("In God We Trust," taken from the national anthem), publicly sponsored Ten Commandments monuments, crosses erected on public property, and the like. The reality is that these expressions simply do not fit compatibly with the modern doctrine, and yet they are often popular and entrenched, and so the courts have sometimes used procedural obstructions to dodge the issues.[105] When these procedural diversions have failed, the results have been mixed and erratic. Sometimes the religious expressions have been judicially condemned. Sometimes they have been upheld, typically with the rationalization that older expressions have been drained of their religious significance by the passage of time — a rationalization that usually leaves both supporters and critics unpersuaded and unhappy.[106]

The ensuing criticisms of hypocrisy and incoherence were seemingly validated by the Supreme Court when on the same day the Court struck down a Ten Commandments display in a Kentucky courthouse but upheld a Ten Commandments monument on the Texas state capital grounds.[107] The swing vote in the disparate decisions belonged to Justice Stephen Breyer, who admitted that the outcomes were not derived from or susceptible to any general rule or doctrine but instead turned on case-by-case "legal judgment."[108] (Whatever that meant, since Breyer expressly did *not* mean judgment under a legal rule.)

Dis-integrating "the People"
But the new conception has not merely detached Americans from their past; on a continuing basis, the separation of public from private purposes and normative criteria has the same potentially fragmenting

effect for the American people collectively as we saw that it can have for individual officials. If "the people" in their public deliberations and decision-making are not supposed to speak and act on the same normative criteria that they embrace and live by in their private and personal lives, then how *are* they supposed to talk, deliberate, and decide?[109] And insofar as Americans in their personal lives operate on different normative criteria from those they use in performing their public duties, does it make sense to say that these are really the same "people" at all?

The problem of how to talk with each other has proven difficult in recent decades. In their separate communities and subgroups, Americans seem capable, on occasion anyway, of conducting probing and sophisticated debates about vital matters. Toss some issue of public importance—welfare, immigration, abortion, marriage, capital punishment—into a gathering of libertarians, or trolley-enthralled analytical philosophers, or natural law theorists, or evangelical Christians, and you may generate a vigorous and searching discussion. But place such questions into the public sphere, instruct people that they are not supposed to invoke their religious beliefs or (on Rawlsian premises) other "comprehensive doctrines,"[110] and what are people supposed to say? How are they supposed to reason with each other?

Some issues—how to reduce unemployment, for example, or improve the balance of trade—will seem to involve mostly instrumental and technical questions, and these issues can be debated on, for example, economic grounds. There is a natural tendency, consequently, to instrumentalize issues so that they can be debated in rational-sounding terms. But when issues have a strong dimension of morality or justice, the challenge becomes more severe. How can citizens meaningfully debate such issues when they are admonished not to invoke what they most fundamentally believe?[111]

Thus, by the early twenty-first century, critics were lamenting that reasoned public discourse in America had almost entirely disappeared. Describing ours as an "age of American unreason," Susan Jacoby perceived a "conscious degradation of standards for political self-presentation and discourse."[112] Ronald Dworkin was if possible even gloomier. Deploring "the lack of any decent argument in American political life," Dworkin contended that political discourse is in an "appalling state." "[O]ur politics are now so debased that they threaten our standing as a genuine democracy."[113]

Increasingly, much of the public debate seemingly consisted of efforts to cram an advocate's particular position into a capacious and honorific but substantively empty term like "equality"[114] — as when contentious and complex questions about the nature of marriage came to be framed as a simple matter of "marriage equality," thereby appearing to render the answer obvious and irresistible.[115] Or else it consisted of appeals to the one thing that everyone still mostly agrees on — namely, that it is wrong to act from mere hatred, malevolence, or (as the courts like to say) "animus." This latter tendency naturally generates what has been called a "discourse of denigration": righteously indignant advocates try to carry their point by accusing their opponents of being bigoted, racist, sexist, homophobic, or transphobic.

Such a discourse is destructive, divisive, and unseemly — and yet almost inevitable. As John Coleman has noted,

> the strongest American voices for a compassionate just community always appealed in public to religious imagery and sentiments, from Winthrop and Sam Adams, Melville and Lincoln of the second inaugural address, to Walter Rauschenbusch and Reinhold Niebuhr and Frederick Douglass and Martin Luther King. . . . The American religious ethic and rhetoric contain rich, polyvalent symbolic power to command commitments and of emotional depth, when compared to "secular" language.[116]

But when this "rich, polyvalent" language is deemed inadmissible, and when many of people's most fundamental convictions are ruled publicly out of bounds — relegated to the private domain — the rhetorical resources admissible for public purposes dry up. And advocates naturally resort to the small if unsavory set of resources still available to them. Even the Supreme Court has been unable to resist the lure of — or perhaps, given our dearth of moral and rhetorical resources, the necessity of — this sort of denigrating discourse.[117]

Beyond informing these maladies of public discourse, however, the conception of the republic as strictly secular, with religion relegated to the private realm, introduces a kind of potentially schizophrenic or disintegrated condition into the American people, just as a similar compartmentalization can do for particular individuals who adopt it. In the domain of their private lives, "the people" may think and live in one way; in the public domain "the people" become almost a different entity, believing and speaking in quite different ways. And then we can ask: in what sense are these "people" really the same entity at all?

To appreciate the lurking problem, start with a hypothetical and simplified situation: imagine that a large majority of people in the United States consists of conscientious and committed Christians or devout Jews or Muslims who are, however, committed to "public reason" or to Brennan-style compartmentalization. A question arises about, say, the ethics of abortion, and "the people"—many of them, anyway, or a sizable consensus—say that abortion is a serious moral evil. Now suppose the same question arises in the public domain, and "the people," dutifully compartmentalizing to keep their religious convictions out of their public deliberations, now give the opposite answer: there is no good reason—no *publicly admissible* reason, anyway—to restrict abortion, and so the freedom to have an abortion should be legally protected.[118] But are these opposing answers actually coming from the same "people"? Or is the private "the people" now a quite separate entity from the public "the people"?

Such fragmentation may subtly but fundamentally undermine the system's democratic credentials. Think of it this way: democracy, we say, means government "of the people, by the people, for the people," but which "the people" are we talking about? The most eligible answer, it seems, would be *the people*—the full, flesh-and-blood people as they actually are and live and believe, with their full panoply of convictions, practices, and commitments. By contrast, the public "the people" seems a more bloodless construction or entity—one crafted by taking the actual living, breathing people and then refashioning them for public purposes by stripping them of their religious convictions and "comprehensive doctrines" in accordance with the precepts of a Brennan or a Rawls, and endowing them instead with a commitment to something like secular or "public reason." But what would be the attraction of a government that is of, by, and for that artificial and uninspiring concoction? Is governance by this constructed and denatured "the people" really so different from governance by a class of imposed officials or bureaucrats?

And in any case, just as a practical matter we might wonder about the viability of a government designed to respond to and to be run not by the flesh-and-blood people but rather by that artificial makeover—the stripped down and refashioned "the people." "The people" meet in their public assemblies, suppose, and, using "public reason," they debate various and sundry matters and reach and enact various conclusions. And then they go home in the evening and, as the full-bodied "the people" they are, contemplate what that other entity—the public "the people"—has done. And they are dissatisfied, even appalled. The legislation enacted by "the people" does not at all meet with the approval of "the people."

They might be told, of course, by the proponents of compartmentalization, that they have no standing to complain because the legislation they now criticize is their own work. For a while this rationalization may confound and silence them. But for how long?

To be sure, this analysis has used a simplified and hypothetical scenario to consider the disintegrating effects of compartmentalization on the collective "the people," or on the republic as a whole. The conclusions of the analysis accordingly have a somewhat artificial quality; that is because in the actual world the compartmentalizing prescriptions of the Supreme Court, or of philosophers like Rawls, have been imperfectly assimilated at best. Properly or not, both citizens and officials *do* often consult and invoke their religious and other philosophical convictions, surreptitiously perhaps, even in public deliberation and decision-making (although they may thereby subject themselves to criticism and may also risk having their decisions invalidated for failing constitutional secularism requirements).[119] Other citizens or officials (including, as noted, people like John Kennedy and William Brennan) easily adhere to the restrictions of public reason, feeling little or no disintegrating tension, because they have little attachment to any religious or other inadmissible comprehensive doctrines anyway. Consequently, the actual world is messy, and the divide between the private "the people" and the public "the people" is not nearly as clean and sharp as in our hypothetical scenario.

This real-world messiness makes the problems that accompany compartmentalization both less but also more vexing than our discussion has suggested. The problems are less severe because the divide is not as sharp and the constraints on public discourse are not as straitening as they would be if everyone conscientiously honored prescriptions calling for religion to be confined to the private domain. Who knows? Maybe even William Brennan himself was unable to leave his religious convictions outside the doors of the courtroom and the judicial chamber. Although Brennan may have scrupulously honored his commitment to keep his judicial performance insulated from his church's teachings on specific matters like abortion, contraception, and aid to religious schools, his biographers suggest that he was nonetheless beholden to his religious beliefs in his general, often-professed commitment to "human dignity."[120] More generally, people do find things to say — deviating from public reason, they *do* invoke their religious and philosophical beliefs in public debates — and public deliberations are thus neither as impoverished nor as insulated from people's personal beliefs as the official compartmentalization would prescribe.

And yet it is awkward to argue that compartmentalization is not actually the disintegrating force it might seem to be in the abstract because, in practice, people mostly don't compartmentalize. A doctor could hardly excuse herself for issuing a lethal prescription to a patient by surmising with a shrug that this particular patient usually forgets to take her medicine anyway. Moreover, in a different sense, the reality of noncompliance and the resulting messiness may make the problems worse. Insofar as compartmentalization is still the ideal — and even, ostensibly, the constitutional requirement — perceived deviations from such compartmentalization will naturally provoke resentment. Those who come out on the wrong side of a public decision will feel justly aggrieved. Not only was the decision misguided, they will think; it was the result of fundamentally unjust or undemocratic or illegal processes and deliberations.

Isn't this sort of mutual suspicion and hostility pervasively apparent in the polarized controversies of our day?

In sum, the reconception of the republic implicit in the compartmentalization imposed by *Schempp* and later decisions posed the risk of a disintegration, both historical and contemporaneous, of the American political community. We might thus wish for some means of overcoming that fragmentation and of binding the nation together. Of connecting the pre-1960s America with the new secular republic, and of uniting the private "the people" with the public "the people."

So, is there any such means? Any resource that could serve to unify the nation against the disintegrating effects of compartmentalization?

In considering the possibility of fragmentation on the individual level, we noticed the possibility—one suggested by John Kennedy in his talk to the Baptist ministers—that conscience might serve to unify the private person and the public person. Although an individual official might work from different normative scripts in her private and public capacities, she is still a unified person because in each realm she acts on the basis of the same ultimate normative authority—namely, her conscience.

Might an ongoing and overarching commitment to the sanctity of conscience similarly connect the pre-*Schempp* America to the "secular republic" announced by the school prayer decisions? And might such a commitment somehow keep "the people" from splitting into private and public entities that can no longer be regarded as a single "the people" at all? James Madison did not prescribe the kind of compartmentalization that Brennan and others favored but, as we saw in the last chapter, he did promote a legally established commitment to conscience as a way of preserving a kind of unity in a religiously pluralistic nation. Maybe a similar commitment might serve to save "the people" from the debilitating fragmentation that Justice Brennan's compartmentalization portended?

IV

Exalting/Reconstituting Conscience

Maybe. Whether conscience could serve this unifying function, thereby countering the disintegrating effects of compartmentalization, is hardly clear. Even so, the possibility at least suggests that the relegation of religion to the private sphere might make it all the more urgent to give public recognition and legal protection to conscience.[121] And in any case, the Supreme Court during Justice Brennan's tenure attempted to do just that—beginning, fittingly, in the same year that the Court officially adopted the "secular republic" compartmentalization.

And yet in purporting to uphold conscience, the Court—and, more generally, the modern age—also turned conscience upside down. As we will see.

Conscience, to be sure, is not expressly mentioned in the Constitution at all. But freedom of conscience has historically been closely associated (or even synonymous) with the free exercise of religion, which of course *is* protected by the First Amendment. Brennan himself seemed to regard the ideas as interchangeable: he would refer, for example, to "the First Amendment guarantees of speech and conscience."[122] And during the Brennan years, the Supreme Court took a more affirmative stance (at least in its official doctrine, if not in its actual results) regarding the free exercise of religion than it had done previously, or than it did after Brennan's retirement. At the same time, the Court pushed free exercise doctrine in the direction of protecting generic conscience, as opposed to "religion" understood in a stricter sense.

Thus, the Court began to say that anyone whose religion would be burdened by conformity to a particular law should be excused from complying with the law unless the government had a compelling interest in requiring such compliance. This idea was not new, to be sure— the courts had often required some such accommodation from the beginning of the republic[123]—but the Court now elevated accommodation into explicit constitutional doctrine. And Brennan himself was the leading proponent of this doctrine, which began with his seminal opinion in *Sherbert v. Verner*,[124] decided the same year as *Schempp*. In later years, he would dissent in important cases in which the Court declined to require accommodation of religious minorities.[125] And he would dissent again in 1990, his last year on the bench, when the Court retreated to a less protective doctrine that permitted government to restrict the exercise of religion so long as it did so under generally applicable and religiously neutral laws.[126]

And yet the revised conception of the political sphere as secular and religiously neutral, though perhaps creating a greater need for the protection of the free exercise of religion, also created a disturbing tension that subtly served to undermine that same commitment. The revision also implicitly dictated a transformation in the conception of conscience.

The most conspicuous manifestation of the tension was on the level of constitutional doctrine. As noted, beginning in the school prayer cases, Brennan was the Court's leading proponent of an establishment clause doctrine mandating that government must be strictly neutral toward religion and must act only for secular purposes.[127] Beginning in the same year, he also became the preeminent advocate of a free exercise doctrine which required government to accommodate religion by excusing religious objectors from burdensome laws unless government had a compelling interest in requiring their compliance. But how could these doctrines—one requiring neutrality toward religion, the other requiring special treatment for religion—be reconciled? What is the secular purpose in singling out religious objectors for legal accommodation? How can accommodating religious objectors but not equally earnest nonreligious objectors be deemed "neutral" toward religion?

Brennan's *Schempp* concurrence already noticed this question,[128] and over the next decades justices and scholars would regularly worry about "the conflict between the clauses"—between the clauses thus interpreted—without producing any very satisfactory resolution. The ingenious solution proposed by one scholar—that the First Amendment means that government is constitutionally *forbidden* to aid religion (establishment clause) except when it is constitutionally *commanded* to do so (free exercise clause)—is indicative of the internal tensions.[129]

A more subtle but perhaps more serious manifestation of the tension was on the level of justification. Madison and Jefferson, as we saw in the last chapter, primarily justified special protection for religious exercise on religious grounds. No duty to society or state could prevail over our prior duty to God, Madison had argued in the "Memorial and Remonstrance." "Almighty God hath created the mind free," Jefferson had declared in his "Virginia Statute for Religious Freedom";[130] coercion in matters of religion violates "the plan of the holy Author

of our religion." But in a regime now committed to confining government to the secular sphere and keeping government strictly neutral in matters of religion, these rationales seemed inadmissible.[131] So,
could the theological justifications in which the constitutional commitment was historically based be replaced by some persuasive secular
substitute?

The practically oriented Brennan[132] seemingly did not worry much
about this question, or perhaps even notice it: he took as a given the
received constitutional commitment to free exercise of religion, apparently unconcerned or unaware that the Court's more secular conception of the republic was digging the historical foundation out from
under that commitment. However, later theorists increasingly did concern themselves with the question. Not surprisingly, they have disagreed
about the answer. But if there is any dominant opinion among scholars
today, it is that there is no adequate justification for protecting religion
per se[133] — and certainly not *theistic* religion in the way Madison had
articulated — and so the constitutional principle needs to be broadened
to include comparable nontheistic or nonreligious personal commitments. Some theorists or jurists draw this conclusion explicitly; others
(including the Court itself) have arrived at much the same position by
defining "religion" broadly to encompass much more than theistic belief and practice, and indeed more than would conventionally be thought
of as "religion" at all. Sometimes this broader subject of protection is
described as "conscience."[134]

But "conscience" in this new context is necessarily something quite
different from what Thomas More or James Madison meant by the
term — namely, the duties that we owe to "the Creator," as Madison
put it. Now conscience means, and needs to mean, something like a
person's deeply felt convictions or commitments regarding how he or
she should live. As Marie Failinger has observed, freedom of conscience
"began as an argument that government must ensure a free response
by the individual called distinctively by the Divine within" but by now
"has come to mean very little beyond the notion of personal existential
decision-making."[135]

This revision was in effect made official by the Court during the
Vietnam War era in two notable cases addressing the scope of the

conscientious objector exemption from compulsory military service. In 1965, when the first of these cases was decided by the Court, the applicable statute reflected a Madisonian conception of conscience: it provided an exemption for young men whose objection to war was grounded in a belief in a "Supreme Being."[136] Daniel Seeger disclaimed any such theistic belief but asserted a sincere and categorical objection to war on essentially moral grounds. And the Court ruled in Seeger's favor, construing the statutory exemption to cover objections based either on theistic belief or commitment or on some other nontheistic belief or commitment that held a "parallel place" in the life of the conscientious but nontheistic objector.[137] This interpretation was reaffirmed five years later in *Welsh v. United States*.[138] Not only did the cases read the statutory exemption more broadly than its wording plausibly allowed; they effectively read the exemption to cover instances that the statute explicitly said it did *not* cover—namely, objections based on "essentially political, sociological, or philosophical views or a merely personal moral code."[139]

Seeger and *Welsh* thus suggested that although government cannot accommodate theistic religion as such—to do so would violate the requirement of religious neutrality—government *can* accommodate conscience (including religiously informed conscience). This conclusion maintained a kind of verbal continuity with the positions held by Madison and Jefferson. But it also involved a significant reconceiving— even in one sense a complete reversal—of what conscience is and why it is deserving of respect.

In what sense, after all, does a sincere but nontheistic objection to war hold a place for the nontheist that is "parallel" to that of the theistic objector's belief that God forbids him to go to war? In terms of their basic logic or substance, these beliefs are *not* parallel: the theist is acting from a morally and ontologically hierarchical view of the universe and of obligation that the nontheist does not accept. Or we could say that Madison's primary rationale for protecting conscience—that we have a prior duty to the Creator that trumps all other duties—simply does not apply to the nontheist's objection.[140] The objections *are* arguably parallel, however, in terms of their subjective or psychological importance to the objector. And it is evidently this subjective element that has now become the beneficiary of the Court's protection.

Or we could frame the inquiry by asking *why* conscience should be entitled to any special respect by outsiders, or by governments, who disagree with a citizen's sincere but (in their view) mistaken judgment? For both Thomas More and James Madison, once again, the gravity and authority of conscience traced back to the transcendent authority of God. A person should do as God commands. And given human fallibility, the duty to do as God commands can only mean that people should do what *they believe* God commands: this was the theologically grounded practical tautology at the core of conscience. Indeed, God commands that humans should do as (they believe) He commands, even if they are mistaken; in that sense, as we saw in the previous chapters, conscience has the paradoxical power to consecrate error. And the government surely should not set itself in opposition to God, as it would do if it compelled its citizens to act contrary to what God requires of them.

Under the more secular regime signaled in the school prayer cases, this sort of rationale became unavailable (and close to incomprehensible). So then, why *is* conscience so weighty or so authoritative? And, more troublingly, why should government respect and attempt to accommodate the consciences of people whom government necessarily believes to be mistaken or misguided in their judgments?

Unable now to answer that question by appealing to the authority of God, *Seeger* and *Welsh* instead suggested that respect for conscience is based on respect for the individual subject. The sincere objector should not be forced to violate, or to be unfaithful to, . . . *himself*.

Elliot believes, let us say, that war is always profoundly wrong. His belief may or may not have a religious basis; either way, he is sincere in his objection. The political community as a whole plainly does not share Elliot's opinion; if it did, the community would not be fighting the war for which it is conscripting young men like Elliot to fight. In the widely shared view of society, in short, Elliot's judgment is mistaken: war (including *this* war) is sometimes justified, even necessary. Nor does the community believe that forcing Elliot to fight would somehow violate God's will; indeed, within the community's now secularized public vocabulary, any such claim is hardly even cognizable. Even so, to force Elliot to act contrary to his sincere conviction would somehow violate *him*—would violate Elliot himself, his integrity, or his personality, or (in the increasingly common vocabulary) his "identity."[141] Something like this—some sort of concern for Elliot's personality or integrity or identity as a subject—must now be the reason for excusing Elliot from serving in the military even though (society believes) Elliot is mistaken in his convictions.

This account of conscience is in one sense like those of More and Madison in prescribing respect for the right of an individual to do as he believes is right. In a more fundamental sense, however, the modern conception is almost the opposite of theirs. Instead of being based on respect for the supreme authority of God, or even on acknowledgment of some objective moral law that is independent of but binding upon particular persons, the protection of conscience in the modern view reflects a recognition of the inviolability or sanctity of individual human beings. Or, we might say, the sanctity of the self.[142] With Thomas More, and even with James Madison, conscience signified submission of the humble, dependent creature before the transcendent Creator. By contrast, in the modern conception, as reflected in *Seeger* and *Welsh*, conscience signifies the elevation of the independent individual subject or self.[143]

This elevation of the self was also a sort of culmination of a development denied and yet hinted at in Thomas More's ideas and somewhat more self-consciously adopted in Madison's—namely, the detachment of conscience from a commitment to *truth*. For More, as we saw in chapter one, the duties of conscience derived from obligations to live in accordance with truth. And yet, in tacitly recognizing the power of conscience to consecrate error, as More did when he permitted his family to take an oath that he understood (but they did not) to be based on pernicious error, More showed how conscience could justify even actions grounded in mistaken beliefs. This possibility was more fully embraced in Madison's conception of conscience which, as we saw in the previous chapter, was attractive precisely because it promised to consecrate a whole variety of contradictory religious opinions. The modern conception, as reflected in *Seeger* and *Welsh*, completes and ratifies this development: what matters is not whether a person's beliefs are true but instead whether the person is acting sincerely.

And, increasingly, this version of what conscience means and requires would come to be described in the vocabulary of—and would modulate into—a new concept: "authenticity."[144]

CONSCIENCE AND AUTHENTICITY

In this respect, *Seeger* and *Welsh* reflected and reenforced a change in the conception of conscience and the person that had already become part of the broader culture. Historian Doug Rossinow explains how the quest for authenticity was central to the social and political movements of the 1960s. Politically active young people "talked all the time about becoming 'real' or 'natural' or 'authentic.'"[145] The Port Huron Statement, a 1962 manifesto of the Students for a Democratic Society (SDS), asserted that the "goal of man and society should be . . . finding a meaning in life that is personally authentic."[146] Although initially associated with the countercultural left, the ideal became more generalized. Writing in the late 1990s, Rossinow commented that "[t]he search for authenticity has become so pervasive a yearning in the United States . . . so as to render it less clearly a dissident, much less a specifically leftist, resource."[147]

Among the many manifestations of this ideal, and of its relation to the traditional commitment to conscience, let us notice two. The first occurred concurrent with the beginning of William Brennan's tenure on the Supreme Court, while the second coincided with the end of that tenure.

Robert Bolt's acclaimed play about Thomas More, *A Man for All Seasons*, was written at about the same time that William Brennan was being appointed to the Senate, and was first performed in the year that John Kennedy was declaring the supremacy of his conscience to the Baptist ministers. Unlike more recent fictional depictions (in particular Hilary Mantel's *Wolf Hall* novels), Bolt's play and the Oscar-winning film adaptation present More in his devotion to conscience as an admirable and indeed heroic figure. And yet Bolt, who explained that he himself was not in any meaningful sense a Christian, admired More not as a saint or a faithful Christian but rather as "a hero of selfhood." More was a man with "an adamantine sense of his own self."[148]

And the play's portrayal reflects this reconception. Thus Bolt has More explain to his daughter Meg why he cannot take King Henry's oath: "When a man takes an oath, Meg, he's holding his own self in his own hands, like water. . . . And if he opens his fingers then—he needn't hope to find himself again."[149] At another point in the play, More de-clares—enigmatically (and, it seems, incoherently)—that "what matters to me is not whether [the papal claim to authority] is true or not but that I *believe* it to be true, or rather, not that I believe it, but that *I* be-lieve it."[150] The movement is from objective truth (which, Bolt's mod-ern More says, is *not* what matters to him) to subjective belief (and doesn't the very concept of "belief" still imply some reference to truth?) to the simple, self-asserting subject or *I*—seemingly now the ultimate normative criterion. The sovereign, "adamantine" self or *I* may express itself in belief, but it is the *I* that counts, not the belief, much less the truth of the belief.

Toward the end of the play, More responds to Henry's henchman Thomas Cromwell, who exclaims disdainfully that More's invocation of conscience is nothing more than "a noble motive for frivolous self-conceit!," in this way:

> MORE: (Earnestly) It is not so, Master Cromwell—very and pure necessity for respect of my own soul.
> CROMWELL: Your own self, you mean!
> MORE: Yes, a man's soul is his self![151]

More's biographer John Guy comments that Bolt's play is "sump-tuous drama but appalling history."[152] More himself, if he could be re-vived and forced to sit in the audience, would likely concur: the play, while depicting him as an admirable man of courage, integrity, and conscience, makes his conscience not the faculty by which he would obey God above all else, even at the cost of his life, but rather his com-mitment to being true to his own "self"—a self which would somehow mysteriously disappear if he violated an oath in the way water slips through open fingers. And yet if this topsy-turvy depiction grossly distorts the historical More's commitments, it nicely captures a preva-lent modern conception of conscience—one that is readily discernible in decisions like *Seeger* and *Welsh*.

A similar development was described by the philosopher Charles Taylor in a book published the year after Brennan stepped down from the Court. Taylor noted that critics of modernity sometimes assail its individualism for being permissive and selfish, but this criticism, Taylor argued, fails to discern that "there is a powerful moral ideal at work here"—namely, "the moral ideal . . . of being true to oneself."[153] This ideal was "something relatively new and peculiar to modern culture."[154] The modern ideal, "part of the massive subjective turn in modern culture," was in some ways akin to older moralities in which "being in touch with some source—God, say, or the Idea of the Good—was considered essential to full being." (That was the view, as we have seen, contained in Thomas More's conception of conscience—and arguably, in attenuated form, in Madison's as well.) But there was a fundamental difference, Taylor explained: "Only now the source we have to connect with is deep in *us*."[155] Closely linked to "the modern notion of dignity, . . . where we talk of the inherent 'dignity of human beings'"— as William Brennan did throughout his career—this modern notion reflects "a radical anthropocentrism."[156]

This commitment to being "true to oneself" may have a genealogical connection to the conscience of Thomas More ("I leave every man to his own conscience" and everyone should "leave me to mine").[157] As we saw in chapter one, the core meaning of conscience to More—and also to Luther—could be expressed in two propositions: first, that you should do what is right, which was equivalent to saying that you should do God's will; and, second, that you should be true to yourself. For More, these propositions converged. God was your Creator and the source of your being—He knew you far better than you knew yourself, and loved you far more than you loved yourself—so to do God's will *was* to be true to yourself.[158] In the modern compartmentalized conception, the "do God's will" proposition has been edited out, at least from the public domain. But the second proposition—to be true to yourself—has been retained, now as a stand-alone obligation. This view, Carter Snead explains, "equates being fully human with finding the unique truth within ourselves and freely constructing our individual lives to reflect it."[159]

This imperative to be true to oneself can still be and often is described in the vocabulary of conscience. But it can also and perhaps better be described in the vocabulary of "authenticity." The philosopher Simon Feldman explains that "[o]n this conception of authenticity, the moral self is the true self, so in acting on conscience, we live authentically."[160] And thus the title of Taylor's book: *The Ethics of Authenticity*. To be authentic is to be true to oneself, which is to be true to one's self.

Taylor argues that, as a historical and political matter, "we can practically *define* the cultural mainstream of Western liberal society in terms of those who feel the draw of this [ideal of authenticity] and other main forms of individualism."[161] Confirmation of Taylor's assessment might be found in an eloquent statement by Barack Obama, in a video addressed to young gay people: "As a nation, we're founded on the belief that all of us are equal and each of us deserves the freedom to pursue our own version of happiness; to make the most of our talents; to speak our minds; to *not* fit in; *most of all, to be true to ourselves.*"[162]

V

CONSTITUTIONALIZING THE CONSECRATED, AUTHENTIC SELF

Conscience has by this point followed a curious course to reach some sort of upside-down culmination. Beginning in a humble acknowledgment of the transcendent goodness and authority of God, it has evolved or devolved into "radical anthropocentrism" — into a commitment to the sanctity or inviolability or dignity of the human person or self. And this "ideal of authenticity" has arguably become the central normative commitment of modern America, and of modern liberal democracies generally; it has become, as Simon Feldman puts it, a "cultural juggernaut."[163]

Justice Brennan seems to have been riding or even helping to drive this juggernaut when he wrote or spoke effusively, as he was wont to do, about "the dignity of man," as he put it in his James Madison Address at NYU in 1961,[164] or "the essential dignity of man," which was the title of another talk he gave in 1961,[165] or "human dignity" as he later put it in a much noted speech at Georgetown in 1985.[166] Conscience is to be valued, Brennan maintained, because it is a manifestation or implication of this more fundamental human dignity.

But not the only implication. On the contrary, Brennan suggested that all of the rights that he is celebrated for having recognized and promoted were manifestations of this same basic value: they are thus closely related to rights of conscience, albeit not so much as offspring but rather as siblings, with "human dignity" as the common source or progenitor. Brennan made the point clear in his Georgetown talk. The "rights of expression and conscience" are of course fundamental to human dignity. But criminal procedure rights (such as the right to receive a "Miranda warning")[167] likewise grow out of "a vision of human dignity." So do electoral rights—as in the "one person one vote principle" established in *Reynolds v. Sims*[168]—and the procedural due process rights attached to government entitlements and benefits. Constitutional rights of equality—and in particular equality for women, which Brennan played a leading role in developing[169]—"ensure[ ] that gender has no bearing on claims to human dignity."

More generally, Brennan viewed the Constitution itself as "a sparkling vision of the supremacy of the human dignity of every individual." Less imaginative observers who simply read the words of the document might find this effusion perplexing; encountering few or no textual expressions of lofty principles and ideals, they might conclude that the Constitution reads more like a legalistic, technical manual for the operations of government.[170] Not so for Brennan (who, as noted, as a Harvard law student had not elected to take the course in constitutional law). For him, as he told the Georgetown audience, the Constitution was "a sublime oration on the dignity of man."

And if *the Constitution itself* in its mundane and lawyerlike text contains little to warrant that description, *constitutional law* as developed during the Brennan years became just such an "oration." Indeed, probably the more far-reaching constitutional consequences of the modern conception of the self as possessed of an innate and inviolable "dignity" lay not in free exercise jurisprudence, which though nominally protective rarely resulted in victories for religious dissenters,[171] but rather in other constitutional domains that lawyers place under the headings of due process, equal protection, privacy, and criminal procedure. By informing decisions like *Roe v. Wade*,[172] *Eisenstadt v. Baird*,[173] and *Craig v. Boren*,[174] Brennan's vision of human dignity contributed to a transformation of American life and culture. And, as Brennan himself insisted, that transformation had been motivated and guided by his conception of "human dignity."[175]

"Human dignity," to be sure, can sound like a noble but nebulous term, but Brennan's construal made at least two things clear. First, human dignity meant the dignity of individuals. It did not contemplate Marxist or fascist ideas glorifying some collective humanity or "the people" in the aggregate. Thus, Brennan talked of "the ideal of *libertarian* dignity," of "the presumed worth *of each individual*," and of "the supremacy of the human dignity of every individual."[176] In this respect, Brennan's "human dignity" was consistent with More's and Luther's and Madison's "conscience," which also inhered in individuals.

Second, the human dignity of the individual clearly meant the dignity of each individual *as understood by that individual.* If the individualist aspect of Brennan's conception of dignity distinguished his ideal from Marxist and fascist commitments to collective humanity, this subjectivist aspect separated him from, for example, the position of his church. Thus, the Catholic Church has been as insistent as any modern institution in proclaiming the importance of human dignity. And the church has surely understood dignity to inhere in every individual person, each of whom is deemed to be a child of God, fashioned in the divine image.[177] Perhaps the most poignant modern exemplification of this idea was Mother Theresa, ministering selflessly for decades to the humblest specimens of humanity in the ghettoes of Calcutta. But dignity as understood in Catholicism would not promote the ability of individuals to degrade themselves by, for instance, reveling in pornography, or inflicting death upon the unborn or themselves.[178] Thus, Mother Theresa, no compartmentalizer, made it clear that abortion is emphatically not a matter for private choice.[179]

For Brennan, by contrast—or if not for Brennan as a Catholic "private citizen" then for Brennan *as Supreme Court justice*—if an individual chooses to terminate the life of an unborn child that she is carrying, or to terminate his own life in painful or unhappy circumstances, that choice must be honored and legally protected. This is what a respect for "dignity" demands.

The most famous declaration of this subjectivist conception of dignity, written two years after Brennan left the Court but in full accordance with his own notions, came in the much discussed "mystery passage" in the case of *Planned Parenthood v. Casey*. A plurality of justices including Brennan's successor and admirer, David Souter, wrote that "[a]t the heart of liberty is the right to define one's own concept of existence, of meaning, of the universe, and of the mystery of human life."[180] This right evidently contemplated not merely a right to *believe* in one's concept of the universe—the state of Pennsylvania had not attempted to regulate what anyone *believed*—but rather some kind of right to have one's conception respected, or not interfered with, by the government. The sentence in a sense perfectly and poetically captures the idea of "human dignity" as Brennan championed it in creating and upholding the rights of individuals to choose whether to utter or indulge in expression that is ennobling or vulgar (at least by societal standards),[181] whether to terminate the life of an unborn child or to bring that child into the world,[182] whether to terminate one's own life or to continue it.[183]

One can imagine a revivified Thomas More, confronted with the "mystery passage," erupting with amazement and anger. The statement is blasphemous, More might insist, because it assigns to individual mortals portentous powers that belong only to God. More would thus agree with Yale professor Arthur Leff's characterization in a famous essay: modern jurisprudence purports to regard human beings within the constitutional system as millions of little "Godlets."[184] The *Casey* passage is also preposterous, More might think, to the point of being comical. The universe is what it is, he might say, and means whatever it means: human beings may indeed have the freedom to acknowledge those realities or not, but no human being has the power to alter them— or to define them for himself or herself. True, a person might delude himself—might imagine that the universe is what he wants it to be, or has the meaning that he wishes it to have. But the delusion will not make it so. And the power to indulge in such delusions is emphatically not the source or meaning of "dignity" (which derives from the fact that humans are created in the image of God, and are created with an orientation to truth) but rather a matter calling for pity, instruction, and correction.

In Brennan's and the Court's compartmentalized public world, by contrast, blasphemy was no longer a cognizable category and God was inadmissible (except perhaps for limited "ceremonial" purposes).[185] The only active and cognizable agents left to wield, or at least purport to wield, the universe-conceiving and meaning-conferring powers formerly exercised by God were . . . human beings. Individual selves creating their own individual universes with their own meanings.[186] Leff's "Godlets." And even though the modern notion stood the older conception on its head, the image of such sovereign selves can still be perceived as a distant descendent—exalted, perhaps, or perhaps bloated and debased—of Thomas More (that "hero of selfhood," as Bolt would have it) compelled by his conscience to stand against all the powers of England. Or of Martin Luther defying empire and church with his "Here I stand! I can do no other."

William Brennan's personal declaration of official independence from his religion and his church, announced to the Senate and then projected onto the nation's fundamental law, thus foreshadowed a republic reconceived as the secular home of millions of liberated and newly elevated and empowered subjects, or selves. For many, this exalting of the individual self or identity has seemed a noble and exhilarating achievement—one that works to liberate human beings, especially those who have been historically oppressed, to be and to express their true, full selves. And Brennan has received his share of adulation for that achievement.[187]

Moreover, this achievement can be seen as a working out of the implications hidden away in or closely associated with the venerable commitment to conscience. In that respect, Jack Rakove makes a cogent observation when he says, as we saw in the last chapter, that James Madison's ideas of freedom of conscience represented "the birth of the modern self."[188] Even if in a different sense the modern reconception of conscience and the person has also turned Madison's understanding upside down, endowing the human self with the normative authority that Madison (like Thomas More in this respect) ascribed to "the Creator."

VI

THE INSOLVENCY OF THE SOVEREIGN SELF

And yet if the elevation of the self could be exhilarating, it could also be unsettling, even disintegrating. Thomas More had worried that the individualistic conception of conscience reflected in Martin Luther's defiant "Here I stand!" would operate as an acidic solvent, dissolving the ties that bind society together and indeed that bind an individual's own life into a meaningful whole. And, as we saw in chapter one, More was surely right up to a point: the developments he decried did indeed work to dissolve the world as he knew it and as it had existed for the previous millennium. Similarly, the distant offspring of that early modern conscience—namely, the modern self, possessed of an inherent "dignity" and bound by an obligation to be "authentic," or true to itself—likewise carries with it a solvent power that, ironically, threatens to subvert and dissolve the very world which has elevated that self to such unprecedented power and stature.

More specifically, the modern commitment to the self and to conscience conceived of as personal authenticity, even as it exalts the self, also threatens to dissolve the self, in three ways. The modern commitment subverts the justifications for respecting dignity and the self. It undermines the social conditions and institutions upon which a secure personal identity depends. And, paradoxically but most fundamentally, the commitment to the self has a tendency to dissolve the self itself.

Let us consider each of these subversive influences more closely.

DISSOLVING THE FOUNDATIONS OF DIGNITY

We have already noticed, in this chapter and the previous one, the irony by which a commitment to religious freedom can work in self-cancelling fashion to subvert its own justifications. As a historical matter, that commitment was centrally grounded in religious rationales—Jefferson's "Almighty God hath created the mind free"—but at least as interpreted in modern times, the commitment entails that religious rationales are inadmissible as bases for public policies or legal principles.

Much the same self-subverting dynamic is apparent with respect to the modern commitment to "human dignity."

What is the justification, after all, for asserting that every human being is possessed of some sacrosanct "dignity" that requires him or her to be treated as "inviolable" and with "equal concern and respect"? Let us be honest: few of those human beings behave in ways indicative of any such dignity. On the contrary, many of them—of us—speak and live in ways that exude mediocrity, or vulgarity, or selfishness. Or depravity: did Stalin or Hitler—or Jeffrey Dahmer—exude a "dignity" entitling them to equal concern and respect?

In antiquity the idea that every individual has a dignity that endows him or her with some kind of moral "inviolability" or right to "authenticity" would have seemed preposterous, or perhaps simply unintelligible.[189] In the Roman Empire, for example, slavery was pervasive, and masters were thought to be entitled to use their slaves in any way they chose, sexually or otherwise. Women were likewise subordinated—confined to the home or consigned to prostitution. And undesired babies were routinely abandoned—left on a street corner or outside the city where, as Philo of Alexandria observed, "all the beasts that feed upon human flesh visit the spot and feast unhindered on the infants."[190]

So then how did the notion come about that every individual, however lowly or uncouth, enjoys some sort of innate "dignity" deserving of respect? The historical evolution was complex, to be sure, but one development seems to have been crucial—namely, the widespread communication and acceptance of the Hebrew and Christian belief that every human being (even "the least among us") is made "in the image of God" and indeed is in some real sense a child of God.[191] Thus, in an essay carefully assessing the ancient sources and influences, historian Kyle Harper shows that "[n]one of the classical political regimes, nor any of the classical philosophical schools, regarded human beings as universally free and incomparably worthy creatures. Classical civilization, in short, lacked the concept of human dignity." This concept was introduced by the biblical concept of the *imago dei*. In this way, "Christianization created the grounds for the development of human rights."[192]

But that biblical and theistic rationale for human dignity and human rights is inadmissible in the modern secular republic. And perhaps even offensive, since it would make the dignity of the human person derivative of the dignity of some higher source.[193] So then, what *is* the warrant for declaring that every human being, even the most ignorant or abandoned or apparently depraved, is possessed of some ennobling dignity?

Perhaps some modern, secular rationale has developed to replace the older theological rationale? But in fact intellectual developments over the last two centuries serve more to debunk than to confirm claims about inherent dignity. Perhaps no intellectual advance has been as influential in shaping modern thought as the evolutionary perspective associated with Darwinism.[194] Conflicts (real or spurious) between evolution and traditional theistic religion are a familiar feature of modern life and thought; the Scopes trial, sensationally publicized at the time by H. L. Mencken and conveyed in slanted form to later generations through the popular movie and play *Inherit the Wind*, is perhaps the most notorious instance.[195] But of course a standard and even stereotypical traditionalist objection to Darwinism—one that Darwinism's proponents have mercilessly mocked—is that by making human beings descendants of "lower" primates or apes, the theory deprives humans of their distinctive dignity.[196] The mockery may be deserved, and yet the traditionalists also have a point: Darwinism does undermine the case for any sort of special "human dignity."

Thus, in the evolutionary view, human beings are not children of God but rather a particular species of evolved primate—the unplanned byproduct of a vast series of accidental selections in the struggle for survival of the fittest. In this vein, the atheist philosopher John Gray observes that "the belief that humans are marked off from all other animals by having free will is a Christian inheritance."[197] By contrast, "Darwin's theory shows the truth of naturalism: we are animals like any other."[198]

And William Brennan's conception of the secular republic led to decisions ensuring that public school students would *not* be taught the biblical account of humanity and *would* be taught the Darwinian account. Thus, while allowing that schools might teach *about* the Bible— in, for example, a literature or history class[199]—*Schempp* forbade the traditional practice of reading the Bible in a devotional or authoritative way. That use of the Bible was relegated to the private sphere, just as Brennan had promised to relegate his own religion to the private sphere. Five years later, in *Epperson v. Arkansas*,[200] the Court struck down a Scopes-era law forbidding the teaching of evolution in schools as a violation of the recently announced constitutional requirement of "absolute" neutrality in matters of religion. Concurring, Justice Black (author of the first school prayer decision and hardly a friend of publicly sponsored religion) wondered how constitutional decisions prohibiting the states from either teaching the Bible or refusing to teach evolution could be deemed "neutral" toward religion.[201] But it was clear that for the Court—and in particular for Justice Brennan—"neutral" meant "secular" in the sense of "not religious."

The completion of this pedagogical transvaluation of values occurred in *Edwards v. Aguillard*,[202] in which the Court struck down a state's "balanced treatment" law mandating the teaching of *both* "creationism" and Darwinism. Writing for the majority, Justice Brennan rejected as a "sham" the state's contention that the law's purpose was to ensure that schools would present competing views and evidence so that students could make up their own minds. The real purpose, Brennan was sure, was to promote a religious view, and this purpose was forbidden under Brennan's secularist Constitution. The result of the decision was that public school students would be instructed only in the Darwinian conception of the origins and nature of human beings; they would be taught the biblical view, if at all, only in the private sphere.

But perhaps human dignity might be grounded not in the *imago dei* rationale but rather in the Enlightenment conception of humans as creatures capable of and guided by their own autonomous "reason"?[203] A second major modern intellectual development, associated with the thinking of Freud, has undermined that possibility. Even as Freud's particular theories have been subjected to debilitating criticisms, his general conception of human beings as the product to a significant extent of subconscious processes and impulses has achieved widespread purchase.[204] The Freudian version emphasizes subconscious sexual impulses; other currently fashionable versions point to other subconscious factors centering on race or gender. In this view, people who sincerely believe they are neither racist nor sexist are today routinely deemed to be acting on and acting out dark underlying psychological prejudices and motivations that they are not even aware of.[205] And this account undermines the depiction of humans as enjoying some special dignity by virtue of being self-aware, self-directed creatures who are defined by and who live in accordance with "reason."

In short, claims about some universal and equal "human dignity," such as those that motivated William Brennan's whole judicial career, are ubiquitous today, but the assertions also seem difficult to justify— and incongruent with the overall modern intellectual climate of opinion. Francis Fukuyama observes that none of the world's constitutions "define[ ] what dignity is, and scarcely a politician in the Western world if pressed could explain its theoretical basis."[206] Philosophers of course continue to struggle with the problem.[207] Increasingly, though, the proposition of "human dignity" seems to function as a sort of "noble lie" or ennobling fiction. A fiction that goes mostly unchallenged insofar as it is in everyone's interest to affirm it, but one that is fragile nonetheless—like a gaudy puffed-up balloon that might be punctured at any moment.

To be sure, fictions can be powerful, and even self-validating.[208] If everyone says that Maryanne is queen, she *will* be; if everyone agrees that a particular piece of flimsy green paper is worth $100, you will be able to exchange it for that amount of food or gasoline. But not all propositions are of this nature: if we all agree that sickness and death are illusory, people will continue to ail, age, and expire nonetheless. Moreover, self-validating fictions cling to a tenuous existence, because if saying something is so can make it so, then saying it is *not* so can likewise make it not so. If everyone rejects Louis's claim to be king, he won't be king any longer; indeed, he may not even persist in possession of his head. If everyone says that the green piece of paper bearing Washington's image is worthless, it *will* be worthless.

And surely there will be those inclined to deny the fiction (if that is what it is) of human dignity. We have seen over the last century instances—the Third Reich, the Pol Pot regime, the current treatment in China of the Uighurs—in which the proposition of human dignity has been brazenly and brutally denied.[209] In the contemporary United States, it increasingly seems that rival cultural and political factions are more eager to demonize than to respect the dignity of their political and cultural opponents. In these circumstances, the fragility of the proposition of human dignity becomes more than an academic concern.

But the exaltation of the self implicit in modern ideas of authenticity, human dignity, and conscience not only subverts the idea of human dignity specifically; more generally, it undermines commitments to truth itself. We saw in the previous chapter that Madison's detachment of conscience from its traditional grounding in Christianity subtly undermined the importance of truth. If what matters is not whether you are living by beliefs that *are* true but rather by beliefs that *you believe* to be true, then actual truth becomes of lesser importance and your motivation to seek a potentially unsettling truth may slacken. The modern emphasis on authenticity reenforces this tendency away from concerns about actual truth. Indeed, *Casey's* proposition that every person has a solemn right to define his or her own conception of the universe and its meaning already reflects this detachment: the idea that there might be an actual truth about the universe and meaning—a truth that individuals might get right or wrong—is not even acknowledged.

And this relaxation of commitments to truth is ubiquitous in modern culture.[210] It is evident in the pervasive "fake news" and the flagrant disregard for actual facts so often detectable in contemporary journalism and politics. It is evident in the Rawlsian commitment to prioritize "reasonableness"—a term of art, of course—over truth.[211] It is evident in a recent study which found that almost three-quarters of American millennials agreed with the statement: "whatever is right for your life or works best for you is the only truth you can know."[212] In this cultural context, both the possibility but also the expectation of serious justifications, not only for human dignity but also for any other important proposition, are severely compromised.

Dissolving the Social Order

Thomas More worried that individualistic conscience would dissolve society as he knew it. Today, the distant descendant of individualistic conscience—namely, the sovereign self with its claims and duties of authenticity—is working to undermine the social order as *we* know it. Exactly how far that process of dissolution will go remains uncertain, and there is always a possibility that the process will provoke a reaction—perhaps of increasing authoritarianism? Indeed, albeit paradoxically, both processes—toward dissolution and toward authoritarianism—may be in operation simultaneously.

For present purposes, what matters is that the solvent process is apparent, in at least two ways; the first of these is quite obvious while the other is slightly less so.

Clash of the Titans

Most obviously, exalting or sanctifying the individual subject or self can pose the same sort of problem created by polytheism, or by international relations in a global situation with multiple "sovereigns." Almost inevitably, the multiple gods are going to disagree with each other (as they do quite vividly in, for example, the *Iliad* and the *Odyssey*) or the various national sovereigns are going to make conflicting claims, and such conflicts can result in hostilities and in destructive violence and warfare. A parallel possibility arises if many millions of individuals—Leff's "Godlets"—are deemed to be in some sense sacred repositories of the dignity and authority formerly assigned to a transcendent God. If every individual is deemed to have the right to define his or her own "concept of existence, of meaning, of the universe, and of the mystery of human life," some of these concepts and universes are inevitably going to collide. What to do then?

To be sure, in any human entity comprised of more than one person—in a family, a community, a nation—opinions will sometimes differ, and interests will sometimes come into competition. This was as true in Thomas More's and James Madison's times as it is in ours. A viable society will necessarily find ways to deal with such differences. In the American republic and other modern democracies, a principal mechanism for dealing with such differences has been law, enacted in popular assemblies and interpreted by courts.

And yet the modern jurisprudence of "human dignity" that developed under the tenure and sponsorship of William Brennan endows this perennial challenge with a new and more intractable quality. In the modern conception, individuals are not just agents with different

opinions and interests. Instead, as we have seen, they are more like
sovereign subjects or selves possessed of "dignity" and endowed with
a right, once again, to define for themselves a "concept of existence, of
meaning, of the universe." In that sense, they are more like smaller
versions of the gods of antiquity or the supposedly sovereign nations
of the global situation. Except that instead of a few hundred or so such
sovereigns there are now hundreds of millions of them.

In addition, the statement of their basic right makes explicit what
the compartmentalization of public and private and the resulting relegation of religion and other "comprehensive doctrines" to the private
domain had already indicated: for public purposes there is not supposed to be any official overarching truth or creed or orthodoxy under
which the competing visions and claims can be adjudicated.[213] Or perhaps there will be such an encompassing orthodoxy—of necessity—but
its enforcement will seem a violation of the basic and cherished proposition that every individual has the right to define for himself or herself
the meaning of the universe and of existence. That right, after all, could
never have been meant or understood as merely a right to *believe* what
one chooses. Surely the *Casey* pronouncement was promising more
than that: if the justices meant only that individuals were free to *believe*
what they wanted about existence and the universe, how was their portentous dictum even relevant to the result reached in *Casey*? What
is the good of a right to define one's own conception of meaning, existence, and the universe if that conception can simply be overridden
and effectively crushed by some other conception proclaimed and
enforced by society or the government?

These difficulties became increasingly apparent as the jurisprudence of human dignity advanced over the latter part of the twentieth
century and the early twenty-first century in what is sometimes described as a "rights revolution" or, as Jamal Greene has recently put
it, "rightsism."[214] A sense of entitlement became widespread. Claims
of rights proliferated, and intensified. Inevitably, some of the claimed
rights conflicted with other claimed rights, and often there seemed no
principled way to reconcile such conflicts. During the Brennan years,
the Court purported to resolve such conflicts through what it called
"balancing," although astute critics pointed out that the Court never

even pretended to address the formidable empirical and conceptual problems that any serious attempt at "balancing" competing rights and interests inevitably presented.[215] Not surprisingly, resolution by "balancing" seemed like resolution by judicial fiat, and the conclusions of such "balancing" were rarely satisfying to the parties who did not prevail.[216]

The current polarization that so obviously and alarmingly afflicts the nation is in part the product of that development, as clashing constituencies each struggle with righteous zeal under the banners of one or another ostensible "right." So is the often-remarked paralysis, or "gridlock," that seems to afflict the traditional means of adjusting and compromising competing interests through legislative action. As Jamal Greene explains:

> Our opponent in the rights conflict becomes not simply a fellow citizen who disagrees with us, but an enemy out to destroy us.... With stakes this high, polarization should not just be expected but is indeed the only sensible response.... Conflict over rights can encourage us to take aim at our political opponents instead of speaking to them. And we shoot to kill.[217]

Greene thus concludes that "[w]e . . . are hurtling toward tragedy."[218]

The Dissolution of Institutions

But the jurisprudence of dignity and the ideal of authenticity have operated as an acid eating at the social order in an even more fundamental if slightly more subtle sense. Although the modern commitments to the authentic self can claim an ancestry in notions of conscience, they are also in the lineage, as Carl Trueman and others have shown, of Rousseau and the Romantic poets like Wordsworth and Shelley.[219] In this romantic vision, the natural and authentic self is perceived as in opposition to the artificial customs and institutions of society that engulf the individual person and seek to condition or compel her into a stifling conformity. The achievement of authenticity thus centrally entails emancipation from, or even rebellion against, established practices and institutions.[220]

In his Charles Eliot Norton Lectures, given at Harvard in 1970 (the same year as *Welsh*), the distinguished literary scholar and critic Lionel Trilling described a similar mindset: "At the behest of the criterion of authenticity, much that was once thought to make up the very fabric of culture has come to seem of little account, mere fantasy or ritual, or downright falsification."[221] Speaking specifically of Joseph Conrad's *Heart of Darkness* but with reference to a common motif in modern literature, Trilling discerned a view of "civilization as fraudulent and shameful."[222]

In a seminal study produced during Brennan's last decade on the Court, Robert Bellah and his associates cited an American source on the same basic idea—to Ralph Waldo Emerson, who in his influential essay "Self-Reliance" "declared the individual and society to be in opposition." Bellah quoted Emerson's assertion that "[s]ociety is everywhere in conspiracy against the manhood of every one of its members."[223] The modern American ideal, Bellah and his associates reported, is in the Emersonian tradition: it is to break free of traditions and culture so as to discover "the self in all its pristine purity."[224] "[T]he meaning of life for most Americans is to become one's own person, almost to give birth to oneself. . . . It involves breaking free from family, community, and inherited ideas."[225]

The theme has been endlessly repeated and celebrated in countless writings, songs, poems, theories, academic studies, and popular slogans. ("Be yourself." "Do your own thing." "Think for yourself.")[226] In the 1960s, Brennan's jurisprudence was developing alongside and in sync with an ideal of nonconformity and individual authenticity that was powerfully reshaping the general culture.[227]

In 1972, Brennan's opinion in *Eisenstadt v. Baird*[228] both typified and officially reenforced this development. Earlier, in the controversial case of *Griswold v. Connecticut*,[229] the Court's legalistic "emanations" and "penumbras" rationale for a right to contraceptives was anchored in a more substantive justification—in the nation's commitments to an *institution*. Namely, marriage. On this point the Court, through Justice Douglas, had waxed eloquent:

> We deal with a right of privacy older than the Bill of Rights—older than our political parties, older than our school system. Marriage is

a coming together for better or for worse, hopefully enduring, and intimate to the degree of being sacred. It is an association that promotes a way of life, not causes; a harmony in living, not political faiths; a bilateral loyalty, not commercial or social projects. Yet it is an association for as noble a purpose as any involved in our prior decisions.[230]

Connecticut's regulation of contraceptives was unconstitutional, in short, because it intruded the government into the "sacred" and "intimate" "association" of marriage.

On that rationale, a Massachusetts law regulating the distribution of contraceptives to *unmarried individuals* might have seemed unproblematic. But in *Eisenstadt*, Justice Brennan summarily brushed that construction aside. "[T]he marital couple is not an independent entity, with a mind and heart of its own," he wrote, "but an association of two *individuals*, each with a separate intellectual and emotional makeup. If the right of privacy means anything, it is the right of the individual, married or single, to be free from unwarranted governmental intrusion."[231] And thus, in a quick and peremptory paragraph, *Griswold's* solemn and eloquent profession of reliance on the institution of marriage was reduced to surplusage: it was *the individual* who was the subject of constitutional protection.

This ideal of individual self-determination and anti-institutional authenticity has persisted and has become if anything even more entrenched and pervasive. In a perceptive recent study of various new religiosities or spiritualities that in one form or another encompass probably half of all Americans,[232] Tara Isabella Burton emphasizes the anti-institutional common core of these religiosities.[233] Burton explains that in this by now almost ubiquitous view, "[t]he solution to the problem of society comes . . . through struggle, tearing down the bastions of what has come before. All of society is the script that must be rewritten."[234] For both of what she regards as the leading candidates to replace the nation's older and biblical civic religion—namely, the social justice culture and the Silicon Valley "techno-utopian ethos"—"expectations and institutions exist solely to be torn down."[235]

From this perspective, established institutions are viewed with suspicion and resentment—as stifling constraints upon individual freedom and authenticity. Law, business, the government, the church, the family, often the schools—in general, "the establishment" (or "the Man")—all fall under suspicion. And indeed, in recent decades all of these institutions have been the subject of relentless critical attack, most typically for their oppressive or "authoritarian" tendencies to suppress the individual in his or her quest to live an authentic life.

Not surprisingly, in this cultural environment, respect for institutions has declined precipitously, beginning in approximately the period in which Justice Brennan's jurisprudence of individual dignity was reshaping American life.[236] The traditional family has lost its formerly almost sacrosanct status: consequently, the percentage of people who marry has declined significantly in recent decades[237] while the percentage of children born to unmarried women has soared.[238] And critics assail what they describe as "family privilege," "marriage fundamentalism," and "the supremacy of the married family."[239] Other institutions have fared similarly. John Hillen reports that

> multiple polls, taken with great deliberation over the past decades, show a shocking decline in the confidence and trust Americans have in their institutions. This applies across the board—government institutions, commercial institutions, educational institutions, religious institutions, and non-profits. Hardly any institution has been spared this collapse in trust.[240]

Thus, Bruce Ledewitz observes that "no institution feels like a source of renewal. . . . [I]n terms of American society as a whole, all institutions have failed."[241]

Perceiving this institutional deterioration to be at the center of current social ills, Yuval Levin urgently prescribes a renewal of institutional life. His appeal resembles the plea for a renewal of "civic membership" made a quarter century earlier, during Justice Brennan's last decade on the Court, by Robert Bellah and his associates.[242] And yet since Bellah's time, the problem of institutional mistrust and alienation has evidently gotten worse.[243] So, is there any realistic hope that the trajectory will be reversed? Levin explains that his proposal for institutional renewal "begins with the premise that human beings are born as crooked creatures prone to waywardness and sin, that we therefore always require moral and social formation, and that such formation is what our institutions are for."[244] But it is of course precisely this premise that the Rousseauian and Emersonian ideal of the authentic self rejects. On the contrary: in this view, it is society and its institutions that are "crooked" and that seek to impose their crookedness on naturally benign and authentic selves.

Institutions are thus something that needs to be overcome in the pursuit of authenticity. And hence the dissolution of the social order continues apace.

"THE AGE OF THE LOST SELF"

The third way in which the solvent power of the modern self is at work is perhaps the most subtle and ironic, but it is also the most fundamental.[245] Beyond its contributions to dissolving the justifications for dignity and also the institutions that comprise the social order, the modern conception of the self also has a tendency to dissolve . . . the self itself.

This proposition is paradoxical, to be sure. How can a movement to exalt the self lead to the dissolution of the self? More fundamentally, how could the self be vulnerable to dissolution? Our "selves" might after all seem to be the most secure element in our world, and the thing we know most surely and intimately. How could we think and communicate at all—as we are doing at this moment, aren't we?—except as the "selves" that we are?

And yet the self can also appear to be a fragile and fleeting phantom. The most searching examinations of modern philosophers tend to conclude that the self is a "fiction," as David Hume put it,[246] or a shifting self-construction.[247] And, again ironically, the modern elevation of the self undermines the conditions needed for a solid and stable self.

"The self, a very nebulous entity indeed."

What, after all, is a "self"?[248] I speak of my "self," or of "myself," and so do you. We use such talk for various necessary purposes. One is to distinguish us from each other: I am not you and you are not me

because we each have our own "self." We also need to establish continuity—something to connect the wizened seventy-year-old with the
grinning gap-toothed kid in the first-grade class photo. Although their
physical appearance, their beliefs, and their mode of life may seem utterly different, they are somehow the same person, we think, connected
by some kind of continuous "self."

And we *need* to think this. Otherwise, for example, it might seem
profoundly unjust to punish someone for a crime committed ten or
twenty years previous, and then to hold that entity—that person, that
"self"—in prison for a period of decades.

But what exactly is that "self"? What does it consist of? We are obligated by the dictum "To thine own self be true," Lionel Trilling observed, "[b]ut we are still puzzled to know not only the locus of the self
to which we are to be true, but even what it is that we are to look for."[249]

Another need is to distinguish what is essential as opposed to what
is merely incidental to who each of us is.[250] Trilling quoted the Oxford
English Dictionary's definition, which defined "self" as "that . . . in a
person [which] is really and intrinsically *he* (in contradistinction to
what is adventitious)."[251] But how is that distinction to be drawn? Surely
you can clip your fingernails or cut your hair and still be the same person, the same "self." Those things are not *you*; they are "adventitious,"
as Trilling and the OED put it. Probably you could even lose a limb,
or even all your limbs, and still be yourself. Same for at least some
mental changes: you are still yourself—aren't you?—even if you alter
your opinions or switch political parties or change religions or forget
a lot of stuff. And yet there are presumably some things that are essential to the self. If your consciousness and memories were somehow
removed and you were implanted with someone else's consciousness
and memories, we would see the same body as before but we would
not likely think that this is *you*.

So what exactly is essential to make you *you*—essential to your
"self," or to your particular personhood?

The modern jurisprudence of conscience and dignity seems to depend on this assumption—namely, that there are features of a person
that are essential to his or her self or personhood and other features
that are merely incidental, or adventitious. So we may think that forc-

ing a man to fight in Vietnam or Iraq even though he is a committed pacifist violates his conscience, his dignity, his personhood. But forcing him to fight even though he would really, really prefer to be golfing or studying frustrates his desires but does *not* violate his conscience, his dignity, or his personhood.

More generally, our freedom to live as we choose may be—and is—restricted in all sorts of ways. We are told by the powers that be that we cannot walk around naked in the courthouse or the shopping mall, that we cannot use particular drugs we might want to use, that we must wear our seatbelts (and facemasks), and on and on and on. These restrictions constrict our freedom but they evidently do not infringe upon our basic personhood or our dignity. Conversely, government *cannot* forbid us to use contraceptives, or to have sexual relations with a person of the same sex, or to sell or watch videos depicting the violent destruction of animals.[252] Because, it seems, these restrictions would violate our "dignity"—the foundation of all of our constitutional rights, in Justice Brennan's view—by somehow violating our personhood or our selves.

So then, what determines which of our desires or interests or commitments are essential to our selves or our personhood, and hence our dignity, and which are merely incidental or adventitious, so that they can be restricted if the government thinks it has a good reason to do so?

In sum, modern culture and modern jurisprudence have made the individual person or "self" more central and elevated—and thus in a sense more important and necessary—than those things have been in the past. But with respect to the question "Okay, but what *is* the 'self'?," modern culture offers more questions than answers. Robert Bellah and his associates concluded that "much of the thinking about the self of educated Americans, thinking that has become almost hegemonic in our universities and much of the middle class, is based on inadequate social science, impoverished philosophy, and vacuous theology."[253]

Indeed, contemporary culture seems confused not only about what the answer to that question is but about what it even wants the answer to be. Take one fundamental dichotomy: Is a person's "self"—what the person essentially is, what makes the person who he or she is—something that is *chosen* or something that is *given*? Or some

combination of the two? The answer is unclear. Moreover, emphasiz-
ing either the chosenness of the self or its givenness leads to awkward
consequences.

Suppose we want to say that the self, or the features or qualities
that make a person who she essentially is, are chosen. That answer has
its attractions. After all, why should something as overwhelmingly,
existentially momentous as "who I am" just be imposed on me, whether
I like it or not? Doesn't it seem more fitting that I should get to choose
"who I am"? Whether I will be male or female, for example, or something else? What sense would it make to take such costly and elaborate care to establish all sorts of freedoms allowing people to make
their own choices in large areas of life and yet not give them any choice
about the most important matter that is presupposed in (and, arguably,
determinative of) all of those other protected choices—namely, who
they actually are?

But this answer is also inconvenient for other purposes. To the extent that the self is chosen, there may be less reason for society to respect or accommodate those whom society finds objectionable than
there is if we suppose that people to a large extent didn't choose and
can't help who they are. Thus, a central claim repeatedly made by proponents of gay rights has been that sexual orientation is an essential
feature of identity that is *not* chosen.[254] Consequently it is unfair to
blame or punish or restrict people for something that they did not
choose and for which they accordingly are not responsible.[255]

The idea of personhood or self as chosen also poses an awkward
conceptual question: If I get to choose my own self, who is the "I"
that does the choosing? Doesn't the proposition that every person
does or should choose who he/she/they/it is contradict itself by (necessarily) positing a chooser (presumably with some sort of identity)
to begin with?

Suppose then that we turn to the other answer: the self is *given*—
by genetic endowment, maybe, or family and social formation, or early
education, or some combination thereof. You just are who and what
you are, and I am who and what I am; we don't get to choose. We may
of course work to mold our character over time, or our lifestyle, but

even those efforts will reflect the movements of a basic self that was just given to us.

This answer might seem more empirically plausible than the answer that emphasizes choice. Most people seem placed in life in particular situations with particular endowments over which they have little choice. Which of us really had any choice over our parents, our place and time of birth, our height, our intelligence or aptitudes, our early upbringing? By the time we may have seemed to have any actual choices of importance, we were already pretty much formed.

Moreover, the "given self" answer is convenient, as noted, for some purposes, such as the advancement of gay rights. But the answer may be inconvenient for other purposes, such as claims for a right to choose or alter one's sex or gender.[256] More generally, the givenness answer seems in tension with the modern notion of "human dignity" with its insistence on the right of every person to define for himself or herself a concept of the universe, existence, and meaning. What good is it to be able to choose what your universe will be like if you can't even choose who you yourself are, and thus you cannot choose who is fashioning that universe? It would be like saying that a person has the right to choose what kind of house he or she will occupy but has no choice over who the architect and builders will be.

Modern culture and discourse seem to offer few solid answers to these kinds of questions. The culture places great normative emphasis on "the person," "the individual," "the self." But it provides precious little insight into what the person or the self is, exactly. Instead, the discourse seems to hop around opportunistically. For one purpose the self is *given*—by what is not exactly clear. For another purpose the self is *chosen*, though it is not exactly clear who or what is doing the choosing.

These are abstract questions—fodder for philosophers, perhaps— but they have their practical and existential dimension as well. And we often encounter that dimension. A person reports that he is having "an identity crisis," or that she "has been living a lie," or that "I'm not sure who I really am" or "I'm not myself" or "The way I'm living, my job, my relationships . . . it's just not me." "[T]he question *Who am I?* is now one of the most fraught of our time," Mary Eberstadt reports.[257]

The Traditional Sources of Personal Identity

Though familiar enough today, such existential angst is arguably a feature of modernity.[258] For people living in Thomas More's day, or James Madison's, the questions might have seemed academic, even unmoored, like the philosopher's question: "How can I know that the world actually exists—that I'm not just some sort of brain in a vat?" Through much of history, your identity—or who you were—was pretty much determined by two principal sources: one theological in nature and the other social.

So, in the first place, throughout the period of Christendom, you were the person you were because you were possessed of an immortal soul, created by and known to God. It was your soul that made you *you* and not someone else, that made the seventy-year-old you the same person as the one-year-old you, and indeed that would make you the same person after your death and resurrection as you were while living on this earth. That soul was recognized and reenforced by consecrating sacraments, as we saw in chapter one—baptism, christening, marriage, last rites. And, as noted, it was the fact that you were made by God in His image that gave you an inherent sacred dignity, without respect to the wretchedness of your circumstances or the waywardness of your life.[259]

But in a more immediate and mundane sense, who you were was also determined by your relations to other people, and especially to your family.[260] Asked to identify yourself, you would likely respond with something like, "I'm John, the son of William and Marian, of the Williamson clan or family." Such relationships not only helped to identify who a person was at any given moment, they also answered the question of continuity, explaining how the seventy-year-old John was the same person as the one-year-old or ten-year-old John. After all, the essential relationships will remain the same throughout the person's life, even after the identifying progenitors have long since passed beyond this mortal sphere.

The philosopher David Velleman contends that such family relationships are for most people a crucial element of identity. The self-knowledge gained through relationships with biological progenitors,

Velleman argues, "is of irreplaceable value in the life task of identity-formation."[261]

These traditional forms of fixing identity persisted into the modern world, and for many they are likely still formative.[262] For William Brennan in particular, such factors seem to have provided a secure sense of identity. Thus, although Brennan's Catholicism may have been less than fervent, there is no reason to doubt that it was sincere as far as it went. And of course Catholicism would have taught him the reality and importance of an immortal soul, created by and known to God. In addition, Brennan was the product of strong parents and a close family that made him the person he was.

His father in particular was a formidable and formative figure. "Everything I am," Brennan observed late in life, "I am because of my father."[263] At six feet tall, father towered over son, who only attained 5'8".[264] Bill senior dominated the household and "brooked no dissent from his children," as Brennan's biographers report.[265] It was his father who determined that Bill junior would go to college at the University of Pennsylvania, would prepare for a practical career in business and later law, would attend Harvard Law School: "[I]t did not seem to occur to [Bill junior] that he might have a say" in such matters.[266] Coming to America from Ireland as an impoverished young man and with only six years of schooling, Bill senior had worked and scraped and finagled his way to prosperity and political prominence in New Jersey,[267] and Bill junior was the beneficiary of that prosperity and prominence. Thus, it was his father's connections that secured for Bill junior his job at the New Jersey law firm where his legal career was shaped.[268]

In 1930, while the future justice was a second-year student at Harvard Law School, his father contracted a fatal case of pneumonia. Bill junior hurried home, but arrived too late to say goodbye to his father. Even so, his father's stature—and his father's expectations for him—were likely reenforced by the experience of watching as forty thousand admiring citizens lined up overnight to pay their respects at the rotunda of the Newark City Hall, and the next day as the procession to St. Patrick's Church stretched on for a mile.[269] Years later, now in his eighties, when asked whether his father would have been surprised to see his son as a Supreme Court justice, Brennan would reply, "No, he would have expected it."[270]

The extraordinary authority of parents and family was manifest in the fact that when Bill junior, the future justice, decided to marry his sweetheart Marjorie, the couple feared family disapproval—Bill was headed off to Harvard, in fulfillment of his father's wishes, and marriage at this point might interfere with his professional advancement—and so they married secretly and lived apart while Bill was in law school. As graduation approached, and with his father now deceased, Bill and Marjorie made plans to go public with a second wedding without telling the family that they had actually already been married for three years. (The plan was foiled, to Bill's mortification, when the priest who had initially married them inadvertently produced a copy of the earlier marriage certificate.)[271]

In short, William Brennan Jr. didn't have to wonder about his identity: that was firmly conferred upon him by his faith and his family. His name itself—including the *Jr.*—served as a perpetual reminder of that identity. Might his often-remarked quiet confidence and personal warmth have been a reflection of the fact that Brennan was a person with a secure sense of who he was?

The Decline of the Traditional Sources

But if faith and family could give someone like Brennan a definite sense of his identity, those sources would become increasingly unavailable to many in the emerging secular republic that the justice was helping to shape. Summarizing the findings of their intensive sociological study in the 1980s, Robert Bellah and associates reported that "the notion that one discovers one's deepest beliefs in, and through, tradition and community is not very congenial to Americans. Most of us imagine an autonomous self existing independently, entirely outside any tradition and community."[272]

So although the notion of an immortal soul created by and known to God surely persists for many, that notion is out of place in the public domain which, again, is supposed to maintain a secular quality. Bellah's study found that "[t]oday religion represents a frame of reference for the self as conspicuous in its absence as in its presence."[273]

The familial basis of identity is likewise much impaired.[274] In part this is because the traditional family structure has been significantly unsettled by modern developments. Another disruptive modern development has been the massive turn to artificial reproductive technologies—the opposition of, for instance, Brennan's church has of course had no influence over policies in the secular republic—which ensure that many thousands of people no longer even know who their biological parents are. Mary Eberstadt explains:

> Who am I? An illiterate peasant of the Middle Ages was better equipped to answer that question than many people in advanced societies in this century. He may only have lived until age thirty—but he spent his days among family and in towns, practicing a shared faith, and thus developed a vivid sense of those to whom he was elementally connected, not just in the course of his life but before birth and after death.[275]

But an even more fundamental problem, probably, is the fact that both the theistic and the familial bases of identity seem incompatible with the modern determination to treat each individual as possessed of his or her own self, autonomy, and intrinsic dignity. You are *you*, yourself. To suggest that your dignity is merely derivative from that of a divine source or creator is to question that dignity. And suppose you do happen to come from a solid and stable family, like Brennan's; even so, it would be demeaning—wouldn't it?—to have to identify yourself primarily as somebody else's son or daughter or spouse. What sense would it make for the very identity of a being with the exalted power and right to form its own conception of meaning, existence, and the universe—for a veritable Godlet—to be determined by the unchosen accident of having been born to Bob the plumber and Mary the baker? Or by the fact of being wedded to Paolo or Elizabeth? Thus, even insofar as community and institutions persist, their capacity to be a basis for personal identity has waned.

But then the questions return. Who are you, exactly? Among the millions of Godlets, what is it that makes you who you distinctively are?

In these circumstances, it would not be surprising if many people experienced a sense of disorientation about who they are.[276] And there are signs of such disorientation. Data indicates that loneliness,[277] depression,[278] and suicide[279] are escalating. These are complex phenomena, to be sure, but they are likely not unrelated to the demoralization that accompanies a breakdown in social trust, social institutions, and a loss of sense of self and identity. In this vein, Aaron Kheriaty, professor of psychology at the University of California, Irvine, describes the dramatic increase in suicide in recent years, especially among younger people, and explains the connection between this trend and the decline in the family structures and social networks which "help form our identities and give our lives a strong sense of purpose and belonging."[280] The huge growth in ancestry research—and, more specifically, in people who are searching for their biological parents,[281] "impelled," as David Velleman explains, "by what they describe as a deep and unrelenting need"[282]—likewise suggests an urgent effort to establish a grounding for personal identity.[283] Velleman adds that "[w]hen adoptees go searching for their biological parents and siblings, there is a literal sense in which they are searching for themselves."[284]

Perhaps even more ominous has been the rise of what is sometimes described as "tribalism."[285] At a time in which the long-established "ties that bind" have been stretched and severed, and delegitimated, is it surprising that people increasingly strive to find some anchor for their personhood in race, or nationalism?[286] Or in fandom—self-identifying attachment to a sports team, a rock band, or a popular fiction or character like Harry Potter (or Severus Snape!)?[287] Or in some political party or religious cause that is fervently embraced not so much because it is true but because it provides some stable grounding for an "identity"?

Perhaps the most conspicuous such development is the escalation of so-called "identity politics."[288] "[T]he political trend [of identity politics] expresses a quest for authenticity," explains Doug Rossinow, a historian of American leftist movements. "Identity politics seeks to clear a space for the fulfillment of a particular group's authenticity and for its political organization. These actions may lead to political change, but even if they do not, this space clearing is still considered desirable, for it can alleviate individuals' estrangement from their genuine identity."[289] Rossinow was writing in the late 1990s, but the prevalence and power of identity politics have surely become even more intense since then.[290] Thus, Mary Eberstadt observes that "identitarianism is now the heart and soul of politics for many people."[291]

VII

"THE PRESENT AGE IS DEMENTED."

So, looking backward, and then looking forward: How would this situation of what is often described as "post-modernity" appear from the early modern perspective of Thomas More? Would More perceive in our situation a sad vindication of his fears for the breakdown of the social order?[292]

A provocative reflection on the question was offered in the comically exaggerated and yet eerily prescient novel *Love in the Ruins*,[293] by the writer and physician Walker Percy. Narrated by its fictional protagonist, Dr. Thomas More, a proud descendant of the sixteenth-century lawyer and knight ("that great soul, the dearest best noblest merriest of Englishmen"),[294] the novel was published in the same year as *Lemon v. Kurtzman* and Rawls's *A Theory of Justice*, a year before *Eisenstadt v. Baird*, and two years before *Roe v. Wade*. Published, in other words, as the America contemplated by Justice Brennan's jurisprudence was taking shape.

In a speech given upon publication of the novel, Percy explained that it was motivated by a concern about "certain elements of self-hatred and self-destructiveness which have surfaced in American life."[295] The novel thus sought "to investigate ... how the boat might go under at the very time everybody is talking about the dignity of the individual and the quality of life." Projecting forward to the future in which the novel was set, Percy predicted that "we will still be using words like 'freedom,' 'the dignity of the individual,' the 'quality of life,' and so on. But the meanings will have slipped."[296]

The America of Percy's novel in some ways seems healthy enough — and much like present-day America. The story in that sense is unlike some other apocalyptic fiction, such as *A Canticle for Leibowitz* or the movie *The Postman*. In the America described by Percy, political rallies are held, scientific research continues apace, people receive professional counseling for despondency and sexual impotence, professional golf tournaments continue to be played, and the GDP continues to rise. Cultural and religious pluralism prevails: there are still a few orthodox Christians (like More himself, in his beliefs if not in his conduct), highly moral religious agnostics (like More's secretary and lover Ellen), new-agey pantheists who believe that they along with everything else are God,[297] secular naturalists who devoutly seek for sightings of the revered ivory-billed woodpecker,[298] and scientific materialists who believe that only what is visible and measurable is real.[299] (In Percy's novel, these last two categories overlap.)

Despite this appearance of prosperity and normalcy, Dr. More senses impending doom. He cannot persuade his tanned, fit, and optimistic colleagues to share in what they perceive as his morbidity. And yet the signs of decay are evident. The country has become badly fragmented — politically, culturally, religiously, racially. "Americans have turned against each other, race against race, right against left, believer against heathen."[300] The Republican Party has degenerated into the Knothead Party (with the slogan "No Man Can Be Too Knotheaded in the Service of His Country"), while the Democratic Party has devolved into the Left Party, or LEFTPAPASANE (for "Liberty, Equality, Fraternity, The Pill, Atheism, Pot, Anti-Pollution, Sex, Abortion Now, and Euthanasia").[301] There are "Left states and Knothead states, Left towns and Knothead towns, but no center towns" — also "Left networks and Knothead networks."[302] The Catholic Church has split into three separate sects.[303] Radicalized Blacks, encouraged and assisted by honored and well-compensated Ivy League professors, are rising in "creative nonviolent violent" revolt.[304]

But this outward fragmentation is merely a manifestation of an inner fragmentation or dissolution of the self. To be sure, the elites remain verbally committed to human dignity and to the idea of "above all every man's sacred right to choose his own destiny and realize his own potential."[305] But this ideal is mocked by actual realities, which reflect a pervasive loss of the integrated self. Given medical advances, people can live to be ninety or one hundred, "as spry as can be, limber-jointed, smooth-faced, supple of artery," and yet become "inexplicably sad" and "despondent in their happiness."[306] Many people fluctuate between angelism and bestialism.[307] One of More's outwardly confident colleagues is "a self successfully playing at being a self that is not itself."[308] More tells another colleague that "[i]t's not even the U.S.A., it's the soul of Western man that is in the very act of flying apart HERE and NOW."[309]

More understands this loss of the self from the inside because he himself is Exhibit A, alternately elated and despondent, wholly fragmented between what he believes and how he actually lives. Although he partially resembles his ancestor and namesake in that he is a reflective and committed Catholic in his beliefs,[310] Percy's Dr. More is also a scientist and a "bad Catholic," given to excessive drinking and serial adultery. He is modern enough to feel no guilt for his philandering and yet still traditional enough to feel guilty for not feeling guilty.[311] At one point, desperate and lost, he attempts suicide, and is temporarily confined to a mental institution. "Who am I?," he wonders.[312] "How can a man spend forty-five years as a stranger to himself?"[313] And he appeals to his ancestor and namesake and pleads with the saint to pray for him and his soul.[314]

Dr. Thomas More, Percy's protagonist, thinks that this combination of social and personal dissolution portends "the hemorrhage and death by suicide of the old Western world."[315] "For the world is broken, sundered, busted down the middle, self ripped from self and man pasted back together as mythical monster, half angel, half beast, but no man."[316]

"[B]roken, sundered, busted down the middle . . ." Or might we put it more gently? "Compartmentalized," perhaps?

And yet Dr. More does not despair utterly. With specific reference to himself and a scientific gadget he has invented for ministering to fractured psyches, but perhaps more generally to "the terrible God-blessed Americans," he mutters desperately: "Don't give up. It is not too late. You are still the last hope. There is no one else. Bad as we are, there is no one else."[317]

But is there truly no one else? If More's ingenious invention fails to fix the problem (as it does), is there still some hope of help from a transcendent source? Perhaps. "Christ have mercy on me," he pleads.

"Sir Thomas More, pray for me. . . . Lord have mercy on your poor church."[318]

Percy himself elsewhere explained the situation in this way:

> [T]he self finds itself ever more conspicuously without a place in the modern world. . . . The act of the self in the very age which was itself designed for the self's understanding of all things and to please the self through the consumption of goods and services—the face of the self is the face of fear and sadness, because it does not know who it is or where it belongs.[319]

And "the 'normal' denizen of the Western world . . . , I think it is fair to say, doesn't know who he is, what he believes, or what he is doing."[320]

And thus, at least from one perspective, we observe the culmination, or the comeuppance, of conscience. Of conscience—that ennobling but also disintegrating faculty that has served to uplift, dignify, and even consecrate humanity. But it also sunders a man from his society and family (Sir Thomas More), from the tradition and church that shaped him (Luther), from the commitment to theological truth (Madison). And finally, in its modern version, it sunders a man (Brennan, Kennedy, Dr. Thomas More, Joe Biden, and so, so many others) from himself, or from his "self," separating the public persona or performer from what ostensibly are, or at least *were*, his deepest and constitutive convictions, and thereby leaving him ignorant of "who he is, what he believes, or what he is doing."

Epilogue

Looking Backward, Looking Forward

We began this drama by contemplating Jacques Barzun's pronouncement that "in the West the culture of the last 500 years is ending."[1] Barzun elaborated on this doleful prognosis by tracing the playing out, and the unraveling, of about a dozen principal themes, including emancipation, individualism, and secularism. In this book we have considered, in more limited and episodic fashion, developments in only one major and related theme: conscience.

Claims of conscience—by men like Thomas More, Martin Luther, even Henry VIII—were conspicuous and formative at the beginning of the modern age. And such claims are conspicuous still, at what Barzun and others have regarded as the end of that age. But although the genealogies may be traceable and the family resemblances discernible, the modern conscience is something quite different from what Thomas More invoked. In comparison with its progenitors, the modern conscience is no humble servant of God and the church or the scriptures; it is proud, inflated, and freestanding. It is closely entwined with the associated and even more conspicuous modern themes of "authenticity" and "dignity." And its implications bear out More's fears that conscience as it was coming to be understood contained the seeds of social and even personal disintegration.

Today, observing the destructive fruit of such seeds in the frightening polarization and fragmentation of our time, we might look back and wonder what went wrong. How did commitments that promised such gains for freedom and human dignity, and that have in some respects delivered on those promises in spectacular fashion, come to have such corrosive consequences of late? Where did conscience go off the rails? Who was, or who is, to blame?

Was it Luther? More seems to have thought so. Madison? Today there is a small but growing body of critics, sometimes clustered around an ideal of "integralism," who would not hesitate to indict the "Father of the Constitution" for some of the evils we face today.[2] Brennan? Though much admired, the justice surely has had his share of critics. One younger reader tells me that Brennan is not nearly the cultural icon today that he was, say, a quarter century ago.

But this is not the place either to accuse or to absolve any of these men or their fellows. And indeed, considered against the broad backdrop of the history we have been reflecting on, there may seem to be a kind of exonerating inevitability to these developments. Our examinations may thus support a sort of darker version of "Whig history." Whig history is usually understood to be optimistic in character, viewing the past as somehow leading inexorably to the enlightened and humane state of affairs that we enjoy today. By contrast, the history we have considered here seems to run in the opposite direction—promising and for a time providing enlightenment and emancipation, but culminating in fragmentation. And the label "Whig history" is usually thought to denote a kind of fallacy. But in this case *are* we dealing with a fallacy? In the men and events that we have studied, doesn't there seem to be a kind of tragic inevitability?

So Luther no doubt played an important role in the breakup of Christendom, as Thomas More believed. And yet, from a distance, doesn't that breakup seem pretty much foreordained? Hadn't history been heading in that direction for some time, with Wycliffe and Ockham and Hus? And could the tenuously maintained, patched-together unity of Christendom really have persisted given the expansion of Western civilization into the Americas and elsewhere, and also given the scientific revolution that ("Enlightened" critics notwithstanding) medieval Christianity itself was bringing about?[3] Moreover, as we saw in chapter one, Thomas More himself was unable to contain the inherently subjective and subversive dimensions of conscience.

In retrospect, therefore, the operations of conscience in supporting the proliferation of pluralism, and the accompanying fragmentation, seem irrepressible. By James Madison's time, that pluralism was already far advanced: it was not something that Madison mischievously concocted as part of a subtle, long-range plan of social subversion. And given such conditions, wasn't Madison's effort to enshrine conscience as a unifying ideal by partially detaching it from its Christian foundations—and, more subtly but ominously, from the historical commitment to formulated theological truth—a necessary response to such pluralism? Notwithstanding the corrosive consequences of that detachment over the longer term? What else could he have done?

In the same way, William Brennan's compartmentalization relegating religious truth to the private domain—first for himself and then for the nation as a whole—may well have portended the kind of social and personal fragmentation we have considered in the last chapter. But Brennan and so many others—political figures like John Kennedy, philosophers like John Rawls—have thought this compartmentalization to be necessary. Necessary and also just, given the country's religious pluralism. Is it clear that they have been wrong on that point? What was the alternative, exactly?

So-called integralists may regret the loss of a more unified relation of church, state, and society.[4] We may (or may not) sympathize with, even share in, their regret. But, seriously, has such deep unity ever been a viable possibility, at least in America? How successful were the Massachusetts Puritans in maintaining such a unity? Or even if unity might have been a possibility in some version of early America, by the time Brennan came on the scene was there even the slightest prospect of restoring it?

In any case, we are what we are, and where we are. So what comes next? Like Barzun, the discussions in this book have not been cheerful. The trajectories we have charted would seem to portend further fragmentation, culminating in . . . who knows what? Better not to say, perhaps, for fear that naming what awaits us might help to bring it about.

And yet maybe this gloom is gratuitous. Maybe our reflections in this book have all been misguided, and our tentative projections misconceived. Those of us who have children or grandchildren may well hope so. And history can surprise. Maybe our unfolding history will suddenly change course in some unexpected way. Maybe some new religion or philosophy, or some revitalized version of an old religion or philosophy, will direct us onto a different and more hopeful course? Current trajectories may not portend anything of that sort. Then again, Tara Isabella Burton's recent fascinating survey of the various spiritualities springing up in the culture (and by her estimate encompassing over half of the population) suggests a widespread yearning for something more meaningful and fulfilling than modern consumerist and professional cultures provide.[5]

Or suppose the darker projections are *not* mistaken. What then? Thomas More thought that the audacious assertions of "conscience" by men like Luther were bringing about the destruction of his world—a world that in broad terms had persisted for a millennium. We can see in retrospect that he was right. More also believed that the loss of that world would be an unmitigated evil. On that point we may well disagree. Even if More was correct in sensing the disintegrating potential of the unmoored conscience over the long run, most of us would say that the intervening five centuries have been filled with evils and atrocities, yes—but also with unnumbered glorious political and economic and scientific advances that we would not want to do without.

So who knows? The foreseeable continuing fragmentation of the social order is a terrifying prospect, to be sure. But the resulting disorder and disorientation, if that is what we are in for, may well have their accompanying blessings.

This is, to be sure, an uncertain and unsatisfying conclusion. I have been told by more than one critic (and by myself) that a book like this needs to conclude with a more positive prescription about where we go from here. And yet if we are in a "fulcrum moment" in history, as Thomas More was, is it realistic to suppose that we can foresee, much less control, what comes after? Or is the wiser course to attempt "amidst the encircling gloom" to conserve what is of value in our present civilization and then, foregoing the pretense that we can "see the distant scene" (as the much-loved hymn "Lead, Kindly Light" puts it), be content to be led?

"One step enough."[6] One step, and then another, taken hopefully in accordance with and under the direction of what we might call (perhaps in a partially revived or recovered sense of the word?) . . . conscience.

NOTES

Prologue

1. Jacques Barzun, *From Dawn to Decadence: 500 Years of Western Cultural Life; 1500 to the Present* (New York: HarperCollins, 2000), xi.
2. Barzun, *From Dawn to Decadence*, xv.
3. Barzun, *From Dawn to Decadence*, xiii.
4. Barzun, *From Dawn to Decadence*, xv.
5. See, e.g., Adam K. Raymond, "How Close Is the U.S. to Civil War? About Two-Thirds of the Way, Americans Say," *New York Intelligencer*, October 24, 2019, https://nymag.com/intelligencer/2019/10/americans-say-u-s-is-two-thirds-of-the-way-to-civil-war.html. See also Mike Allen, "Republicans and Democrats Agree—The Country Is Falling Apart," *Axios*, Jan. 14, 2021, https://www.axios.com/poll-america-falling-apart-4a13376f-f962-46e3-8e2c-174d396f25d1.html. In his article, Allen states: "In a new Axios-Ipsos poll, fourth-fifths of Americans—both Republicans and Democrats—say America is falling apart."
6. For assessments in this vein, see Ross Douthat, *The Decadent Society: How We Became the Victims of Our Own Success* (New York: Avid Reader Press, 2020), 8.

1. Peter Ackroyd, *The Life of Thomas More* (New York: Anchor Books, 1998), 398.
2. John Guy, *Thomas More* (New York: Oxford University Press, 2000), 212.

3. Richard Rex, "More and the Heretics: Statesman or Fanatic?," in *The Cambridge Companion to Thomas More*, ed. George M. Logan (Cambridge: Cambridge University Press, 2011), 93, 108.

4. The judgment was Samuel Johnson's. Quoted in Robert Bolt, *A Man for All Seasons* (London: Heinemann, 1960), v.

5. Erasmus, who knew More well, described him in this way: "I do not think . . . that Nature ever formed a mind more present, ready, sharpsighted and subtle, or in a word more absolutely furnished with every kind of faculty than his. Add to this a power of expression equal to his intellect, a singular cheerfulness of character, and an abundance of wit." Quoted in James Monti, *The King's Good Servant But God's First: The Life and Writings of Thomas More* (San Francisco: Ignatius Press, 1997), 27. Historian Derek Wilson offers a different portrayal: More was "cynical," "a bigot, a fanatic, a man whose piety led him into such impious actions as vulgar abuse, lying, and persecution," "exquisitely cruel," and a self-promoter who "picked up perks as a modern ex-public servant picks up company directorships." Derek Wilson, *In the Lion's Court: Power, Ambition, and Sudden Death in the Reign of Henry VIII* (New York: St. Martin's Press, 2001), 17, 23, 58, 60, 224.

6. Thomas More, *The Last Letters of Thomas More*, ed. Alvaro de Silva (Grand Rapids, MI: Eerdmans, 2001), 61. Hereafter, this title will be referred to as *Last Letters*.

7. Ackroyd, *Life of Thomas More*, 399.

8. See Guy, *Thomas More*, 189. "In More's case, the lack of counsel was no impediment, since he could equal or outshine the best legal minds. His disadvantage was that the jury appears to have been rigged."

9. J. J. Scarisbrick, *Henry VIII* (New Haven, CT: Yale University Press, 1997), 167.

10. Thomas More, *The Sadness of Christ and Final Prayers and Instructions*, ed. Gerard Wegemer, trans. Clarence Miller (Strongsville, OH: Scepter Publishers, 1993), 152–55.

11. William Roper, "The Life of Sir Thomas More," in *Saint Thomas More: Selected Writings*, ed. John F. Thornton and Susan B. Varenne (New York: Vintage Books, 2003), 179, 242.

12. Roper, "Life of Sir Thomas More," 242.

13. Ackroyd, *Life of Thomas More*, 406.

14. Carlos M. N. Eire, *Reformations: The Early Modern World, 1450–1650* (New Haven, CT: Yale University Press, 2016), 325.

15. Peter Ackroyd reports that Margaret "was undoubtedly the most learned woman of her day, at least in England." Ackroyd, *Life of Thomas More*, 147.

16. John Guy, *A Daughter's Love: Thomas More and His Dearest Meg* (Boston: Houghton Mifflin Harcourt, 2008), 3–4.

17. Wilson, *In the Lion's Court*, 11.

18. Susan Brigden, *New Worlds, Lost Worlds: The Reign of the Tudors, 1485–1603* (New York: Penguin Books, 2000).

19. Monti, *King's Good Servant*, 117, 139.

20. See Ackroyd, *Life of Thomas More*, 282.

21. See Glenn A. Moots, "Was the Protestant Reformation a Radical Revolution?," *Law & Liberty* (October 29, 2021), https://lawliberty.org/was-the -protestant-reformation-a-radical-revolution/. "Luther refers to the conscience over five hundred times, identifying it as the 'coram deo'—that which puts us before the face of God—to distinguish it from the ethical and political rules of society."

22. Heiko A. Oberman, *Luther: Man Between God and the Devil*, trans. Eileen Walliser-Schwarzbart (New Haven, CT: Yale University Press, 1989), 203. Noah Feldman argues that Luther's stance was one of the foundations of modern freedom of conscience. Noah Feldman, "The Intellectual Origins of the Establishment Clause," *New York University Law Review* 77 (2002): 357–59.

23. Quoted in Paul Strohm, *Conscience: A Very Short Introduction* (Oxford: Oxford University Press, 2011), 19.

24. See Richard Marius, *Thomas More: A Biography* (Cambridge, MA: Harvard University Press, 1999), 358. See also Brigden, *New Worlds, Lost Worlds*, 112: "This was a king with the power and will to advance his private conscience as a principle to bind not only the bodies but the souls of his subjects, and to set that private conscience against the whole of Christendom."

25. For a valuable history of these developments, see Andrew R. Murphy, *Conscience and Community* (University Park: Pennsylvania State University Press, 2001), 276–91.

26. Strohm, *Conscience*, 1.

27. Barzun's gloomy prognosis is discussed in the prologue.

28. See Guy, *Thomas More*, 212, which observes that "More loved [Margaret] more than anyone except God."

29. Hilaire Belloc, *Characters of the Reformation* (Rockford, IL: Tan Books, 1992), 65.

30. *Last Letters*, 64.

31. See Brad S. Gregory, *Salvation at Stake: Christian Martyrdom in Early Modern Europe* (Cambridge, MA: Harvard University Press, 1999), 104. "Certain devout Christians, particularly within post-Tridentine Catholicism, actively yearned for martyrdom."

32. More, *Sadness of Christ*, 12.

33. *Last Letters*, 87.

34. *Last Letters*, 63.

35. *Last Letters*, 67.

36. *Last Letters*, 89.

37. Ackroyd, *Life of Thomas More*, 346.

38. Guy, *A Daughter's Love*, 72.

39. See *Last Letters*. For example, on page 45: "Therefore let us give Him as many thanks as we can (for certainly we can never give Him enough); and in our agony remembering His (with which no other can ever be compared), let us beg Him with all our strength that He may deign to comfort us in our anguish by an insight into His; and when we urgently beseech Him, because of our mental distress, to free us from danger, let us nevertheless follow His own most wholesome example by concluding our prayer with His own addition:

'Yet not as I will but as you will.' If we do these things diligently, I have no doubt at all that just as an angel brought Him consolation in answer to His prayer, so too each of our angels will bring us from His Spirit consolation that will give us the strength to persevere in those deeds that will lift us up to heaven."

40. Ackroyd, *Life of Thomas More*, 367.

41. Roper, "Life of Sir Thomas More," 230. See also *Last Letters*, 74, 86.

42. *Last Letters*, 58.

43. See Peter Marshall, "The Last Years," in *The Cambridge Companion to Thomas More*, ed. George M. Logan (Cambridge: Cambridge University Press, 2011), 116, (quote on) 126: "The confiscation of More's property also reduced his family to conditions of poverty. Although Lady Alice eventually secured a government pension, it is possible that some estrangement from her husband came about as a result of her inability to understand why he would force them all to suffer for a principle which few appeared to share."

44. Guy, *A Daughter's Love*, 244.

45. *Last Letters*, 65.

46. More's *Utopia* had begun with praise of "my friend Cuthbert Tunstall, an excellent person [whose] . . . learning and moral character . . . are too remarkable for me to describe adequately." Thomas More, *Utopia*, trans. Paul Turner (London: Penguin Books, 1965), 37. *Utopia* was first published in 1516.

47. *Last Letters*, 87.

48. *Last Letters*, 73.

49. Bolt, *A Man for All Seasons*, 140. This exchange in the play appears to be based on the following passage from the most extended prison letter, which reports More's conversation with Meg as follows: "And some may be peradventure of that mind, that if they say one thing and think the while the contrary, God more regardeth their heart than their tongue, and that therefore their oath goeth upon that they think, and not upon that they say. . . . But in good faith, Marget, I can use no such ways in so great a matter: but like as if mine own conscience served me, I would not let to do it." *Last Letters*, 79.

50. See Sissela Bok, *Lying* (New York: Pantheon Books, 1978), 32–46.

51. Bok, *Lying*, 38.

52. For discussion and defense of Augustine's categorical position, see Paul J. Griffiths, *Lying: An Augustinian Theology of Duplicity* (Eugene, OR: Wipf & Stock, 2010).

53. Monti, *King's Good Servant*, 74. See also Louis L. Martz, *Thomas More: The Search for the Inner Man* (New Haven, CT: Yale University Press, 1990). Indeed, as a young man in his twenties, More had given a series of acclaimed lectures on *City of God*, Augustine's magnum opus. Monti, *King's Good Servant*, 29.

54. See Ackroyd, *Life of Thomas More*, 184, 190, 216, 220, 243, 321, 331, 350.

55. Ackroyd, *Life of Thomas More*, 168.

56. Ackroyd, *Life of Thomas More*, 156.

57. See Belloc, *Characters of the Reformation*, 63. "He could foresee no fruit following upon his great example. In fact, during all the four hundred years from his day to ours, no apparent political fruit has been borne by it."

58. Monti, *King's Good Servant*, 115.

59. Brigden, *New Worlds, Lost Worlds*, 43.

60. *Last Letters*, 74–75.

61. For a collection of Christian teachings on the subject, see Jill Haak Adels, *The Wisdom of the Saints: An Anthology* (New York: Oxford University Press, 1987), 153–55.

62. Marius, *Thomas More*, 467.

63. John T. Noonan, Jr. and Edward McGlynn Gaffney, Jr., *Religious Freedom: History, Cases, and Other Materials* (New York: Foundation Press, 2001), 111 (emphasis added). See also *Last Letters*, 90: "leaving every man to their own conscience, myself will with good grace follow mine."

64. Peter Ackroyd observes that "[h]is opponents were genuinely following their consciences," but More "truly believed Lutherans to be 'daemonum satellites' ('agents of the demons') who must, if necessary, be destroyed by burning." Ackroyd, *Life of Thomas More*, 302, 248.

65. Monti, *King's Good Servant*, 32–34.

66. Ackroyd, *Life of Thomas More*, 50.

67. Marius, *Thomas More*, 54.

68. His son-in-law William Roper reported that "because he [More] was of a pleasant disposition, it pleased the King and Queen after the council had supped, at the time of their supper, for their pleasure commonly to call for him to be merry with them. Whom when he perceived so much in his talk to delight that he could not once in a month get leave to go home to his wife and children, whose company he most desired." Roper, "Life of Sir Thomas More," 185. In addition, "for the pleasure he [the king] took in his company would his grace suddenly sometimes come to his house at Chelsea to be merry with him" (191).

69. Ackroyd, *Life of Thomas More*, 294–97.

70. John Guy explains that although More's first wife is commonly called "Jane" by modern writers, in family documents her name is given as "Joanna" or sometimes "Joan." Guy, *A Daughter's Love*, 9.

71. Thornton and Varenne, *Saint Thomas More*, 246–47; Guy, *A Daughter's Love*, 39.

72. See More, *Sadness of Christ*, 54, observing that in the "dark silence of the night, [we] will find that it is more receptive to divine consolation than it is during the daytime, when the noisy bustle of business on all sides distracts the eyes, the ears, and the mind and dissipates our energy in manifold activities."

73. Monti, *King's Good Servant*, 57–60; Ackroyd, *Life of Thomas More*, 255–56.

74. Roper, "Life of Sir Thomas More," 209.

75. See Thomas More, *The Four Last Things, The Supplication of Souls, and A Dialogue on Conscience*, rendered in modern English by Mary Gottschalk (New York: Scepter Publishers, 2002).

76. See More, *Sadness of Christ*.

77. Ackroyd, *Life of Thomas More*, 35.

78. More reported that he had been told that "you are in the habit . . . of looking so serious when you mean something in jest that many times people

think you might be joking when you are dead serious." Thomas More, *Dialogue Concerning Heresies*, rendered in modern English by Mary Gottschalk (New York: Scepter Publishers, 2006), 92.

79. Ackroyd, *Life of Thomas More*, 87–95.
80. More, *Dialogue Concerning Heresies*, 92.
81. Ackroyd, *Life of Thomas More*, 95.
82. Ackroyd, *Life of Thomas More*, 260.
83. Roper, "Life of Sir Thomas More," 201.
84. He was "of an amiable joyousness, and even an incipient laughter." "Since his boyhood he has so delighted in merriment that it seems to be part of his nature." The observations by Erasmus are taken from a letter he wrote in 1519. "Description of Thomas More by Erasmus," in Thornton and Varenne, *Saint Thomas More*, 244–47.
85. Ackroyd, *Life of Thomas More*, 282.
86. Monti, *King's Good Servant*, 56–63.
87. On one such procession, when he was offered a horse because of his rank as a knight, More replied: "My Lord went on foot; I will not follow him on horseback." As a lawyer, More provided substantial *pro bono* services. Monti, *King's Good Servant*, 77–78.
88. Ackroyd, *Life of Thomas More*, 255–56.
89. Ackroyd, *Life of Thomas More*, 188.
90. This was a standard procedure for initiating a debate or "disputation." See Craig Harline, *A World Ablaze: The Rise of Martin Luther and the Birth of the Reformation* (New York: Oxford University Press, 2017), chap. 1.
91. Monti, *King's Good Servant*, 120–23.
92. See Ackroyd, *Life of Thomas More*, 63. "More recognized instinctively that [Luther] was mounting an attack upon the whole medieval polity as constituted by the Catholic Church."
93. Monti, *King's Good Servant*, 122.
94. See Ackroyd, *Life of Thomas More*, 279, 248, 307, 310–11, and at 230.
95. For an account of Tyndale and his achievements (and a caustic treatment of More), see Brian Moynahan, *God's Bestseller: William Tyndale, Thomas More, and the Writing of the English Bible—A Story of Martyrdom and Betrayal* (New York: St. Martin's Press, 2003).
96. For a careful review of the critical and more apologetic interpretations of More's conduct in this respect, see Guy, *Thomas More*, 106–25. Guy concludes that, in the end, there are tensions in More's advocacy of tolerance in *Utopia* and his persecution of heretics that cannot be fully resolved (122).
97. See Martz, *Thomas More*, 4: "More did pursue rigorously those suspected of heresy. . . . That was what his duty required under the statutes of the realm." See also Guy, *Thomas More*, 122, which observes that "More was set to the anti-Lutheran campaign by Henry VIII. . . . In attacking heresy as Lord Chancellor, he was continuing the King's agenda."
98. Martz, *Thomas More*, 5–6. Richard Rex argues, however, that More's vigor in persecuting heretics is not fully reflected in the mere number of actual executions. Between 1527 and 1533, More was involved in police or judicial

proceedings against approximately forty suspected heretics. Rex, "More and the Heretics," 106.

99. See, e.g., Michael Moreland, "Thomas More Was Not 'Unnaturally Fond of Torturing Heretics,'" *Mirror of Justice* (May 29, 2012), https://mirror ofjustice.blogs.com/mirrorofjustice/2012/05/thomas-more-was-not-unnaturally -fond-of-torturing-heretics.html. "Thomas More generally shared in the preju- dices of his age and was complicit in practices (most especially the use of state coercion with regard to religious belief) that we would today regard as morally odious. That's just to say that he lived in the early sixteenth century and not the early twenty-first century."

100. See generally Alexandra Walsham, *Charitable Hatred: Tolerance and Intolerance in England 1500–1700* (New York: Manchester University Press, 2006). Ethan Shagan observes that "[b]efore the 1640s, the state's prerogative to punish religious deviance was almost unanimously praised as moderate, while broad claims for religious toleration were almost unanimously condemned as extremist." Ethan H. Shagan, *The Rule of Moderation* (New York: Cambridge University Press, 2011), 288.

101. Marius, *Thomas More*, 391–95.

102. Marius, *Thomas More*, xxiv. In a similar vein, John Guy argues that More was enforcing the law against heretics and carrying out the king's pro- gram. But More also repeatedly expressed his loathing of heretics, and he asked that his epitaph record that he had been "grievous" to "thieves, murderers and heretics." Guy concludes that "[t]his is too extreme. There is too much passion, even satisfaction." Guy, *Thomas More*, 217.

103. See Martz, *Thomas More*, 4, which discerns in More's expressions "not . . . a note of hysteria or rejoicing, but rather a tone of fearsome warning and somber satisfaction at finding justice done." More himself argued that "what the Church law on this calls for is good, reasonable, compassionate, and chari- table, and in no way desirous of the death of anyone." More, *Dialogue Con- cerning Heresies*, 464.

104. See generally Robert Louis Wilken, *Liberty in the Things of God* (New Haven, CT: Yale University Press, 2019).

105. Bede, *The Ecclesiastical History of the English People* (Oxford World Classics ed., 1994), chap. 26, p. 41. Bede's history is dated to 731 AD.

106. See More, *Utopia*, trans. Turner, 117–23, esp. 119, 121.

107. The point is emphasized in Strohm, *Conscience*.

108. See Ian Christopher Levy, "Liberty of Conscience and Freedom of Religion in the Medieval Canonists and Theologians," in *Christianity and Free- dom*, ed. Timothy Samuel Shah and Allen D. Hertzke, vol. 1, *Historical Per- spectives* (Cambridge: Cambridge University Press, 2016), 149, 162, 171. See also Brian Tierney, "Religious Rights: A Historical Perspective" in *Religious Liberty in Western Thought*, ed. Noel B. Reynolds and W. Cole Durham, Jr. (Atlanta: Scholars Press, 1996), 29, 37. In good scholastic fashion, the medieval analysis could become technical in its distinctions and vocabulary. See Charles E. Cur- ran, "Conscience in the Light of the Catholic Moral Tradition," in *Conscience*, ed. Charles E. Curran (New York: Paulist Press, 2004), 6–8.

109. See, e.g., Michael S. Moore, "Good Without God," in *Natural Law, Liberalism and Morality*, ed. Robert P. George (New York: Oxford University Press, 1996), 221, 229.

110. See Germain Grisez and Russell Shaw, "Conscience: Knowledge of Moral Truth," in Curran, *Conscience*, 39, (quote on) 41. "Most fundamentally, conscience is one's awareness of moral truth—or that which is truly right and good to do."

111. Although, technically, the logic of conscience suggests that if you do what *is* right believing it to be wrong, you are guilty of doing wrong.

112. Explaining the meaning of conscience in the Catholic tradition, Germain Grisez and Russell Shaw articulate the point clearly: "We ought always to follow our consciences, and we are always wrong if we do not. This is so even if conscience is mistaken, erroneous. For if conscience—one's last, best judgment that something is morally right or wrong—is mistaken, one is in no position to know it. . . . In short, if we violate conscience, we think we are doing wrong. To do what one thinks is wrong, however, is always morally wrong. Thus, conscience must be followed even if it is erroneous." Grisez and Shaw, "Conscience," 43.

113. In saying that these propositions would have been practically equivalent, we need not enter here into any interpretation of exactly where these men stood on the debate between so-called rationalists and voluntarists regarding the exact relationship of God's will to goodness—a question on which major Christian thinkers like Thomas Aquinas, Duns Scotus, and William of Ockham had developed different views.

114. See Acts 17:28.

115. Mark 8:36.

116. Thomas à Kempis, *The Imitation of Christ*, bk. 2, chap. 6. Ackroyd, *Life of Thomas More*, 101.

117. Thomas à Kempis, *The Imitation of Christ*, bk. 2, chap. 6.

118. *Last Letters*, 58.

119. Eire, *Reformations*, 185.

120. See Moots, "Was the Protestant Reformation a Radical Revolution?," which stresses that for Luther, conscience was entirely subservient to God's will as known through scripture.

121. See Oberman, *Luther*, 204, which explains that for Luther conscience "is not the autonomous center of man's personality, it is always guided and is free only once God has freed and 'captured' it."

122. See Ackroyd, *Life of Thomas More*, 229, which says that Luther "possessed the authentic voice of the free and separate conscience."

123. See, e.g., Nicholas P. Miller, *The Religious Roots of the First Amendment* (New York: Oxford University Press, 2012), 1, 91–94.

124. Drawing on the conceptions of conscience held by Luther, Kierkegaard, Newman, Barth, and even (somewhat more problematically) More, Helen Costigane asserts that "there has been a common strand in the history of conscience which stresses personal responsibility, a standing-apart from the collective stance if it conflicts with one's innermost truth." Helen Costigane SHCJ, "A History

of the Western Idea of Conscience," in *Conscience in World Religions,* ed. Jayne Hoose (Notre Dame, IN: University of Notre Dame Press, 1999), 3, 14.

125. See Immanuel Kant, "An Answer to the Question: What Is Enlightenment?," reprinted in *What is Enlightenment?,* ed. James Schmidt (Berkeley: University of California Press, 1996), 58.

126. *Last Letters,* 84.

127. *Last Letters,* 84, 82, 83. See also on page 60 that authority lies in "the general council of Christendom."

128. More, *Dialogue Concerning Heresies,* 59.

129. For the argument that More came to accept papal sovereignty, see Belloc, *Characters of the Reformation,* 63, and Ackroyd, *Life of Thomas More,* 228, 270. For the contrary view, see Marius, *Thomas More,* 432–33, 458, 517. John Guy argues that all the available evidence shows that More believed in papal primacy but not papal supremacy; whether More changed his mind at the end of his life cannot be known. Guy, *Thomas More,* 201–3, 222.

130. *Last Letters,* 82–83.

131. See Eamon Duffy, "'The comen knowen myltytude of crysten men': A Dialogue Concerning Heresies and the Defense of Christendom," in *The Cambridge Companion to Thomas More,* ed. George M. Logan (Cambridge: Cambridge University Press, 2011), 191, (quote on) 199. "[T]his appeal to the common life of the Church as the ultimate criterion of Christian authenticity never becomes merely or mainly an appeal to hierarchy or to the teaching authority of the clergy. . . . More never once appeals to the teaching of a pope or council to clinch his argument."

132. *Last Letters,* 85.

133. More, *Dialogue Concerning Heresies,* 59.

134. Guy, *Thomas More,* 199–200, 197.

135. For a detailed review and assessment of the competing arguments and interpretations, see Scarisbrick, *Henry VIII,* 13–197.

136. Scarisbrick, *Henry VIII,* 164.

137. See Strohm, *Conscience,* 19. "Who can say whether Henry was *really* troubled in his conscience, or (as seems more likely) in some other part of his body."

138. *Last Letters,* 85.

139. *Last Letters,* 85.

140. See John Finnis, "Faith, Morals, and Thomas More," in *Religion and Public Reasons,* Collected Essays 5 (New York: Oxford University Press, 2011), 164, which contends that although More declined to explain his position, it is "clear and not in doubt" that "More believed, in 1534 as in 1529 when he became Lord Chancellor, that Henry's marriage to Catherine was consistent with divine law and perfectly valid."

141. More, *Dialogue Concerning Heresies,* 153, 177.

142. See More, *Dialogue Concerning Heresies,* 146–47.

143. See Rex, "More and the Heretics," 100–101. "From first to last, [More's] argument is a *reductio ad absurdum*: namely, that Christ promised to send the

Holy Spirit to guide the Church in all truth, and that if the teachings of the evangelicals were true, then Christ's promise, the guidance of the Spirit, and the Church must all have turned out to be false."

144. An important qualification is that it seems that More was not convinced that the Protestants were actually sincere in their beliefs. Or so he said, repeatedly. See, e.g., More, *Dialogue Concerning Heresies*, 488. See also Ackroyd, *Life of Thomas More*, 299–311. Richard Marius reports that More "refused to believe that even those heretics who died in witness to their hope could possibly be sincere." Marius, *Thomas More*, 518. How he could believe this presents an interesting question that we need not pursue here—although it may be worth noting that More's ascription of insincerity to his opponents is hardly without precedent. See, e.g., Timothy L. Hall, *Separating Church and State: Roger Williams and Religious Liberty* (Chicago: University of Illinois Press, 1998), 61–62, which discusses the Puritan view that heretics who persist after having been "convinced" of their errors by adequate arguments do not act from conscience but rather from "wilfulness." And such interpretive dismissals can show up in surprising places—including in the heart of modern liberalism. Thus, Ronald Dworkin argued that virtually no one really believes abortion is murder: the millions of people who say they believe this only think they do. See Ronald Dworkin, *Life's Dominion* (New York: Vintage Books, 1994), 9–19.

145. See Brad S. Gregory, *The Unintended Reformation: How a Religious Revolution Secularized Society* (Cambridge, MA: Belknap Press of Harvard University Press, 2012), 94. "The assertion that scripture alone was a self-sufficient basis for Christian faith and life . . . produced not even rough agreement, but an open-ended welter of competing and incompatible interpretations."

146. Eire, *Reformations*, 193.

147. Eire, *Reformations*, 190.

148. Eire, *Reformations*, 197–210.

149. Eire, *Reformations*, 242–44.

150. Eire, *Reformations*, 271–77.

151. More, *Sadness of Christ*, 81.

152. See More, *Dialogue Concerning Heresies*, 172. "These books are, by the secret counsel of the Holy Spirit, made so plain and simple that everyone can find in them some things that they can understand, and yet so lofty, on the other hand, and so hard, that there is no one so astute that they cannot find in them things far above their grasp, far too profound to penetrate."

153. See Brigden, *New Worlds, Lost Worlds*, 132. "Dissension appeared in every community where the 'new' faith had penetrated, and reports of the trouble reached Cromwell daily from every part of the country."

154. More, *Sadness of Christ*, 62.

155. See Monti, *King's Good Servant*, 16, which describes More's "passionate dedication to the unity of the Church."

156. William Wordsworth, epigraph to "Ode: Intimations of Immortality."

157. The phrase is sometimes attributed, probably incorrectly, to Arnold Toynbee. See "History Is Just One Damn Thing after Another," Quote Investigator, September 16, 2015, https://quoteinvestigator.com/2015/09/16/history/.

158. Charles Taylor, *Sources of the Self* (Cambridge: Cambridge University Press, 1989), 43.

159. See John Bossy, *Christianity in the West, 1400–1700* (New York: Oxford University Press, 1985), 14–56.

160. Kevin Madigan, *Medieval Christianity: A New History* (New Haven, CT: Yale University Press, 2015), xviii.

161. For a valuable presentation, see Eire, *Reformations*, 27–42. See also Benjamin J. Kaplan, *Divided by Faith: Religious Conflict and the Practice of Toleration in Early Modern Europe* (Cambridge, MA: Harvard University Press, 2007), 60–72.

162. See Bossy, *Christianity in the West*; Eamon Duffy, *Saints, Sacrilege and Sedition: Religion and Conflict in the Tudor Reformations* (London: Bloomsbury, 2012); Eamon Duffy, *The Stripping of the Altars: Traditional Religion in England, 1400–1580* (New Haven, CT: Yale University Press, 1992).

163. Bossy, *Christianity in the West*, 14–19. See also Brigden, *New Worlds, Lost Worlds*, 52: "Choosing godparents was a way of creating affinity and formalizing relationships."

164. Bossy, *Christianity in the West*, 19–26.

165. See Bossy, *Christianity in the West*, 66–70; Brigden, *New Worlds, Lost Worlds*, 42–44; Duffy, *Stripping of the Altars*, 91–130.

166. Eire, *Reformations*, 28.

167. Brigden, *New Worlds, Lost Worlds*, 58.

168. Brigden, *New Worlds, Lost Worlds*, 77–78.

169. Eire, *Reformations*, 28. See also Duffy, *Saints, Sacrilege and Sedition*, 129: "parishioners . . . worshipped in buildings which were a dense forest of symbolic reminders of the dead, and of their living kindred, in which ritual objects and the organization of sacred space located the parishioner within a community that articulated itself through time as well as through physical and social space." For elaboration, see Duffy, *Stripping of the Altars*, 301–37.

170. See also Brigden, *New Worlds, Lost Worlds*, 66–68.

171. Bossy, *Christianity in the West*, 32–33.

172. See Brigden, *New Worlds, Lost Worlds*, 38–41.

173. Eire, *Reformations*, 34.

174. Eire, *Reformations*, 33.

175. Alister McGrath, *The Intellectual Origins of the European Reformation* (New York: Oxford University Press, 1987), 69–121, describes the rich diversity of views in late medieval theology.

176. Gregory, *Unintended Reformation*, 84.

177. Mark 12:17.

178. See Eamon Duffy, *Saints and Sinners: A History of the Popes* (New Haven, CT: Yale University Press, 1997), 49–50.

179. Eire, *Reformations*, 603–4.

180. Kaplan, *Divided by Faith*, 2.

181. See R. W. Southern, *Western Society and the Church in the Middle Ages* (New York: Penguin Books, 1970), 18–22, 125. However, Southern stresses that these measures were of limited efficacy.

182. Benedict Anderson, *Imagined Communities: Reflections on the Origin and Spread of Nationalism*, rev. ed. (New York: Verso Books, 2016).

183. See Gregory, *Unintended Reformation*, 2: "On the eve of the Reformation, Latin Christianity comprised for good or ill the far from homogeneous yet institutionalized worldview within which the overwhelming majority of Europeans lived and made sense of their lives." See also Duffy, *Stripping of the Altars*, 4, which observes that "late medieval Catholicism exerted an enormously strong, diverse, and vigorous hold over the imagination and the loyalty of the people up to the very moment of the Reformation."

184. Southern, *Western Society*, 22.

185. See More, *Dialogue Concerning Heresies*, 468, which acknowledges that "the ambition of Christian rulers who desire each other's dominion set them at war and deadly dissensions among themselves, whereby while each of them has aspired to the aggrandizing of his own dominion, they have little cared what became of the common corps of Christendom."

186. More, *Dialogue Concerning Heresies*, 489.

187. See Kaplan, *Divided by Faith*, 37. "In the wake of the reformations, European society was divided in a way it had never previously been. Once a single spiritual community united, if only loosely, as a 'common corps of Christendom,' to many it seemed to have lost all order and coherence."

188. Brigden, *New Worlds, Lost Worlds*, 94, notes that Protestantism had "consequences destructive of the whole sacramental and penitential system of the Church."

189. More, *Sadness of Christ*, 63–64.

190. Brigden, *New Worlds, Lost Worlds*, 98.

191. Duffy, *Saints, Sacrilege and Sedition*, 33. See also Ackroyd, *Life of Thomas More*, 234: "This departure from the customs of a thousand years was part of a general dislocation of values. It can be traced in the attention to privacy in domestic life, the substitution of simple for complex spaces in religious architecture, the abandonment of canon law in the universities, the theory of national empire promulgated by Henry, the word 'state' replacing 'res publica' or 'commonwealth'. What emerged in England was an energetic and male-dominated society of commerce and of progress, together with its own state church; it was a religion of the book and of private prayer, eschewing all the ritual, public symbolism and spectacle which had marked late medieval Catholicism. The age of More was coming to its close."

192. Quoted in Monti, *King's Good Servant*, 117.

193. Yeats, "The Second Coming."

194. More, *Dialogue Concerning Heresies*, 459.

195. Diarmaid MacCulloch, *The Reformation: A History* (New York: Viking, 2004), 154.

196. Ackroyd, *Life of Thomas More*, 248.

197. Eire, *Reformations*, 199–210.

198. Eire, *Reformations*, 208–9.

199. Ackroyd, *Life of Thomas More*, 266–67.

200. G. R. Elton, *Reformation Europe, 1517–1559* (New York: Harper & Row, 1963), 83.

201. See Rex, "More and the Heretics," 103, which suggests that "[p]erhaps the imaginative gap between More's attitude to heresy and ours might be bridged by the realization that he refers to heretics in the way that today [we] refer to drug-dealers, child-molesters and suicide bombers."

202. Rex, "More and the Heretics," 230.

203. Louis Martz discerns in More's later writings "a weariness, a sad realization that the flood of heretical books is sweeping on, despite his careful, lengthy confutations." Martz, *Thomas More*, 43.

204. Eire, *Reformations*, 55.

205. See Steven Ozment, *The Age of Reform, 1250–1550* (New Haven, CT: Yale University Press, 1980), 164–70.

206. Ozment, *Age of Reform*, 150–55. See also Brian Tierney, "Political and Religious Freedom in Marsilius of Padua," in Reynolds and Durham, *Religious Liberty in Western Thought*, 59.

207. In a largely debunking biography, Richard Marius notes that anti-semitic jokes and proverbs were common in More's England, and so it is "a startling fact that we find no hostile remark or metaphor about contemporary Jews in all the works of Thomas More." Marius observes that "Shakespeare's Shylock demonstrates that Englishmen could still hate Jews in the barbarous style of most Christians of the time; it happened that Thomas More did not." Marius, *Thomas More*, 8.

208. The New Testament notes these as disputed issues among early Christians. See Acts 15; I Corinthians 15.

209. *Last Letters*, 58.

210. See, e.g., Ackroyd, *Life of Thomas More*, 86, 230. See also Moynahan, *God's Bestseller*, 249: "The young humanist who wrote *Utopia* had changed into a reactionary."

211. "Christ is also betrayed into the hands of sinners," he wrote, "when His most holy body in the sacrament is consecrated and handled by unchaste, profligate, and sacrilegious priests," adding that "such things . . . happen all too often." More, *Sadness of Christ*, 63.

212. Thus, one of the most eloquent and oft-quoted passages from American constitutional law comes from West Virginia State Board of Education v. Barnette, 319 U.S. 624 (1943): "If there is any fixed star in our constitutional constellation, it is that no official, high or petty, can prescribe what shall be orthodox in politics, nationalism, religion, or other matters of opinion or force citizens to confess by word or act their faith therein."

213. For analysis of how these concepts work to conceal deeper beliefs, and in that sense to frustrate the work of "reason," see Steven D. Smith, *The Disenchantment of Secular Discourse* (Cambridge, MA: Harvard University Press, 2010), chap. 1.

214. Marius, *Thomas More*, 470.

215. In this vein, More suggested that those who took the oath in good conscience might in the last judgment be sent to heaven, whereas he himself, understanding the errors of the oath, would be sent "to the devil" if he were to take it. *Last Letters*, 81.

216. See Gregory, *Salvation at Stake*, 352. "Institutionally and intellectually, our world is one the committed early modern Christians scarcely could imagine. I am certain they would not have wanted to live in it."

217. See Martz, *Thomas More*, 43, which discerns in More's later work "a weariness, a sad realization that the flood of heretical books is sweeping on, despite his careful, lengthy confutations."

218. Roper, "Life of Sir Thomas More," 200–201

CHAPTER TWO

1. For summaries of what happened at the convention, see Edmund Randolph, *History of Virginia*, ed. Arthur H. Shaffer (Charlottesville: University Press of Virginia, 1970; originally written ca. 1810); Ralph Ketcham, *James Madison: A Biography* (Charlottesville: University Press of Virginia, 1990; first published in 1970), 68–75; Irving Brant, *James Madison*, vol. 1, *The Virginia Revolutionist* (Indianapolis: Bobbs-Merrill, 1941), 234–50.

2. For the finished product, see the Virginia Bill of Rights, reprinted in *The American Republic: Primary Sources*, ed. Bruce Frohnen (Indianapolis: Liberty Fund, 2002), 157–58.

3. Thomas Jefferson did not participate in the Virginia convention—he was away serving in the Continental Congress—and the Virginia Declaration was drafted by George Mason. Irving Brant explains: "Mason, who loved credit as well as Jefferson did, knew better than anybody else how great Jefferson's unacknowledged debt to him was. Striking as are the resemblances between the final versions of the Declaration of Independence and the Virginia Declaration of Rights, there is an even greater similarity between Mason's first draft, which was available to Jefferson . . . , and the first draft of Jefferson's document." Brant, *James Madison*, 240.

4. See Thomas E. Buckley, *Establishing Religious Freedom: Jefferson's Statute in Virginia* (Charlottesville: University Press of Virginia, 2013), 56, which observes that "[n]o one in the legislature in 1776 . . . could have envisioned what was in store for church and state in Virginia."

5. Irving Brant discusses claims that the original article was written by Patrick Henry but concludes that Mason was definitely the author. Brant, *James Madison*, 241–43.

6. Brant, *James Madison*, 244.

7. Ketcham, *James Madison*, 69.

8. Brant, *James Madison*, 201–2. See also Richard Brookhiser, *James Madison* (New York: Basic Books, 2011), 4: "He was a small man—just over five feet tall, just over a hundred pounds."

9. See Brant, *James Madison*, 201. "Not only was Madison young, unknown and reserved in a convention of proved leaders and aggressive newcomers, but he was overshadowed physically."

10. Brant, *James Madison*, 202.

11. See Brant, *James Madison*, 205–6.

12. Randolph, *History of Virginia*, 235. In a recent biography, Richard Brookhiser offers this assessment: Madison "was smarter than Monroe, Armstrong, and Winder put together; smarter than Jefferson, perhaps even smarter than Adams." Brookhiser, *James Madison*, 4.

13. Ketcham, *James Madison*, 72.

14. With reference to Madison's proposed prohibition of emoluments, Thomas Buckley comments that "[a]t one stroke that would have disestablished the church." Buckley, *Establishing Religious Freedom*, 53.

15. Brant, *James Madison*, 245–46.

16. Noah Feldman, *The Three Lives of James Madison: Genius, Partisan, President* (New York: Random House, 2017), 59.

17. See John T. Noonan, *The Lustre of Our Country: The American Experience of Religious Freedom* (Berkeley: University of California Press, 1998), 70. "Astonishingly, [Patrick Henry], that bulwark of the established church, introduced the new text to the convention."

18. Rhys Isaac, *The Transformation of Virginia, 1740–1790* (Chapel Hill: University of North Carolina Press, 1999), 279.

19. Brant, *James Madison*, 209.

20. Buckley, *Establishing Religious Freedom*, 54.

21. Buckley, *Establishing Religious Freedom*, 54; Brant, *James Madison*, 247.

22. Brant, *James Madison*, 247.

23. Irving Brant, celebrating Madison's achievement, contended that the amendment had a "drastic" and substantive purpose that was "known to everybody." Brant, *James Madison*, 249. But Brant provided no evidence for this conclusion, and indeed he noted that Madison himself reported that the amendment was readily accepted with little or no discussion (248). Brant discounted Madison's own report as reflecting the young man's modesty. But it seems unlikely that everyone in the convention understood that Madison was offering a "drastic" reconception of church and state but nonetheless easily accepted that reconception, and subsequent events in Virginia hardly support such a characterization.

24. Ketcham, *James Madison*, 73; Noonan, *Lustre of Our Country*, 69–70; Rodney K. Smith, *James Madison: Father of Religious Liberty* (Springville, UT: Plain Sight Publishing, an imprint of Cedar Fort, 2019), 118–23. See also Lynne Cheney, *James Madison: A Life Reconsidered* (New York: Penguin Books, 2015), 59–60: "It was a simple alteration that accomplished a mighty change."

25. Quoted in Ketcham, *James Madison*, 73.

26. Brookhiser, *James Madison*, 23–24.

27. Jack N. Rakove, *Beyond Belief, Beyond Conscience: The Radical Significance of the Free Exercise of Religion* (New York: Oxford University Press, 2020), 10–11.

28. For more detailed accounts of the episode, see Steven Waldman, *Founding Faith* (New York: Random House, 2009), 115–26; Lance Banning, *The Sacred Fire of Liberty: James Madison and the Founding of the Federal Republic* (Ithaca, NY: Cornell University Press, 1998), 88–97; Feldman, *Three Lives of James Madison*, 57–67.

29. James Madison, "A Memorial and Remonstrance against Religious Assessments," reprinted in *Selected Writings of James Madison*, ed. Ralph Ketcham (Indianapolis, IN: Hackett Publishing, 2006), 21.

30. Lance Banning describes the "Memorial and Remonstrance" as "a cornerstone in the American tradition of religious freedom." Banning, *Sacred Fire of Liberty*, 91. Nicholas Miller asserts that the "Memorial and Remonstrance" was "arguably the most important statement on the reasons for disestablishment in American history. The statement is far more extensive and complete than any other that Madison—or any other constitutional founder for that matter—gave on the topic." Nicholas P. Miller, *The Religious Roots of the First Amendment: Dissenting Protestants and the Separation of Church and State* (New York: Oxford University Press, 2012), 144. See also Rakove, *Beyond Belief, Beyond Conscience*, 81, which asserts that "the *Memorial* remains the central statement of the enlightened approach to religious freedom that the sages of Monticello and Montpelier pursued."

31. "A Bill for Establishing Religious Freedom," Virginia, 1779 and 1786, reprinted in *The Sacred Rights of Conscience: Selected Readings on Religious Liberty and Church-State Relations in the American Founding*, ed. Daniel L. Dreisbach and Mark David Hall (Indianapolis, IN: Liberty Fund, 2009), 250.

32. "Bill for Establishing Religious Freedom," Dreisbach and Hall, *Sacred Rights*, 250 (emphasis added).

33. Rakove, *Beyond Belief, Beyond Conscience*, 88.

34. Cheney, *James Madison*, 11.

35. Marbury v. Madison, 5 U.S. 137 (1803).

36. Ketcham, *James Madison*, 10.

37. See Buckley, *Establishing Religious Freedom*, 82–115.

38. Ketcham, *James Madison*, 5–6.

39. Ketcham, *James Madison*, 12.

40. Brant, *James Madison*, 45. "With all outdoor labor and household chores performed by slaves, there were no physical tasks whatever imposed upon the growing boy."

41. Lynne Cheney emphasizes this affliction and tries to make it a significant factor in Madison's thinking on matters like religion. Cheney, *James Madison*, 4, 6.

42. Ketcham, *James Madison*, 51–52.

43. Ketcham, *James Madison*, 17–19. On the importance of dancing in Virginia culture, see Isaac, *Transformation of Virginia*, 81–87.

44. Ketcham, *James Madison*, 19.

45. Ketcham, *James Madison*, 20.

46. Feldman, *Three Lives of James Madison*, 5–6.

47. Rakove, *Beyond Belief, Beyond Conscience*, 69.

48. Ketcham, *James Madison*, 23.

49. Brant, *James Madison*, 73.

50. Feldman, *Three Lives of James Madison*, 6.

51. Brant, *James Madison*, 68–71.

52. Feldman, *Three Lives of James Madison*, 4.

53. Brant, *James Madison*, 72–73.

54. Ketcham, *James Madison*, 34.

55. The facts in this paragraph are taken from Ketcham, *James Madison*, 5–50. Irving Brant, author of a multivolume biography, complained that Madison "has come down through his biographers as a colorless, detached, passionless intellect." Brant attempted to restore "[t]he Madison who was known among his associates as a teller of ribald stories, who wrote obscene satires for public delivery in a college chapel, who left a long pornographic poem . . . among his papers, who satirized some of his neighbors as 'old bigots' and threatened to tar and feather unpatriotic rectors." Brant, *James Madison*, 40.

56. Brookhiser, *James Madison*, 19.

57. Ketcham, *James Madison*, 45. See also Brant, *James Madison*, 78: "An intense student, Madison applied himself with a zeal which created a tradition bordering on the marvelous."

58. Ketcham, *James Madison*, 31.

59. Ketcham, *James Madison*, 38–39, 43.

60. Ketcham, *James Madison*, 43.

61. Ketcham, *James Madison*, 44.

62. Noonan, *Lustre of Our Country*, 65; Smith, *James Madison*, 107.

63. Ketcham, *James Madison*, 55–56.

64. Brant, *James Madison*, 105.

65. Ketcham, *James Madison*, 63.

66. Feldman, *Three Lives of James Madison*, 22.

67. Ketcham, *James Madison*, 64

68. Ketcham, *James Madison*, 65.

69. Cheney, *James Madison*, 49.

70. David L. Holmes, *The Faiths of the Founding Fathers* (Oxford: Oxford University Press, 2006), 93–94; Rakove, *Beyond Belief, Beyond Conscience*, 71, 98.

71. Ketcham, *James Madison*, 13.

72. Ketcham, *James Madison*, 9.

73. Ketcham, *James Madison*, 13.

74. Isaac, *Transformation of Virginia*, 60.

75. Isaac, *Transformation of Virginia*, 60. See also Brant, *James Madison*, 52: "Here news was exchanged, official notices from the colony government were read, family reunions were held, youthful friendships started, courtships got under way."

76. Ketcham, *James Madison*, 46.

77. Brant, *James Madison*, 62.

78. Holmes, *Faiths of the Founding Fathers*, 93.

79. Ketcham, *James Madison*, 52.

80. Brant, *James Madison*, 119.

81. Brant, *James Madison*, 118.
82. Madison, "Memorial and Remonstrance," 24 (para. 7).
83. Madison, "Memorial and Remonstrance," 26 (para. 12).
84. Nearly all Virginians were Christians—mostly Episcopalians, Presbyterians, Baptists, Methodists, and Quakers—but, at least according to historian Rhys Isaac, anticlerical sentiment was also pervasive. Isaac, *Transformation of Virginia*, 146–147, 155–157.
85. Holmes, *Faiths of the Founding Fathers*, 94.
86. Holmes, *Faiths of the Founding Fathers*, 95.
87. Ketcham, *James Madison*, 46–47.
88. For an interpretation attributing greater piety to Madison, see Noonan, *Lustre of Our Country*, 65–68, 86–89. See also generally Smith, *James Madison*.
89. Buckley, *Establishing Religious Freedom*, 34–37.
90. See Buckley, *Establishing Religious Freedom*, 70–72.
91. John T. Noonan, Jr. and Edward McGlynn Gaffney, Jr., *Religious Freedom: History, Cases, and Other Materials on the Interaction of Religion and Government* (New York: Foundation Press, 2001), 159.
92. Isaac, *Transformation of Virginia*, 203.
93. Ketcham, *James Madison*, 55–56.
94. From its earliest days, Virginians had thought of the colony as a Christian commonwealth. Thomas Buckley explains that Virginians "conceived of their society in organic terms. Just as all belonged to a single political entity—the English colony of Virginia governed from Williamsburg—so all should be members of the Church of England, each sitting in his or her proper place in the church on Sunday. Relationships were neatly ordered and hierarchical. Moreover, the church-state relationship was mutually beneficial. The church supported the state by its public worship and by teaching the Christian gospel, the moral law, and the obligations of good subjects of the Crown. The colonial government supports the church by favorable laws, public taxes, and benevolent oversight. Church and state worked together in friendly alliance for the well-being of the whole society." Buckley, *Establishing Religious Freedom*, 8.
95. Noonan, *Lustre of Our Country*, 81.
96. See Miller, *Religious Roots*, 144. "Madison's wording—'and therefore'—shows his belief that disestablishment was an imperative that followed logically from the principles of religious freedom and conscience articulated in the first portion of the clause."
97. Brant, *James Madison*, 244.
98. Brant, *James Madison*, 245.
99. Brant, *James Madison*, 245.
100. Brant, *James Madison*, 246.
101. Brant, *James Madison*, 244.
102. Noonan, *Lustre of Our Country*, 75. "No qualifications whatever on the right and duty to pay homage to God as one sees fit? Surely, in the heat of battle, JM exaggerates! No, his theologicial premises compel these radical conclusions."

103. See, e.g., Chris Beneke, "The Historical Context of the Religion Clauses of the First Amendment," in *The Cambridge Companion to the First Amendment and Religious Liberty*, ed. Michael D. Breidenbach and Owen Anderson (Cambridge: Cambridge University Press, 2020), 140–42; Joseph J. Ellis, *The Quartet: Orchestrating the Second American Revolution, 1783–1789* (New York: Knopf, 2015), 116; Brant, *James Madison*, 246–48; Brookhiser, *James Madison*, 8, 23–24; Banning, *Sacred Fire of Liberty*, 86; Feldman, *Three Lives of James Madison*, 27; Waldman, *Founding Faith*, 114–15.

104. Rakove, *Beyond Belief, Beyond Conscience*, 2–3, 6, 13.

105. Noonan, *Lustre of Our Country*, 69.

106. See generally Rakove, *Beyond Belief, Beyond Conscience*; Brookhiser, *James Madison*, 23–24; Feldman, *Three Lives of James Madison*, 27.

107. See, e.g., L. John Van Til, *Liberty of Conscience: The History of a Puritan Idea* (Nutley, NJ: Craig Press, 1972), 3: "One point that still seems especially important is the distinction between liberty of conscience and toleration. The point has been made time and again in the text, but here it may be noted that toleration is a grant from a government while liberty of conscience is an inherent condition of man given him when he was made in the image of God."

108. In his careful study of the development of notions of conscience and toleration, Andrew Murphy notes that although modern scholars often distinguish between religious "toleration" and "religious liberty" or "liberty of conscience," earlier figures like William Penn typically used the terms interchangeably. "I do not find it helpful to differentiate between the two terms 'toleration' and 'liberty of conscience,'" Murphy explains, "when the historical sources on which my account relies do not do so consistently." Andrew R. Murphy, *Conscience and Community* (University Park: Pennsylvania State University Press, 2001), xi–xii.

109. See, e.g., Brookhiser, 8, 23–24; Ketcham, *James Madison*, 73; Cheney, *James Madison*, 59–60; Martha C. Nussbaum, *Liberty of Conscience: In Defense of America's Tradition of Religious Equality* (New York: Basic Books, 2007), 90; Banning, *Sacred Fire of Liberty*, 86.

110. Rakove, *Beyond Belief, Beyond Conscience*, 3.

111. In his oft-noted letter to a Jewish association in Rhode Island, for example, President Washington observed that "[i]t is now no more that toleration is spoken of, as if it was by the indulgence of one class of people, that another enjoyed the exercise of inherent natural rights." Letter from George Washington to the Hebrew Congregation in Newport, Rhode Island, reprinted in Dreisbach and Hall, *Sacred Rights*, 464.

112. See, e.g., Rakove, *Beyond Belief, Beyond Conscience*, 14: "Communities became tolerant not because they recognized the moral rights of dissenters, but rather because the task of preserving religious uniformity through tested techniques of persecution had grown too costly." See also Van Til, *Liberty of Conscience*, 6: "A government pursues a policy of toleration for reasons of state which are most often expedient reasons."

113. See, e.g., Rakove, *Beyond Belief, Beyond Conscience*, 22, which asserts that toleration "remained a policy that could be abandoned as easily as it could be advanced." See also Van Til, *Liberty of Conscience*, 6, which describes "the implication in *toleration* that the state merely grants as a privilege what it tolerates, a grant that may be withdrawn."

114. Rakove, *Beyond Belief, Beyond Conscience*, 2, 23.

115. The statute's final section acknowledged that the enacting legislature had no power to bind future legislatures but added that any legislature that might repeal the statute would be infringing on a natural right. "Bill for Establishing Religious Freedom," Dreisbach and Hall, *Sacred Rights*, 251.

116. This is the central claim in Nussbaum, *Liberty of Conscience*, 87–97. See also page 91: "Madison's central argument is that any sort of establishment violates the equality of citizens." In a similar vein, see Rakove, *Beyond Belief, Beyond Conscience*, 183; Feldman, *Three Lives of James Madison*, 61.

117. See, e.g., Smith, *James Madison*, 123–24.

118. In addition to providing that *"all Men* should enjoy *the fullest Toleration"* in the exercise of their religion, the Mason version expressly described the only admissible grounds for limiting the freedom entailed by such toleration: government could restrict religious exercise only if "under Colour of Religion, any Man disturb the Peace, the Happiness, or Safety of Society, or of Individuals." Brant, *James Madison*, 244.

119. Nussbaum, *Liberty of Conscience*, 97.

120. See Nussbaum, *Liberty of Conscience*, 90. "Toleration suggested hierarchy . . ."

121. See generally Ethan H. Shagan, *The Rule of Moderation: Violence, Religion and the Politics of Restraint in Early Modern England* (Cambridge: Cambridge University Press, 2011), 288; Alexandra Walsham, *Charitable Hatred: Tolerance and Intolerance in England, 1500–1700* (New York: Palgrave Macmillan, 2006).

122. Lynch v. Donnelly, 465 U.S. 668, 688 (1984) (O'Connor, J., concurring).

123. Thomas Paine, The Rights of Man, in *Reflections on the Revolution in France and The Rights of Man* (Garden City, NY: Anchor Books, 1973), 267, 324 (emphasis in original).

124. Quoted in Benjamin J. Kaplan, *Divided by Faith: Religious Conflict and the Practice of Toleration in Early Modern Europe* (Cambridge, MA: Harvard University Press, 2007), 9.

125. See Joel Harrison, *Post-Liberal Religious Liberty: Forming Communities of Charity* (Cambridge: Cambridge University Press, 2020), 43. "On an equal concern and respect account, neutrality is required because endorsing one religion as true (however provisionally or even moderately) over any other conception of the good is an act of disrespect. Such endorsement may be characterised as infringing equal civic status—that is, as alienating the person from his or her own community, by declaring, through endorsement, that certain beliefs are more valuable than others."

126. Michael Walzer, *On Toleration* (New Haven, CT: Yale University Press, 1997), 52 (footnote deleted).

127. I say "appears to regard" because the celebrated dictum is susceptible to more than one interpretation. See Steven D. Smith, "Fixed Star or Twin Star: The Ambiguity of *Barnette*," *FIU Law Review* 13 (2019): 801.

128. 319 U.S. 624 (1943).

129. "Deism" is sometimes defined as the view that the Creator made the world, set it in motion, and then withdrew from further oversight or participation. Although the founders are often described as having been attracted to deism, the actual evidence is unsupportive. See Mark David Hall, *Did America Have a Christian Founding?* (Nashville, TN: Nelson Books, 2019), 1–18.

130. See Goldring/Woldenberg Institute of Southern Jewish Life, *Encyclopedia of Southern Jewish Communities—Richmond, Virginia*, https://www.isjl .org/virginia-richmond-encyclopedia.html.

131. Madison, "Memorial and Remonstrance," 27 (para. 15).

132. Noonan, *Lustre of Our Country*, 75.

133. Waldman, *Founding Faith*, 125.

134. For a description of the episode, see Buckley, *Establishing Religious Freedom*, 210–15.

135. Nussbaum, *Liberty of Conscience*, 92.

136. Nussbaum's interpretation of Roger Williams involves similar wishful thinking. See Steven D. Smith, "The Wages of Advocacy," *First Things* (February 2008), reviewing Nussbaum, *Liberty of Conscience*, https://www.firstthings .com/article/2008/02/002-the-wages-of-advocacy.

137. Rakove, *Beyond Belief, Beyond Conscience*, 99.

138. Like Nussbaum and Rakove, Howard Gillman and Erwin Chemerinsky want to contend that Madison, Jefferson, and other founders constructed a wholly secular government, and like Orwell's Ministry of Truth, they simply rewrite history to make it conform to their desired description. Thus, they contend that "[b]y the time the American Republic was founded there would be no references in the founding documents to a Supreme Being." Howard Gillman and Erwin Chemerinsky, *The Religion Clauses: The Case for Separating Church and State* (New York: Oxford University Press, 2020), 22. Evidently the Declaration of Independence does not count as one of the "founding documents." And when they come to Jefferson's "Virginia Statute for Religious Freedom," Gillman and Chemerinsky provide an extended quotation from the eloquent preamble but, in Orwellian fashion, edit out the beginning phrase ("Almighty God hath created the mind free") and use ellipses to delete the remaining religious language. Ibid., 33.

139. Daniel Boorstin, *The Lost World of Thomas Jefferson* (Chicago: University of Chicago Press, 1993). First published 1948.

140. Boorstin, *Lost World of Thomas Jefferson*, 194, 196.

141. On Biden's public expressions of religiosity, see generally Massimo Faggioli, *Joe Biden and Catholicism in the United States* (New London, CT: Bayard, 2021).

142. See Stuart Banner, "When Christianity Was Part of the Common Law," *Law and History Review* 16 (1998): 27, 43. "From the United States Supreme Court to scattered local courts, from Kent and Story to dozens of writers no

one remembers today, Christianity was generally accepted to be part of the common law."

143. See Thomas Jefferson, "Whether Christianity Is Part of the Common Law?" (1764), reprinted in Dreisbach and Hall, *Sacred Rights*, 539.

144. Holy Trinity Church v. United States, 143 U.S. 457, 471 (1892).

145. Zorach v. Clauson, 343 U.S. 306, 312 (1952).

146. See David M. Smolin, "Consecrating the President," *First Things* (January 1997), https://www.firstthings.com/article/1997/01/consecrating-the -president.

147. E.g., Elk Grove School Dist. v. Newdow, 542 U.S. 1, 35 (2004); New-dow v. Lefevre, 598 F.3d 698 (9 Cir. 2010); Newdow v. Roberts, 603 F.3d 1002 (D. C. Cir. 2010).

148. Mark DeWolfe Howe, *The Garden and the Wilderness* (Chicago: University of Chicago Press, 1965), 11. See also Rakove, *Beyond Belief, Beyond Conscience*, 9, which asserts that "the success of evangelical Christianity fostered the creation of a 'moral establishment' in which overtly Protestant values continued to suffuse American law"; Jonathan Den Hartog, "Church and State in the Nineteenth Century," in Breidenbach and Anderson, *Cambridge Companion to the First Amendment and Religious Liberty*, 192, 292, which describes the existence of "an informal Protestant establishment."

149. Robert N. Bellah, *The Broken Covenant: American Civil Religion in Time of Trial*, 2nd ed. (New York: Seabury Press, 1975), (emphasis added). For a more recent treatment of the subject, see Philip Gorski, *American Covenant: A History of Civil Religion from the Puritans to the Present* (Princeton, NJ: Princeton University Press, 2019).

150. See, e.g., David Sehat, *The Myth of American Religious Freedom* (Oxford: Oxford University Press, 2011); Frederick Mark Gedicks and Roger Hendrix, "Uncivil Religion: Judeo-Christianity and the Ten Commandments," *West Virginia Law Review* 110 (2007): 275.

151. Noah Feldman explains that "[u]ntil the 1870s, the word 'secular' did not even figure in American discussions of church and state. 'Secularism' in the contemporary sense was a term unknown to the framers and unmentioned by the Reconstruction Congress that drafted the Fourteenth Amendment. As late as the Scopes trial of 1925, 'secularism' was still a term of opprobrium to most Americans, associated as it was with radical atheism and contempt for religion." Noah Feldman, *Divided by God* (New York: Farrar, Straus and Giroux, 2005), 181.

152. See Sidney E. Mead, *The Lively Experiment: The Shaping of Christianity in America* (New York: Harper & Row, 1963), 59.

153. In its constitution of 1776, for example, Pennsylvania required all state legislators to affirm a belief in "one God, the Creator and Governor of the universe," and to "acknowledge the Scriptures of the Old and New Testaments to be given by inspiration." B. F. Morris, "State Constitutional Provisions and Proclamations Related to Religion: The Constitution of Pennsylvania," Dreisbach and Hall, *Sacred Rights*, 257.

154. Ketcham, *Selected Writings*, 3. See also Waldman, *Founding Faith*, 105, which describes Madison's "Pennsylvania -envy."

155. Ketcham, *Selected Writings*, 307.

156. Donald L. Drakeman, *Church, State, and Original Intent* (Cambridge: Cambridge University Press, 2010), 330. Drakeman updates his analysis and defends his interpretation against competitors in Donald Drakeman, "Which Original Meaning of the Establishment Clause is the Right One?" in Breidenbach and Anderson, *Cambridge Companion to the First Amendment and Religious Liberty*, 365. I have argued for a slightly different interpretation of the establishment clause, see, e.g., Steven D. Smith, *The Rise and Decline of American Religious Freedom* (Cambridge, MA: Harvard University Press, 2014), 48–66, but for present purposes the differences are unimportant.

157. Drakeman, "Which Original Meaning," 390.

158. Letter from Thomas Jefferson to Messrs. Nehemiah Dodge, Ephraim Robbins, and Stephen S. Nelson (January 1, 1802) (final version), reprinted in Dreisbach and Hall, *Sacred Rights*, 528.

159. See, e.g., T. Jeremy Gunn, "The Separation of Church and State versus Religion in the Public Square," in *No Establishment of Religion: America's Original Contribution to Religious Liberty*, ed. T. Jeremy Gunn and John Witte, Jr. (New York: Oxford University Press, 2012), 15, 18, which advocates an interpretation that "favors the 'separation of church and state' (or more properly *religion* and the state)" (emphasis in original). See also Gillman and Chemerinsky, *Religion Clauses*, 12, 46; Isaac Kramnick and R. Laurence Moore, *The Godless Constitution: A Moral Defense of the Secular State*, rev. ed. (New York: W. W. Norton, 2005), 200, which asserts that "Jefferson's metaphor . . . is a powerful statement about the need for a secular state."

160. See Federalist 37 (Madison), in *The Federalist Papers*, ed. Clinton Rossiter (New York: Signet Books, 2003), 226–27. "It is impossible for a man of pious reflection not to perceive in [the creation of the Constitution] a finger of that Almighty hand which has been so frequently and signally extended to our relief in the critical stages of the revolution."

161. James Madison, First Inaugural Address (March 4, 1809), https://miller center.org/the-presidency/presidential-speeches/march-4-1809-first-inaugural -address.

162. Although Madison criticized the practice of paying legislative chaplains in a personal writing called the "Detached Memoranda" that remained unpublished during his lifetime, there is no evidence that he opposed the establishment of congressional chaplains when the practice was approved in the First Congress. See Hall, *Did America Have a Christian Founding?*, 82–83.

163. Ketcham, *Selected Writings*, 284–85 (emphasis added).

164. In his second inaugural address, for example, Jefferson declared: "I shall need, too, the favor of that Being in whose hands we are, who led our forefathers, as Israel of old, from their native land, and planted them in a country flowing with all the necessaries and comforts of life; who has covered our infancy with

his providence, and our riper years with his wisdom and power; and to whose goodness I ask you to join with me in supplications, that he will so enlighten the minds of your servants, guide their councils, and prosper their measures, that whatsoever they do, shall result in your good, and shall secure to you the peace, friendship, and approbation of all nations." Thomas Jefferson, Second Inaugural Address (March 4, 1805), reprinted in Dreisbach and Hall, *Sacred Rights*, 530.

165. See, e.g., Letter from Thomas Jefferson to the Reverend Samuel Miller (January 23, 1808), reprinted in Dreisbach and Hall, *Sacred Rights*, 530. For a more detailed elaboration of the point, see Steven D. Smith, "The Establishment Clause and the 'Problem of the Church,'" in *Challenges to Religious Liberty in the Twenty-First Century*, ed. Gerard V. Bradley (Cambridge: Cambridge University Press), 3, 13–16.

166. Rakove, *Beyond Belief, Beyond Conscience*, 9. See also Steven K. Green, *The Second Disestablishment: Church and State in Nineteenth-Century America* (Oxford: Oxford University Press, 2010).

167. See, e.g., Phillip E. Hammond, *Religion and Personal Autonomy: The Third Disestablishment in America* (Columbia: University of South Carolina Press, 1992).

168. These are all propositions set forth in the American revision of the Anglican Thirty-nine Articles, sections I, IX, and XIII. See "The Thirty-Nine Articles of Religion of the Church of England," in *The Creeds of Christendom*, vol. 3, ed. Phillip Schaff, revised by David S. Schaff (Grand Rapids, MI: Baker Book House, 1983).

169. Quoted in Den Hartog, "Church and State in the Nineteenth Century," 192, 199–200.

170. It is sometimes argued that government should maintain neutrality only in the area of religion. But in fact it is no more possible for government to avoid making decisions and adopting policies that are congruent with some religious beliefs, and that reject other religious beliefs, than for government to be neutral with respect to nonreligious beliefs. For elaboration, see Steven D. Smith, "*Barnette*'s Big Blunder," *Chicago-Kent Law Review* 78 (2003): 625.

171. Banning, *Sacred Fire of Liberty*, 4.

172. For example, he argued that an officially preferred church would discourage immigration into the state. This may have been a cogent consideration in Virginia in the 1780s; conversely, the argument would have little force in a political community that viewed immigration as more of a challenge and burden than a blessing. In a corollary argument, Madison suggested that by discouraging immigration, religious establishment would impede the spread of Christianity. He may have been right, but in other contexts—our modern political situation, for one—the idea that public policy should be shaped so as to encourage the spread of Christianity will seem odd and alien.

173. For example, Madison argued that religious establishment undermines the social order because it causes strife and division. Thomas More took an opposing view: as we have seen, he thought that the church, working in cooperation

with the government, performed an essential function not only in holding society together but in consecrating society—endowing it with an intimate connection to the sacred and the eternal. In this disagreement, we today may incline to side with Madison. But it also seems possible that both men were right, albeit in a limited way. In one context—one in which religious pluralism is an accomplished and inextinguishable reality, for example—Madison's position might be persuasive: any attempt to impose an official church will likely be hugely contentious. But in other contexts, More's position might be more cogent. That position had, after all, held Europe together for a thousand years after the collapse of the Roman Empire.

174. Noonan, *Lustre of Our Country*, 81.

175. 1 Samuel 16:7 (KJV).

176. For elaboration, see Steven D. Smith, *Pagans and Christians in the City* (Grand Rapids, MI: Eerdmans, 2018), chap. 3.

177. For extensive documentation, see Robert Louis Wilken, *Liberty in the Things of God: The Christian Origins of Religious Freedom* (New Haven, CT: Yale University Press, 2021).

178. See Noonan and Gaffney, *Religious Freedom* (New York: Foundation Press, 2001), 86–87.

179. See, e.g., Thomas More, *Dialogue Concerning Heresies*, rendered in modern English by Mary Gottschalk (Strongsville, OH: Scepter, 2006); Perez Zagorin, *How the Idea of Religious Toleration Came to the West* (Princeton, NJ: Princeton University Press, 2003), 14–45; Brian Tierney, "Religious Rights: A Historical Perspective," in *Religious Liberty in Western Thought*, ed. Noel B. Reynolds and W. Cole Durham, Jr. (Atlanta: Scholars Press, 1996), 29, 42–55.

180. Zagorin, *How the Idea*, 27–28. See also ibid., 30: Augustine "did not see coercion and free will as opposites in religious choice but claimed that fear plays a part in spontaneous acts of the will and may serve a good end."

181. Kaplan, *Divided by Faith*, 25.

182. Richard Arneson makes a similar argument for coercing people to comply with antidiscrimination laws even if they are conscientiously opposed. "The aim," Arneson explains, "is to change the hearts and minds of men and women and to bring it about that in time people will not only conform their conduct to the aims of antidiscrimination law but will also do so willingly and cease to have racially charged motivations that lead them to do what the laws forbid." Richard J. Arneson, "Against Freedom of Conscience," *San Diego Law Review* 47 (2010): 1038. Arneson suggests that "inducing people to act against their conscientious beliefs may over time alter their conscientious beliefs." Ibid.

183. See Zagorin, *How the Idea*, 44, which explains that heresy was viewed as "a plague, a cancer, an infection, a contagion, a lethal poison, and was compared especially to leprosy." See Murphy, *Conscience and Community*, 44: "[John] Cotton compared the banishment of heretics and other troublemakers to excluding someone with the plague or other infectious diseases." See also Kaplan, *Divided by Faith*, 28: "Aquinas also advanced the argument that heretics would influence and corrupt the orthodox, spreading their crime like a communicable disease."

184. More, *Dialogue Concerning Heresies*, 473, 470.

185. Quoted in Mead, *Lively Experiment*, 60. See Murphy, *Conscience and Community*, 54: "The claim that tolerating religious dissent would lead to chaos, irreligion, and anarchy was repeated again and again by Massachusetts leaders." See also Murphy, *Conscience and Community*, 142: "Antitolerationists . . . stressed the danger that toleration posed to social order and civil peace."

186. See, e.g., More, *Dialogue Concerning Heresies*, 149–55.

187. See Thomas Nagel, *The Last Word* (New York: Oxford University Press, 1997), 130. "It isn't just that I don't believe in God and, naturally, hope that I'm right in my belief. It's that I hope there is no God! I don't want there to be a God; I don't want the universe to be like that."

188. See Rakove, *Beyond Belief, Beyond Conscience*, 57. "Yet by the middle decades of the eighteenth century, the colonials were beginning to inhabit a world of religious pluralism where law and custom were no longer strong enough to preserve communal uniformity and orthodoxy. The very idea of dissent was becoming problematic, as it became ever more difficult to say where orthodoxy resided."

189. See Rakove, *Beyond Belief, Beyond Conscience*, 52, which observes that "Quaker behavior was so offensive that even Roger Williams . . . held them in open contempt."

190. See Reynolds v. United States, 98 U.S. 145 (1878).

191. See West Virginia Board of Educ. v. Barnette, 319 U.S. 624 (1943).

192. See State v. Beagley, 305 P.3d 147 (Ore. App. 2013).

193. See Employment Division v. Smith, 494 U.S. 872 (1990).

194. See Church of the Lukumi Babalu Aye v. Hialeah, 508 U.S. 520 (1993).

195. At this point the discussion might veer off in various directions, but we should stick to what Madison actually says. Thus, anticipating modern First Amendment theory, someone might propose that the truth, in religion as in other matters, is best achieved by a sort of free marketplace of ideas. See, e.g., John H. Garvey, *What Are Freedoms For?* (Cambridge, MA: Harvard University Press, 1996), 51. Or we might say that although you, the ruler, feel certain that the Episcopal beliefs are true and the Baptist beliefs are false, you are still a fallible mortal and you might be wrong. This sort of argument from fallibility had already been urged by Locke and others, and it would be developed in a celebrated essay by John Stuart Mill and would become a commonplace in free speech theory. The argument is problematic because although it is surely true that rulers are fallible, it is not clear why this fallibility has different implications for religion and speech than it has for other matters, where we typically expect our eminently fallible rulers just to be careful and make the best judgments they can. And in any case, although Madison also tried to make something of the fallibility of rulers, this was not his point in article 16 or in the principal argument in the "Memorial and Remonstrance." Instead, he offered a different kind of argument: he suggested, without quite openly asserting, that even a false belief *can* be spiritually efficacious—so long as it is sincere.

196. In this vein, Larry Alexander criticizes a rationale for religious freedom offered by John Garvey that is very much like Madison's argument in the

"Memorial and Remonstrance." See Garvey, *What Are Freedoms For?*, 46–57. Alexander argues that the claim that religious faith must be voluntary—a claim made by Garvey (and Madison, and Locke, and many others) is a rationale only for permitting the exercise of what we or the authorities regard as *true* religion. Conversely, if someone is professing and practicing a false religion, then it may be true that we cannot bring that person around to a saving faith by compulsion, but it is also true that we cannot bring the person to a saving faith by allowing them to continue in their false faith. See Larry Alexander, "Good God, Garvey! The Inevitability and Impossibility of a Religious Justification of Free Exercise Exemptions," *Drake Law Review* 47 (1998): 35.

197. See Acts 5:39.

198. See Harrison, *Post-Liberal Religious Liberty*, 82. "[A] further thought creeps in: that God finds acceptable the individual's construal of belief so long as it is grounded in sincerity."

199. Compare Murphy, *Conscience and Community*, 229, which observes that in early modern defenses of freedom of conscience, "voluntarily worshipping a certain way was considered almost as important as the objective correctness (or lack thereof) of the mode of worship itself."

200. See Charles E. Curran, "Conscience in the Light of the Catholic Moral Tradition," in *Conscience*, ed. Charles E. Curran (New York: Paulist Press, 2004), 3, 5 (footnote deleted): "A conscience that is sincere but invincibly erroneous can and should be followed without any guilt on the agent's part. . . . Aquinas held that such an act of conscience is not wrong. Alphonsus maintained that such an act is not only not wrong but it is also good and even meritorious."

201. See Beneke, "Historical Context," 153. "To our modern eyes, eighteenth-century Protestant denominations appear to be no more than a hair's breadth apart. Yet those differences seemed of vital importance at the time."

202. See Ketcham, *James Madison*, 52.

203. Quoted in Kathleen A. Brady, *The Distinctiveness of Religion in American Law: Rethinking Religion Clause Jurisprudence* (New York: Cambridge University Press, 2015), 105.

204. See note 93, which explains how in Virginia the established church had been regarded as a necessary support for society.

205. Benedict Anderson, *Imagined Communities*, rev. ed. (London: Verso Books, 2016).

206. Thomas Jefferson, Notes on the State of Virginia, Query XVIII. - Manners, in *The Portable Thomas Jefferson*, ed. Merrill D. Peterson (New York: Viking, 1975), 215.

207. George Fletcher, "In God's Image: The Religious Imperative of Equality Under Law," *Columbia Law Review* 99 (1999): 1608, 1611.

208. Madison, "Memorial and Remonstrance," 26–27 (para. 15).

209. Madison's proposal would have included language declaring that "the full and equal rights of conscience [shall not] in any manner, or on any pretext, be infringed," and also that "no State shall violate the equal rights of conscience." Ketcham, *James Madison*, 165.

210. Noonan, *Lustre of Our Country*, 75.

211. See Smith, *Rise and Decline*, 36–38.

212. John Witte, Jr., *God's Joust, God's Justice* (Grand Rapids, MI: Eerdmans, 2006), 16. See also Murphy, *Conscience and Community*, 111: "According to the orthodox view, conscience represented the voice of God within an individual."

213. Joseph Smith, founder of the Church of Jesus Christ of Latter-day Saints (or Mormonism), recalled the religious situation in upstate New York during his teenage years in the early nineteenth century: "[T]he whole district of country seemed affected by [a religious revival], and great multitudes united themselves to the different religious parties, which created no small stir and division amongst the people, some crying 'Lo, here!' and others, 'Lo, there!' Some were contending for the Methodist faith, some for the Presbyterian, and some for the Baptist. . . . [A] scene of great confusion and bad feeling ensued." Joseph Smith– History, extracted in The Pearl of Great Price, verses 5–6.

214. Essay by Elihu, *The American Mercury* (February 18, 1788), reprinted in Dreisbach and Hall, *Sacred Rights*, 352.

215. See James Turner, *Without God, Without Creed* (Baltimore: Johns Hopkins University Press, 1985), 44. "If one disregards the expatriate Barlow just before 1800, America does not seem to have harbored a single individual before the nineteenth century who disbelieved in God. . . . For disbelief in God remained scarcely more plausible than disbelief in gravity."

216. See Charles Taylor, *Sources of the Self* (Cambridge, MA: Harvard University Press, 1989), 309. "Even in the latter part of the eighteenth century, in the era of the high Enlightenment, genuine atheism was very rare."

217. Ketcham, *Selected Writings*, 305–6.

218. See generally Charles Taylor, *A Secular Age* (Cambridge, MA: Belknap Press of Harvard University Press, 2007).

CHAPTER THREE

1. As Sanford Levinson explains, "Brennan in effect claimed that his Catholicism . . . would play no role whatsoever in his understanding of his judicial role." Like other justices who have self-identified as Catholic, Brennan was "forced to proclaim the practical meaninglessness of that identification." Sanford Levinson, *Wrestling with Diversity* (Durham, NC: Duke University Press, 2003), 194.

2. The following facts are distilled from Seth Stern and Stephen Wermiel, *Justice Brennan: Liberal Champion* (Boston: Houghton Mifflin Harcourt, 2010), 71–85, and Hunter R. Clark, *Justice Brennan: The Great Conciliator* (Secaucus, NJ: Carol Publishing Group, 1995), 76–79.

3. See Clark, *Justice Brennan*, 78. Stern and Wermiel find Vanderbilt's version implausible. Stern and Wermiel, *Justice Brennan*, 67.

4. Stern and Wermiel, *Justice Brennan*, 165.

5. Stern and Wermiel, *Justice Brennan*, 90–91.

6. Stern and Wermiel, *Justice Brennan*, 21.

7. His biographers observe that "Brennan's account of being completely dumbfounded upon learning he was Eisenhower's pick for the Supreme Court made for good newspaper copy, but strains credulity. He was much too shrewd not to realize the purpose of his sudden summons to Washington." They add that "Brennan always wanted to be seen as a regular guy rather than an ambitious climber, so he may well have played dumb for the benefit of Brownell and reporters." Stern and Wermiel, *Justice Brennan*, 80–81.

8. John T. McGreevy, *Catholicism and American Freedom* (New York: W. W. Norton, 2003), 166–67.

9. Clark, *Justice Brennan*, 110.

10. Reported in Daniel M. Berman, "Mr. Justice Brennan: A Preliminary Appraisal," *Catholic University Law Review* 7 (1985): 1, 11–12.

11. Stern and Wermiel, *Justice Brennan*, 119.

12. Stern and Wermiel, *Justice Brennan*, 115, 119–20.

13. Brennan's colleague and frequent jurisprudential opponent, William Rehnquist, described Brennan's "legendary warmth and charm." William H. Rehnquist, "Foreword," in *Reason and Passion: Justice Brennan's Enduring Influence*, ed. E. Joshua Rosenkranz and Bernard Schwartz (New York: W. W. Norton, 1997), 11. Jeffery Leeds, formerly a Brennan law clerk and later an interviewer, observed in 1986 that Brennan was "easily the warmest member of the Court, famous for his charm, always linking arms with his colleagues or reaching out for a hand or a shoulder." Jeffrey T. Leeds, "A Life on the Court," *New York Times*, October 5, 1986, https://archive.nytimes.com/www.nytimes.com/books/97/07/06/reviews/brennan-interview.html. See also David Halberstam, "The Common Man as Uncommon Man," in Rosenkranz and Schwartz, *Reason and Passion*, 22, 25: "No one who has ever met [Justice Brennan] can be other than moved by the powerful and enduring quality of his humanity. He is a man defined by his own innate decency and kindness. . . . He has always been unaffected by position, and he remains incapable of posturing. . . . He has always treated everyone he meets, regardless of station, with a human grace that is absolute."

14. The authors of the leading biography observe that Brennan was "the most forceful and effective liberal ever to serve on the Court" and "perhaps the most influential justice of the entire twentieth century." Stern and Wermiel, *Justice Brennan*, xiii.

15. Bernard Schwartz, "How Justice Brennan Changed America," in Rosenkranz and Schwartz, *Reason and Passion*, 31.

16. See Stern and Wermiel, *Justice Brennan*, 418. "By the end of his tenure, Brennan would cite human dignity as 'the basic premise on which I build everything under the Constitution.'" For further discussion, see the beginning of section V: Constitutionalizing the Consecrated, Authentic Self in this chapter.

17. Alan Abramowitz and Steven Webster, "'Negative Partisanship' Explains Everything," *Politico*, September/October 2017, https://www.politico.com/magazine/story/2017/09/05/negative-partisanship-explains-everything-215534/.

18. Lee Drutman, "How Hatred Came to Dominate American Politics," *FiveThirtyEight*, October 5, 2020, https://fivethirtyeight.com/features/how -hatred-negative-partisanship-came-to-dominate-american-politics/.

19. See, e.g., Gary Lawson, "What is 'United' about the United States?" *Boston University Law Review* 101, no. 5 (October 2021): 1793; David French, *Divided We Fall: America's Secession Threat and How to Restore Our Nation* (New York: St. Martin's Press, 2020); Adam K. Raymond, "How Close is the U.S. to Civil War? About Two-Thirds of the Way, Americans Say," New York Intelligencer, October 24, 2019, https://nymag.com/intelligencer/2019/10 /americans-say-u-s-is-two-thirds-of-the-way-to-civil-war.html; Bruce Frohnen, "A Tale of Two Americas," *Chronicles*, July 1, 2021, https://www.chronicles magazine.org/a-tale-of-two-americas/; Nathan Newman, "The Case for Blue State Secession," *Nation*, February 10, 2021, https://www.thenation.com/article /politics/secession-constitution-elections-senate/; F. H. Buckley, *American Secession: The Looming Threat of a National Breakup* (New York: Encounter, 2020). For a gloomy distillation of negative trends, see Nick Bryant, *When America Stopped Being Great: A History of the Present* (London: Bloomsbury, 2021), 329–45. See ibid., 340: "We are no longer talking about decline. . . . This is about disintegration."

20. Nick Bryant, "Joe Biden One Year On: Has the United States Become Ungovernable?," *BBC News*, January 19, 2022, https://www.bbc.com/news /world-us-canada-60036911.

21. Leeds, "A Life on the Court" (emphasis added).

22. Stern and Wermiel. *Justice Brennan*, 16.

23. Stern and Wermiel, *Justice Brennan*, 26–44.

24. Stern and Wermiel, *Justice Brennan*, 13.

25. Stern and Wermiel, *Justice Brennan*, 165.

26. See James Turner, *Without God, Without Creed* (Baltimore: Johns Hopkins University Press, 1985), 44. "If one disregards the expatriate Barlow just before 1800, America does not seem to have harbored a single individual before the nineteenth century who disbelieved in God. . . . For disbelief in God remained scarcely more plausible than disbelief in gravity."

27. See, e.g., Abington School Dist. v. Schempp, 374 U.S. 203, 240 (1963) (Brennan, J., concurring); Goldman v. Weinberger, 475 U.S. 503, 518–19 (1986) (Brennan, J., dissenting).

28. Massimo Faggioli, *Joe Biden and Catholicism in the United States* (New London, CT: Bayard, 2021), 32, which describes "Kennedy's strategy of privatization of his Catholicism."

29. Brennan's distinction, however, is not the only premise on which such officials might and sometimes do rely. In a much-discussed lecture given at the University of Notre Dame, Governor Mario Cuomo presented himself as a sincere Catholic and also a pro-choice politician. But Cuomo did not argue that as an official he should not act on the basis of his religious beliefs. Rather, he argued that religious beliefs must be implemented in accordance with prudential judgment, and that legal restrictions on abortion would be ineffectual, divisive, and imprudent. See Mario Cuomo, "Religious Belief and Public Morality: A Catholic Governor's Perspective," delivered September 13, 1984, as the John A. O'Brien

Lecture in the University of Notre Dame's Department of Theology, https://archives.nd.edu/research/texts/cuomo.htm.

30. See generally McGreevy, *Catholicism and American Freedom*.

31. Sanford Levinson has discussed a similar phenomenon in the professions, particularly the legal profession. Law schools and the legal profession itself, Levinson suggests, train lawyers to set aside important aspects of their personal identities, including "race, gender, religion, or ethnic background," in order to become "almost purely fungible members of the respective professional communities." Levinson, *Wrestling with Diversity*, 125–26. In this way, Levinson argues, the profession strives to produce what he calls a "bleaching out" of the self. Ibid. See also ibid., 24–25.

32. Peter L. Berger, *The Many Altars of Modernity* (Boston: DeGruyter, 2014), 89–90.

33. See generally John Rawls, *Political Liberalism* (New York: Columbia University Press, 1996).

34. See Stern and Wermiel, *Justice Brennan*, 164. "Both Brennan and Kennedy had tried their whole lives to retain their identities as Irish Catholics." With respect to Kennedy, Massimo Faggioli explains: "A practicing Catholic but not visibly devout, Kennedy had nevertheless been formed by the Catholic faith in a life in which he had faced death, in war as well as from health problems that plagued him throughout his life. He received the sacrament of extreme unction three times, in 1947, 1954, and 1955, before he was given the sacrament the last time following that tragic shooting in Dallas on November 22, 1963." Faggioli, *Joe Biden*, 35.

35. McGreevy, *Catholicism and American Freedom*, 148. In his more considered and published response, Smith explained that he was no theologian, but that during his many years of public service, including his four terms as governor of New York, he had never experienced any conflict arising from his Catholicism. Smith's written response also drew upon the learning of a theomagisterial teaching that it cited. Alfred E. Smith, "Catholic and Patriot," *Atlantic*, May 1927, https://www.theatlantic.com/magazine/archive/1927/05/catholic-and-patriot/306522/.

36. Quoted in Faggioli, *Joe Biden*, 23.

37. Stern and Wermiel, *Justice Brennan*, 165.

38. Stern and Wermiel, *Justice Brennan*, 167.

39. William J. Brennan, Jr., "Thomas More: Saint and Judge," *Catholic Lawyer* 4, no. 2 (Spring 1958): 162.

40. See, e.g., "Chief Justice Roberts Statement—Nomination Process," excerpted from *Confirmation Hearing on the Nomination of John G. Roberts, Jr. to be Chief Justice of the United States: Hearings before the Committee on the Judiciary*, United States Senate, 109th Cong. 55–56 (2005), https://www.uscourts.gov/educational-resources/educational-activities/chief-justice-roberts-statement-nomination-process.

41. Alexander M. Bickel, *The Least Dangerous Branch: The Supreme Court at the Bar of Politics* (New Haven, CT: Yale University Press, 1962), 97–98.

42. This is the central theme pursued in Kent Greenawalt, *Religious Convictions and Political Choice* (New York: Oxford University Press, 1987).

43. Judith Jarvis Thomson, "A Defense of Abortion," in *Biomedical Ethics and the Law*, ed. J. M. Humber and R. F. Almeder (New York: Plenum Press, 1976).

44. See below notes 210–12 and accompanying text (discussing loss of commitment to objective truth in contemporary culture).

45. See, e.g., John Paul II, *The Gospel of Life (Evangelium Vitae): On the Value and Inviolability of Human Life* (Washington, DC: United States Conference of Catholic Bishops, 1995), secs. 57–63.

46. "Compartmentalization" is, to be sure, a broader term; it can describe all manner of allocations that humans routinely and necessarily make. You work during the day and sleep at night. You talk in particular terms and on particular subjects with your colleagues at work, and in other terms and on other subjects with your spouse at home. All of these divisions and allocations might be described as forms of "compartmentalization." But the compartmentalization that we are concerned with here, and that Brennan and Kennedy and so many others have committed themselves to, is compartmentalization of the disintegrative kind—the kind that occurs when someone agrees or is told not to consult particular beliefs or values in a particular domain *although those beliefs or values would otherwise be relevant to* or even *determinative of* decisions and actions in that domain. The Rawlsian directive to bracket one's "comprehensive doctrines" in the performance of public duties is this kind of disintegrative compartmentalization pretty much by definition, because if a doctrine is "comprehensive" then it seems that the doctrine *will* speak to matters even in the public domain. Whether a particular person like Brennan or Kennedy actually holds a faith in the "comprehensive" sense that the doctrine purports to carry is of course a different question.

47. John F. Kennedy, "Address to Southern Baptist Leaders" (1960), https://usa.usembassy.de/etexts/democrac/66.htm.

48. "I do not accept the right of any . . . ecclesiastical official, to tell me what I shall do in the sphere of my public responsibility as an elected official." John F. Kennedy, "Greater Houston Ministerial Association Q and A," September 12, 1960, https://www.americanrhetoric.com/speeches/jfkhouston ministerialQ&A.htm. See also Kennedy, "Address to Southern Baptist Leaders."

49. Kennedy, "Greater Houston Ministerial Association Q and A."

50. Engel v. Vitale, 370 U.S. 421 (1962).

51. Abington School Dist. v. Schempp, 374 U.S. 203 (1963).

52. Everson v. Board of Education, 330 U.S. 1 (1947).

53. This point is developed at much greater length in Steven D. Smith, "Constitutional Divide: The Transformative Significance of the School Prayer Decisions," *Pepperdine Law Review* 38 (2011): 945.

54. Abington School Dist. v. Schempp, 374 U.S. 203 (1963) at 344–45.

55. Epperson v. Arkansas, 393 U.S. 97, 103, 106 (1968).

56. Abington School Dist. v. Schempp, 374 U.S. 203 (1963) at 222.

57. Lemon v. Kurtzman, 403 U.S. 602, 612–13 (1971).

58. The Court explicitly repudiated the *Lemon* test, though not the more basic requirement of "neutrality," in Kennedy v. Bremerton School Dist., 597 U.S. __ (2022).

59. Lynch v. Donnelly, 465 U.S. 668 (1984).

60. Engel v. Vitale, 18 Misc.2d 659 (NY Sup Ct Special Term 1959).

61. Bruce C. Dierenfield, *The Battle Over School Prayer* (Lawrence: University Press of Kansas, 2007), 115–16. Though sharply critical of Meyer's conclusion, constitutional scholar Philip Kurland conceded that Meyer's opinion was "exhaustive and erudite." Philip B. Kurland, "The School Prayer Cases," in *The Wall Between Church and State*, ed. Dallin H. Oaks (Chicago: University of Chicago Press, 1963), 149.

62. Dierenfield, *Battle Over School Prayer*, 128.

63. Paul G. Kauper, "Schempp and Sherbert: Studies in Neutrality and Accommodation," in *Religion and the Public Order*, ed. Donald A. Gianella (Ithaca, NY: Cornell University Press, 1963), 3, 6. See also Gerard V. Bradley, "The Judicial Experiment with Privatizing Religion," *Liberty University Law Review* 1, no. 1 (Winter 2006): 32, which says "[t]he [*Engel*] opinion is absolute, peremptory, confident, even strident." Louis Fisher defends the decision but suggests that it provoked misunderstanding and angry reaction in part because of "the clumsy and tactless way it was written and presented." Louis Fisher, *Religious Liberty and America* (Lawrence: University Press of Kansas, 2002), 123.

64. Abington School Dist. v. Schempp, 374 U.S. 203 (1963) at 216–22.

65. Abington School Dist. v. Schempp, 374 U.S. 203 (1963) at 294 (Brennan, J., concurring).

66. Abington School Dist. v. Schempp, 374 U.S. 203 (1963) at 237–41.

67. A classic article advocating such an approach was Herbert Wechsler, "Toward Neutral Principles of Constitutional Law," *Harvard Law Review* 73 (1959), 1, 18–19.

68. For my own criticisms of the emphasis on "principles and purposes," see Steven D. Smith, *Fictions, Lies, and the Authority of Law* (Notre Dame, IN: University of Notre Dame Press, 2021), 67–71. And see generally Steven D. Smith, Larry Alexander, James Allan, and Maimon Schwarzschild, *A Principled Constitution? Four Skeptical Views* (Lanham, MD: Lexington Books, 2022).

69. Abington School Dist. v. Schempp, 374 U.S. 203 (1963) at 243, 299.

70. The establishment clause, Brennan suggested, should be understood to prohibit those involvements of religious with secular institutions which (a) serve the essentially religious activities of religious institutions; (b) employ the organs of government for essentially religious purposes; or (c) use essentially religious means to serve governmental ends where secular means would suffice. Abington School Dist. v. Schempp, 374 U.S. 203 (1963) at 231 (Brennan, J., concurring).

71. Abington School Dist. v. Schempp, 374 U.S. 203 (1963) at 294–304.

72. Abington School Dist. v. Schempp, 374 U.S. 203 (1963) at 299–300.

73. Marsh v. Chambers, 463 U.S. 783, 796 (1983) (Brennan, J., dissenting).

74. Marsh v. Chambers, 463 U.S. 783 (1983) at 802 (quoting *Lemon v. Kurtzman*).

75. See, e.g., Lynch v. Donnelly, 465 U.S. 668 (1984); Allegheny County v. ACLU, 492 U.S. 573 (1989).

76. In Aguilar v. Felton, 473 U.S. 402 (1985), the Court invalidated a federal program; in School District of Grand Rapids v. Ball, 473 U.S. 373 (1985), the Court invalidated a similar state program.

77. Aguilar v. Felton, 473 U.S. 402 (1985) at 424–25 (O'Connor, J., dissenting).

78. Writing at the time, Philip Kurland observed that "[t]he immediate reaction to Engel was violent and gross." Kurland, "School Prayer Cases," 142. Bruce Dierenfield reports that Engel provoked "the greatest outcry against a U.S. Supreme Court decision in a century." Dierenfield, *Battle Over School Prayer*, 72. At a conference of state governors, every governor except New York's Nelson Rockefeller condemned *Engel* and urged passage of a constitutional amendment to overturn it. Dierenfield, *Battle Over School Prayer*, 146. See also Robert S. Alley, *Without a Prayer: Religious Expression in Public Schools* (Amherst, NY: Prometheus Books, 1996), 28, 230, which recalled that the school prayer decisions "sent shock waves through large portions of the citizenry" and "caused an enormous uproar against the Supreme Court"; Julia C. Loren, Engel v. Vitale: *Prayer in the Public Schools* (San Diego, CA: Lucent Books, 2001), 7, 61, which observed that "[t]he public outcry against the Court's ruling was swift and loud" and that "newspaper editorials across the country denounced the ruling." Lucas Powe noted that "Engel produced more mail to the Court than any previous case (and few write to say what a good job the justices are doing)." Lucas A. Powe, *The Supreme Court and the American Elite, 1789–2008* (Cambridge, MA: Harvard University Press, 2009), 260.

79. Bruce Dierenfield remarks that "[i]n a rare moment of political tone-deafness, [Chief Justice Earl] Warren did not anticipate the fallout from the [Engel] case." Dierenfield, *Battle Over School Prayer*, 132.

80. See, e.g., Dierenfield, *Battle Over School Prayer*, 136, which reports Professor Philip Kurland's view that Engel was "important but narrow in breadth." A *New Republic* essay found the critical public reaction "remarkable," adding that "[m]ost authoritative observers believe that the practical consequences of *Engel v. Vitale* in our school system will be negligible." Reprinted in Terry Eastland, *Religious Liberty in the Supreme Court* (Washington, DC: Ethics and Public Policy Center, 1993), 142–43.

81. In this vein, generally moderate University of Chicago law professor Philip Kurland condemned the decisions' critics as "religious zealots" and lumped them together with "racists" and John Birch Society extremists. Quoted in John C. Jeffries, Jr., and James E. Ryan, "A Political History of the Establishment Clause," *Michigan Law Review* 100, no. 2 (November 2001), 279, 325–26.

82. See generally Stephen H. Webb, *American Providence* (New York: Continuum, 2004), 29–50; Michael Novak, *On Two Wings* (San Francisco, CA: Encounter Books, 2002), 8–24; Michael E. Smith, "Religious Activism: The Historical Record," *William & Mary Law Review* 27, no. 5 (1986), 1087.

83. Robert N. Bellah, *The Broken Covenant: American Civil Religion in Time of Trial*, 2nd ed. (New York: Seabury Press, 1975), 2 (emphasis added).

84. Bellah, *Broken Covenant*, 3.

85. Bellah, *Broken Covenant*, 174. See also ibid., 168: "[T]he American republic, which has neither an established church nor a classic civil religion, is, after all, a Christian republic, or I should say a biblical republic, in which biblical religion is indeed the civil religion."

86. Bellah, *Broken Covenant*, 12. For a more recent scholarly treatment of the pervasiveness of civil religion throughout American history, see Philip Gorski, *American Covenant: A History of Civil Religion from the Puritans to the Present* (Princeton, NJ: Princeton University Press, 2019).

87. Throughout the nation's history, more religious interpretations had competed with more secularist interpretations: what I have elsewhere called "the American settlement" was committed to religious freedom but left the exact content of that commitment a matter of ongoing contestation. The school prayer decisions and the modern constitutional jurisprudence suppressed that competition by making the secularist interpretation the official and judicially enforced constitutional doctrine. See Steven D. Smith, *The Rise and Decline of American Religious Freedom* (Cambridge, MA: Harvard University Press, 2014), 76–138.

88. Elton Trueblood, *Abraham Lincoln: Theologian of American Anguish* (New York: Harper & Row, 1973), 135–36.

89. Gary Scott Smith, "Franklin Delano Roosevelt and the Quest to Achieve an Abundant Life," in Gary Scott Smith, *Faith and the Presidency: From George Washington to George W. Bush* (Oxford: Oxford University Press, 2006), chap. 6, para. 2, https://oxford.universitypressscholarship.com/view/10.1093/acprof:oso /9780195300604.001.0001/acprof-9780195300604-chapter-6. Later in that paragraph, Smith adds that "Roosevelt's faith was sincere but not intellectually sophisticated. Like his approach to politics, his faith focused more on action than contemplation, more on results than on principles."

90. The president had famously added "and I don't care what it is." Quoted in Paul Horwitz, "Religion and American Politics: Three Views of the Cathedral," *University of Memphis Law Review* 39, no. 4 (Summer 2009), 973, 978. The statement was not made casually or inadvertently, it seems, but reflected Eisenhower's considered commitment: "The General said over and over during the campaign that when the founding fathers said that men were endowed by the Creator with rights, they showed that the basis or foundation of this nation and form of government lay in a 'deeply felt religious faith.' Our government is the attempt to 'translate' that religion into the political world. He said that no other nation has American's 'spiritual and moral strength.' He said that 'the Almighty takes a definite and direct interest day by day in the progress of this nation.'" William Lee Miller, *Piety Along the Potomac: Notes on Politics and Morals in the Fifties* (Boston: Houghton Mifflin, 1964), 34.

91. Zorach v. Clauson, 343 U.S. 306, 312 (1952).

92. See Martin Luther King, Jr., *I Have a Dream: Writings and Speeches That Changed the World*, ed. James M. Washington (New York: HarperCollins, 1986).

93. For the text of the letter, see King, "Letter from a Birmingham Jail," in King, *I Have a Dream*, 83.

94. Stephen Monsma describes the Regents' Prayer invalidated in *Engel* as "innocuous (some would say insipid)." Stephen V. Monsma, *Positive Neutrality* (Westport, CT: Greenwood Press, 1993), 74.

95. Dierenfield, *Battle Over School Prayer*, 67–68.

96. Noah Feldman, *Divided by God* (New York: Farrar, Straus and Giroux, 2005), 70.

97. Gerard Bradley describes 1984 as the highpoint of the judicial effort to privatize religion, as manifest in the following year's Brennan-authored decisions in Aguilar v. Felton, 473 U.S. 402 (1985), and School District of Grand Rapids v. Ball, 473 U.S. 373 (1985). Bradley, "Judicial Experiment with Privatizing Religion," 17.

98. Mark DeWolfe Howe, *The Garden and the Wilderness: Religion and Government in American Constitutional History* (Chicago: University of Chicago Press, 1965), 154.

99. Thus, when T. Jeremy Gunn argues that the Constitution "favors the 'separation of church and state' (or more properly *religion* and the state)," Gunn seems unaware that his parenthetical is peremptorily making a crucial change in meaning. Rather, he evidently supposes that he is merely offering an obvious and unobjectionable clarification. T. Jeremy Gunn, "The Separation of Church and State versus Religion in the Public Square," in *No Establishment of Religion*, ed. T. Jeremy Gunn and John Witte, Jr. (New York: Oxford University Press, 2012), 15, 18. See also Howard Gillman and Erwin Chemerinsky, *The Religion Clauses: The Case for Separation of Church and State* (New York: Oxford University Press, 2020), 12, 46; Isaac Kramnick and R. Laurence Moore, *The Godless Constitution: Defense of the Secular State*, rev. ed. (New York: W. W. Norton, 2005), 200, which asserts that "Jefferson's metaphor . . . is a powerful statement about the need for a secular state"; John Swomley, *Religious Freedom and the Secular State* (Buffalo, NY: Prometheus Books, 1987), 17, which interprets "[t]he constitutional doctrine of separation of church and state to mean that [t]he Constitution . . . provides for a wholly secular government."

100. See John Ayto, *Dictionary of Word Origins* (New York: Arcade Publishing, 1990), 465: "**secular** Latin *saeculum*, a word of uncertain origin, meant 'generation, age.' It was used in early Christian texts for the 'temporal world' (as opposed to the 'spiritual world'). . . . The more familiar modern English meaning 'non-religious' emerged in the 16th century."

101. For a discussion of how, even during the period of Christendom, government was expected to be "secular" and of how the dominant meanings of the term have changed, see Steven D. Smith, *The Disenchantment of Secular Discourse* (Cambridge, MA: Harvard University Press, 2010), 112–50. See also Nomi Stolzenberg, "The Profanity of Law," in *Law and the Sacred*, ed. Austin Sarat (Stanford: Stanford University Press, 2007), 35.

102. Admitting that their characterization is overstated—or "overdramatic"—Stanley Hauerwas and William Willimon recall sensing that the world changed "on a Sunday evening in 1963." Stanley Hauerwas and William H. Willimon, *Resident Aliens: Life in the Christian Colony* (Nashville: Abingdon Press, 1989), 15. The earlier cultural assumption had been that the nation and the community were fundamentally Christian, and that a person growing up in the culture would naturally be Christian. Now that assumption dissolved in a culture that was deemed to be fundamentally secular. Hauerwas and Willimon associate this alteration in sensibilities with the opening on a particular Sunday of the

Fox Theater in Greenville, South Carolina, in defiance of tradition mandating that such businesses be closed on Sunday. The Fox Theater obviously did not cause the transformation, nor did any other single event. And of course the change did not happen all in one day, or all in one year. And yet Hauerwas and Willimon are perceptive in singling out 1963 as a watershed date. And the *Schempp* decision of that year was significant in both reflecting and officially ratifying the transformation.

103. The point is developed in Steven D. Smith, "Justice Douglas, Justice O'Connor, and George Orwell: Does the Constitution Compel Us to Disown Our Past?," SSRN, May 2005, https://papers.ssrn.com/sol3/papers.cfm ?abstract_id=728663.

104. In the Rawlsian version of the modern compartmentalization, Lincoln's speech appears to run roughshod over the constraints of "public reason." Far from avoiding the invocation of "comprehensive doctrines," the address gains its power precisely from the fact that it does openly and unapologetically discuss the nation and the war under the aspect of a comprehensive doctrine—and a doctrine of providentialism at that. So, then, what should we say? That Lincoln, far from deserving the adulation he has usually received, ought instead to be castigated (and perhaps, in today's terms, "cancelled") for violating at least the spirit of democracy and of the Constitution, if not the actual letter? Rawls struggled valiantly to explain how this embarrassing conclusion would not necessarily follow from his philosophy, but the results were not edifying. For further discussion, see Steven D. Smith, *Pagans and Christians in the City: Culture Wars from the Tiber to the Potomac* (Grand Rapids MI: Eerdmans Publishing, 2018), 356.

105. See, e.g., Salazar v. Buono, 559 U.S. 700 (2010); Elk Grove School District v. Newdow, 542 U.S. 1 (2004) (Pledge of Allegiance).

106. See, e.g., Douglas Laycock, "Comment: Theology Scholarships, The Pledge of Allegiance, and Religious Liberty: Avoiding the Extremes but Missing the Liberty," *Harvard Law Review* 118, no. 1 (November 2004): 155, 235, which observes that "[t]his rationale is unconvincing both to serious nonbelievers and to serious believers."

107. McCreary County v. ACLU, 545 U.S. 844 (2005); Van Orden v. Perry, 545 U.S. 677 (2005).

108. Van Orden v. Perry, 545 U.S. at 700 (Breyer, J., concurring in the judgment).

109. Theorists have debated whether the constraints imposed by Rawlsian public reason should apply not only to officials but also to ordinary citizens in the conduct of their public responsibilities—for example, voting, debating public issues, and so forth. On the one hand, it would be virtually impossible to enforce any constraint directing citizens to bracket their religious convictions when, say, they step into the voting booth. On the other hand, if public decisions and policies are supposed to be based on secular and not religious grounds, that constraint (whether or not it is enforceable) presumably applies to citizens in the discharge of their public responsibilities. In some instances, after all, the citizens *are* the legislators—in cases of issues decided by general referendum, for example. And even in the more standard situations, if a legislator is not supposed

to vote on religious grounds, then surely a legislator cannot escape this constraint by saying "*I* only acted to carry out the desires of my constituents; *they* were the ones who based their political preferences on religious grounds" anymore than a legislator can escape the Constitution's equality constraints by saying "*I* don't have any racial animus; I was merely promoting the (racist) preferences of *my constituents.*"

110. In what is known as "the proviso," Rawls himself later modified his position to allow that reasons based on "reasonable" comprehensive doctrines can be offered in political discourse regarding important public decisions so long as "in due course public reasons, given by a reasonable political conception, are presented sufficient to support whatever the comprehensive doctrines are introduced to support." Rawls, *Political Liberalism*, li–lii. Although the meaning of this "proviso" is subject to interpretation, the most natural reading suggests that religious reasons can be offered in public discourse so long as they do not alter the outcome of a public decision—i.e., so long as they make no practical difference.

111. See R. J. Snell, "God and Public Reason," *Public Discourse*, June 19, 2021, https://www.thepublicdiscourse.com/2021/06/76402/, which states that "a politics [of technological secularism] might be very good at determining interest rates and how to build roads, but it would be all but incapable of asking about the justice of such things."

112. Susan Jacoby, *The Age of American Unreason* (New York: Pantheon Books, 2008), 283.

113. Ronald Dworkin, *Is Democracy Possible Here? Principles for a New Political Debate* (Princeton, NJ: Princeton University Press, 2006), 4, 1, 130.

114. See Smith, *Disenchantment of Secular Discourse*, 29–31. On the emptiness of equality, the classic text is Peter Westen, "The Empty Idea of Equality," *Harvard Law Review* 95, no. 3 (January 1982): 537.

115. See Erwin Chemerinsky, "Keynote by Erwin Chemerinsky," *University of California Davis Law Review* 48, no. 2 (December 2014): 447. On page 464 of this keynote, Chemerinsky says: " I think . . . the rhetoric was important as well when there was this shift to using the phrase 'marriage equality.' The advocates of this right, instead of speaking so much about 'same-sex marriage,' which then puts the focus on 'same-sex,' phrased this instead as being about 'marriage equality.' And equality is such a powerful norm in our society." For criticism, see Steven D. Smith, "The Red Herring of 'Marriage Equality,'" *Public Discourse*, March 27, 2013, https://www.thepublicdiscourse.com/2013/03/7912/.

116. John Coleman, *An American Strategic Theology* (New York: Paulist Press, 1979), 193–94.

117. See Steven D. Smith, "The Jurisprudence of Denigration," *University of California Davis Law Review* 48, no. 2 (December 2014): 675.

118. Whether the reasons for prohibiting abortion are necessarily "religious" is a very contestable point, to be sure. See, e.g., Neal Conan and Garry Wills, "Abortion 'Isn't a Religious Issue,' Author Says," NPR, November 5, 2007, https://www.npr.org/transcripts/16012892. But the compartmentalization relegating "religion" to the private domain is hardly precise in its definitions: for practical purposes, the fact that much of the opposition to abortion comes from

churches and religious thinkers seems enough to cause the position to be classified as "religious."

119. Consider, for example, pre-*Obergefell* decisions striking down traditional marriage laws with the observation that such laws were based on religious considerations. See, e.g., Varnum v. Brien, 763 N.W.2d 862, 904 (Iowa Sup. Ct. 2009), which declared that "[w]hile unexpressed, religious sentiment likely motivates many, if not most, opponents of same-sex civil marriage. . . ." See also Cruzan v. Director, Missouri Department of Health, 497 U.S. 261, 347, 350 (1990) (Stevens, J., dissenting), and Webster v. Reproductive Health Services, 492 U.S. 490, 566 (1989) (Stevens, J., dissenting), in which Justice John Paul Stevens voted to strike down laws regulating suicide and abortion based on his suspicion that the secular rationales offered in support of such laws were really pretexts for more "theological" commitments.

120. Stern and Wermiel, *Justice Brennan*, 166, 418–19.

121. In a similar vein, Abner Greene has argued that religion cannot be the predominant basis for legislation or public policy under the establishment clause, and that it is accordingly important that religion also be accommodated against unfavorable or burdensome legislation. Abner S. Greene, "The Political Balance of the Religion Clauses," *Yale Law Journal* 102, no. 7 (1993): 1611.

122. See, e.g., a speech by Justice William J. Brennan, Jr., "To the Text and Teaching Symposium, Georgetown University," October 12, 1985, https://fed soc.org/commentary/publications/the-great-debate-justice-william-j-brennan -jr-october-12-1985.

123. See, e.g., People v. Phillips, New York Court of General Sessions, June 14, 1813. The decision was privately reported but has been frequently reprinted. See, e.g., Michael W. McConnell, John H. Garvey, and Thomas C. Berg, *Religion and the Constitution*, 3rd ed. (New York: Wolters Kluwer, 2011), 139. Paul Horwitz observes that "[a]ccommodation of religion is an aboriginal feature of American public law. From the earliest days of the Republic, exemptions from legally imposed burdens on religious belief and practice 'were seen as a natural and legitimate response to the tension between law and religious conviction.'" Paul Horwitz, "Comment: The Hobby Lobby Moment," *Harvard Law Review* 128, no. 1 (November 2014): 154–89 at 167, which partially quotes Michael W. McConnell, "The Origins and Historical Understanding of Free Exercise of Religion," *Harvard Law Review* 103, no. 7 (May 1990): 1409–1517 at 1466. See also Clark B. Lombardi, "Nineteenth-Century Free Exercise Jurisprudence and the Challenge of Polygamy: The Relevance of Nineteenth-Century Cases and Commentaries for Contemporary Debates about Free Exercise Exemptions," *Oregon Law Review* 85, no. 2 (2006): 369–442 at 403–23.

124. Sherbert v. Verner, 374 U.S. 398 (1963).

125. Lyng v. Northwest Indian Cemetery Protective Ass., 485 U.S. 439 (1988); Goldman v. Weinberger, 475 U.S. 503 (1986).

126. Employment Division v. Smith, 494 U.S. 872 (1990). In *Smith*, Brennan joined in the dissent written by Justice Harry Blackmun.

127. Scholars and even justices sometimes debated, to be sure, whether the *Lemon* doctrine permitted governments to act for a religious purpose so long as they also had a secular purpose. But the common assumption, and the view

that Brennan himself favored, indicated that only secular purposes were legitimate. Brennan made the point clear in his dissent in Lynch v. Donnelly, 465 U.S. 668, 699 (1984) (Brennan, J., dissenting), where he argued that even if a creche in a Christmas display had a permissible secular purpose, the display was nonetheless unconstitutional if the display also had a religious element and if the secular purpose could be achieved with a purely secular display.

128. Abington School Dist. v. Schempp, 374 U.S. 203 (1963) at 296–99 (Brennan, J., concurring).

129. See Gary Simson, "The Establishment Clause in the Supreme Court: Rethinking the Court's Approach," *Cornell Law Review* 72, no. 5 (July 1987): 905–35 at 913.

130. A Bill for Establishing Religious Freedom, Virginia, 1779 and 1786, reprinted in *The Sacred Rights of Conscience: Selected Readings on Religious Liberty and Church-State Relations in the American Founding*, ed. Daniel L. Dreisbach and Mark David Hall (Indianapolis, IN: Liberty Fund, 2009), 250.

131. See Kathleen A. Brady, *The Distinctiveness of Religion in American Law: Rethinking Religion Clause Jurisprudence* (New York: Cambridge University Press, 2015), 93: "The problem with James Madison's argument . . . has been that it seems to rest on religious premises that do not appeal to the increasing numbers of Americans who are not religious believers or who do not share Madison's eighteenth-century Protestant theology." However, Brady argues that Madison's argument can be formulated in more general terms—in terms of "openness to the divine"—that should be acceptable today. Ibid., 80–99.

132. See Halberstam, "Common Man as Uncommon Man," 26. "Brennan was a man whose intelligence was practical rather than abstract."

133. See, e.g., Kenneth Einar Himma, "An Unjust Dogma: Why a Special Right to Religion Wrongly Discriminates Against Non-Religious Worldviews," *San Diego Law Review* 54, no. 2 (May–June 2017): 217; Brian Leiter, *Why Tolerate Religion?* (Princeton, NJ: Princeton University Press, 2012); Micah Schwartzman, "What If Religion Is Not Special?," *University of Chicago Law Review* 79, no. 4 (Fall 2012): 1351; Gemma Cornelissen, "Belief-Based Exemptions: Are Religious Beliefs Special?," *Ratio Juris* 25, no. 1 (March 2102): 85; Christopher L. Eisgruber and Lawrence G. Sager, *Religious Freedom and the Constitution* (Cambridge, MA: Harvard University Press, 2007); Anthony Ellis, "What is Special about Religion?," *Law and Philosophy* 25, no. 2 (March 2006): 219; James W. Nickel, "Who Needs Freedom of Religion?," *University of Colorado Law Review* 76, no. 4 (2005): 941.

134. For elaboration of this description, see Smith, *Pagans and Christians in the City*, 328–33.

135. Marie Failinger, "Wondering After Babel," in *Law and Religion*, ed. Rex J. Ahdar (Aldershot, Hampshire, UK: Ashgate Publishing, 2000).

136. United States v. Seeger, 380 U.S. 163 (1965).

137. United States v. Seeger, 380 U.S. 163 (1965) at 166.

138. Welsh v. United States, 398 U.S. 333 (1970).

139. Welsh v. United States, 398 U.S. 333 (1970) at 342–43.

140. The point is developed in McConnell, "Origins and Historical Understanding," 1409, 1488–1500.

141. See, e.g., Christie Hartlie and Lori Watson, "Political Liberalism and Religious Exemptions," in *Religious Exemptions*, ed. Kevin Vallier and Michael Weber (New York: Oxford University Press, 2018); Jocelyn Maclure, "Conscience, Religion, and Exemptions: An Egalitarian View," in Vallier and Weber, *Religious Exemptions*, 9, 12; Douglas Laycock, "The Wedding Vendor Cases," *Harvard Journal of Law & Public Policy* 41, no. 1 (Winter 2018): 49, 61; Thomas C. Berg, "Religious Accommodation and the Welfare State," *Harvard Journal of Law & Gender* 38, no. 1 (Winter 2015): 113–18; Robert Audi, *Democratic Authority and the Separation of Church and State* (New York: Oxford University Press, 2011), 42, 71; Alan Brownstein, "Gays, Jews, and Other Strangers in a Strange Land: The Case for Reciprocal Accommodation of Religious Liberty and the Right of Same-Sex Couples to Marry," *University of San Francisco Law Review* 45, no. 2 (Fall 2010): 389, 400–402; Troy L. Booher, "Finding Religion for the First Amendment," *John Marshall Law Review* 38, no. 2 (Winter 2002): 469, 471–72; Jane Rutherford, "Religion, Rationality, and Special Treatment," *William & Mary Bill of Rights Journal* 9, no. 2 (February 2001): 303, 344–45. See also Obergefell v. Hodges, 135 S. Ct. 2584, 2593 (2015) (Constitution protects right of "persons, within a lawful realm, to define and express their identity"); Town of Greece v. Galloway, 134 S. Ct. 1811, 1853 (2014) (Kagan, J., dissenting) ("A person's response to [religious] doctrine, language, and imagery . . . reveals a core aspect of identity—who that person is and how she faces the world.").

142. See Carl Trueman, *The Rise and Triumph of the Modern Self* (Wheaton, IL: Crossway, 2020), 93, which describes an "inward turn, the turn to the individual, [that] gave the individual a value—a dignity—that eventually came to stand independent of any sacred order."

143. In this vein, Ronald Beiner criticizes David Richards's use of conscience to ground a variety of legal rights. "The spuriousness of this recurrent appeal to the sacredness of conscience is very clearly displayed," Beiner argues, "in [Richards's] discussion of pornography. How can this possibly be a matter of conscience? What is at issue here, surely, is the sacredness of consumer preferences." And Beiner goes on to scoff that "[b]y [Richards's] contorted reasoning, the decision to snort cocaine constitutes an act of conscience." Ronald Beiner, *Philosophy in a Time of Lost Spirit* (Toronto: University of Toronto Press, 1997), 30.

144. For a helpful discussion of this development, see Andrew R. Murphy, *Conscience and Community* (University Park: Pennsylvania State University Press, 2001), 276–91.

145. Doug Rossinow, *The Politics of Authenticity: Liberalism, Christianity, and the New Left in America* (New York: Columbia University Press, 1998), 5.

146. Rossinow, *Politics of Authenticity*, 5.

147. Rossinow, *Politics of Authenticity*, 340.

148. Robert Bolt, *A Man for All Seasons* (London: Heinemann, 1960), xii–xiv.

149. Bolt, *Man for All Seasons*, 140.

150. Bolt, *Man for All Seasons*, 91.

151. Bolt, *Man for All Seasons*, 153.

152. John Guy, *Thomas More* (New York: Oxford University Press, 2000), 223.

153. Charles Taylor, *The Ethics of Authenticity* (Cambridge, MA: Harvard University Press, 1991), 15.

154. Taylor, *Ethics of Authenticity*, 25.

155. Taylor, *Ethics of Authenticity*, 26 (emphasis added).

156. Taylor, *Ethics of Authenticity*, 46, 58.

157. Thomas More, *The Last Letters of Thomas More*, ed. Alvaro de Silva (Grand Rapids, MI: Eerdmans, 2001), 61.

158. For a contemporary expression of this idea, see Joseph Cardinal Ratzinger, "Conscience and Truth," in Joseph Ratzinger, *On Conscience: Two Essays* (Philadelphia: Ignatius Press, 2007), 33. Ratzinger argues against "modern liberal notions of autonomy" in favor of "the much deeper sense that nothing belongs less to me than I myself. My own 'I' is the site of the profoundest surpassing of self and contact with him from whom I come and toward whom I am going."

159. O. Carter Snead, *What It Means to Be Human* (Cambridge, MA: Harvard University Press, 2020), 5. Later in this book (68–96), Snead provides a valuable critique of this conception and an insightful discussion of its effects in undermining community and a sense of purpose and meaning.

160. Simon Feldman, *Against Authenticity: Why You Shouldn't Be Yourself* (Lanham, MD: Lexington Books, 2015), 11. Feldman distinguishes several different conceptions of authenticity, and argues that none of them provides an appropriate ethical ideal.

161. Taylor, *Ethics of Authenticity*, 75 (emphasis in original). See also Tara Isabella Burton, *Strange Rites: New Religions for a Godless World* (New York: PublicAffairs, 2020), 33, 145.

162. Quoted in Feldman, *Against Authenticity*, 182 (second emphasis added).

163. Feldman, *Against Authenticity*, 189. See also ibid., 192, which remarks on "the problematic authenticity fetishism that saturates so much of our contemporary normative discourse."

164. William J. Brennan, Jr., "The Bill of Rights and the States," *New York University Law Review* 36, no. 4 (April 1961): 761, 771. (This article was originally presented as the James Madison Lecture at the New York University School of Law on February 15, 1961.)

165. William J. Brennan, Jr., "The Essential Dignity of Man" (remarks to the Morrow Citizens Association on Correction, Newark, New Jersey, November 21, 1961).

166. Brennan, "To the Text and Teaching Symposium," https://fedsoc.org/commentary/publications/the-great-debate-justice-william-j-brennan-jr-october-12-1985.

167. From Miranda v. Arizona, 384 U.S. 436 (1966).

168. Reynolds v. Sims, 377 U.S. 533 (1964).

169. See Ruth Bader Ginsburg and Wendy Webster Williams, "Court Architect of Gender Equality: Setting a Firm Foundation for the Equal Status of Men and Women," in Rosenkranz and Schwartz, *Reason and Passion*, 185, 186.

"Justice Brennan stepped forward as the Court's clearest, most constant speaker for women's equality."

170. See, e.g., Gary Lawson and Guy Seidman, "Originalism as a Legal Enterprise," *Constitutional Commentary* 23, no. 1 (Spring 2006): 47, 53. "[T] he Constitution on its face presents itself to the world as an instruction manual for a form of government. It is simply too dry, technical, and boring to be anything else." And see generally Smith, Alexander, Allan, and Schwarzchild, *Principled Constitution*.

171. See Gillman and Chemerinsky, *Religion Clauses*, 108–10, 113, 135.

172. Roe v. Wade, 410 U.S. 113 (1973).

173. Eisenstadt v. Baird, 405 U.S. 438 (1972).

174. Craig v. Boren, 429 U.S. 190 (1976).

175. See William J. Brennan, "My Life on the Court," in Rosenkranz and Schwartz, *Reason and Passion*, 17, 18. "I will say . . . that high on the list of the Court's accomplishments during my tenure were a panoply of opinions protecting and promoting individual rights and human dignity."

176. Speech by Justice William J. Brennan, Jr., "To the Text and Teaching Symposium, Georgetown University," October 12, 1985, https://fedsoc.org /commentary/publications/the-great-debate-justice-william-j-brennan-jr -october-12-1985.

177. See, e.g., John Paul II, *Gospel of Life*, sec. 34. See also *Catechism of the Catholic Church* (Città del Vaticano: Libreria Editrice Vaticana, 1994; English trans., Mahwah, NJ: Paulist Press, 1994), 424 para. 1700. "The dignity of the human person is rooted in his creation in the image and likeness of God."

178. See, e.g., *Catechism*, 432 para. 1740. "The exercise of freedom does not imply a right to say or do everything. . . . By deviating from the moral law man violates his own freedom, becomes imprisoned within himself, disrupts neighborly fellowship, and rebels against divine truth."

179. See, e.g., Mother Theresa, "Speech at the Cairo International Conference" (September 9, 1994): "I have said often, and I am sure of it, that the greatest destroyer of peace in the world today is abortion. If a mother can kill her own child, what is there to stop you and me from killing each other? The only one who has the right to take life is the One who has created it. Nobody else has that right: no conference, no government."

180. Planned Parenthood v. Casey, 505 U.S. 833, 851 (1992) (plurality opinion by Justices O'Connor, Kennedy, and Souter).

181. Although, in an early case decided in his first year on the Court, Justice Brennan recognized that obscenity was a constitutionally unprotected category (Roth v. United States, 354 U.S. 476 [1957]), he later came to the view that regulation of obscenity was impermissible except perhaps to protect children and unconsenting adults. Brennan was emphatic that the community has no interest in preventing consenting adults from obtaining and viewing materials that the community deems offensive, immoral, or obscene. See Paris Adult Theatre I v. Slaton, 413 U.S. 49, 108–13 (1973) (Brennan, J., dissenting).

182. For example, Roe v. Wade, 410 U.S. 113 (1973), overruled in Dobbs v. Jackson Women's Health Organization, 597 U.S.__ (2022).

183. See, e.g., Cruzan v. Director, Missouri Department of Health, 497 U.S. 261, 301, 311 (1990) (Brennan, J., dissenting), which grounded a right to refuse life-sustaining food or hydration in human dignity.

184. Arthur Allen Leff, "Unspeakable Ethics, Unnatural Law," *Duke Law Journal* 1979, no. 6 (December 1979): 1237, 1246.

185. Lynch v. Donnelly, 465 U.S. 668, 715–17 (1984) (Brennan, J., dissenting). See also Elk Grove School Dist. v. Newdow, 542 U.S. 1, 35 (2004) (O'Connor, J., concurring), which maintained that religion can be used for purposes of "solemnizing public occasions, expressing confidence in the future, and encouraging the appreciation of what is worthy in our society."

186. See Jean Bethke Elshtain, *Sovereignty: God, State, and Self* (New York: Basic Books, 2008), 159–60: "[W]ith the emergence of sovereign selves, the sovereign God stands as a provocation: man must himself become a God against the Creator God in order to strip himself of any indebtedness, whether to Creator or other persons." See also Charles Taylor, *Sources of the Self: The Making of the Modern Identity* (Cambridge, MA: Harvard University Press, 1989), 249: "The disengaged subject . . .takes over some of the prerogatives accorded God in Occamist theology. Indeed, in some ways the new outlook can be seen as a kind of anthropological transposition of this theology."

187. See, for example, the various mostly adulatory essays in Rosenkranz and Schwartz, *Reason and Passion*.

188. Jack N. Rakove, *Beyond Belief, Beyond Conscience: The Radical Significance of the Free Exercise of Religion* (New York: Oxford University Press, 2020), 10–11.

189. For discussion, see Larry Sidentrop, *Inventing the Individual: The Origins of Western Liberalism* (Cambridge, MA: Belknap Press of Harvard University Press, 2014), 7–42.

190. Quoted in O. M. Bakke, *When Children Became People* (Minneapolis: Fortress Press, 2005), 112.

191. See, generally, Sidentrop, *Inventing the Individual*; Tom Holland, *Dominion: How the Christian Revolution Remade the World* (New York: Basic Books, 2019). See also Francis Fukuyama, *Identity: Contemporary Identity Politics and the Struggle for Recognition* (London: Profile Books, 2019), 52, which acknowledges the "Christian origins of the right to dignity."

192. Kyle Harper, "Christianity and the Roots of Human Dignity in Late Antiquity," in *Christianity and Freedom*, vol. 1: *Historical Perspectives*, ed. Timothy Samuel Shah and Allen D. Hertzke (Cambridge: Cambridge University Press, 2016), 123, 127, 130.

193. See Elshtain, *Sovereignty*, 170. "God is a problem, . . . for any notion of God's sovereignty clashes with our presuppositions of self-sovereignty."

194. See, e.g., Daniel C. Dennett, *Darwin's Dangerous Idea: Evolution and the Meanings of Life* (New York: Simon & Schuster, 1996).

195. For an excellent review of the trial and its effects on American culture, see Edward J. Larson, *Summer for the Gods: The Scopes Trial and America's Continuing Debate over Science and Religion* (New York: Basic Books, 1997).

196. See, e.g., Epperson v. Arkansas, 393 U.S. 97 n. 10 (1968). The point was hotly contested in perhaps the first major debate on the subject—the 1860 Oxford "Great Debate" between Bishop Samuel Wilberforce and Thomas Huxley (a.k.a. "Darwin's bulldog"). See "The Great Debate," Museum of Natural History website, University of Oxford, https://oumnh.ox.ac.uk/great-debate.

197. John Gray, *Straw Dogs: Thoughts on Humans and Other Animals* (London: Granta Books, 2002), xii.

198. Gray, *Straw Dogs*, 31. See Trueman, *Rise and Triumph*, 189, which observes that in the evolutionary view "humans are relativized in relation to other creatures. Descent from a prior species excludes special creation of man and woman, and natural selection renders teleology unnecessary as a hypothesis."

199. Abington School Dist. v. Schempp, 374 U.S. 203 (1963) at 300 (Brennan, J. concurring).

200. Epperson v. Arkansas, 393 U.S. 97 (1968).

201. Epperson v. Arkansas, 393 U.S. 97 (1968) at 113 (Black, J., concurring).

202. Edwards v. Aguillard, 482 U.S. 578 (1987).

203. See, e.g., Taylor, *Sources of the Self*, 315, which describes the development in Descartes, Locke, and Kant of the idea of "our dignity as rational agents."

204. See Trueman, *Rise and Triumph*, 266. "Freud's ideas . . . have come to shape the social imaginary of Western culture in profound ways. One might ask why this is so, given that his psychoanalytic theories are now largely discredited."

205. Trueman, *Rise and Triumph*, 275, which describes "the basic contention that it is the unconscious that is the real bedrock of individual identity, the thing about the person that is most real." See Charles R. Lawrence III, "The Id, the Ego, and Equal Protection: Reckoning with Unconscious Racism," *Stanford Law Review* 39, no. 2 (January 1987): 317.

206. Fukuyama, *Identity*, 51–52.

207. See, e.g., George Kateb, *Human Dignity* (Cambridge, MA: Belknap Press of Harvard University Press, 2011).

208. The point is developed at length in Steven D. Smith, *Fictions, Lies, and the Authority of Law.*

209. Various instances are described and reflected on in Joseph Vining, *The Song Sparrow and the Child: Claims of Science and Humanity* (Notre Dame, IN: University of Notre Dame Press, 2004).

210. See Ratzinger, "Conscience and Truth," 26. "Here we come into contact with the really critical issue of the modern age. The concept of truth has been virtually given up."

211. See, e.g., Michael Pakaluk, "Rawls and the Rejection of Truth," *Law & Liberty*, April 23, 2021, lawliberty.org/forum/rawls-and-the-rejection-of -truth/. Rawls's political philosophy makes no appeal to truth: "in public reason, ideas of truth based on comprehensive doctrines are replaced by the idea of the politically reasonable." "The search for reasonable grounds of agreement rooted in our conception of ourselves replaces the search for moral truth interpreted as fixed by a prior and independent order of objects and relations, whether natural or divine. Rawls says such things repeatedly, but it seems hardly anyone grasps the point. What is Rawls's legacy? What is the condition of a society

which, following his lead, rejects truth as a criterion?" See also Jody S. Kraus, "Political Liberalism and Truth," *Legal Theory* 5, no. 1 (March 1999): 45, 55: "Political liberalism's preferred strategy is to substitute the idea of reasonableness for truth."

212. Burton, *Strange Rites*, 164.

213. See West Virginia Board of Education v. Barnette, 319 U.S. 624 (1943), which famously asserts that "if there is any fixed star in our constitutional constellation, it is that no official, high or petty, can prescribe what shall be orthodox in politics, nationalism, religion, or other matters of opinion or force citizens to confess by word or act their faith therein." For consideration of different interpretations of the dictum, see Steven D. Smith, "'Fixed Star' or Twin Star: The Ambiguity of *Barnette*," *FIU Law Review* 13, no. 4 (Spring 2019): 801.

214. Jamal Greene, *How Rights Went Wrong: How Our Obsession with Rights is Tearing America Apart* (Boston: Houghton Mifflin Harcourt, 2021), 58.

215. See T. Alexander Aleinikoff, "Constitutional Law in the Age of Balancing," *Yale Law Journal* 96, no. 5 (April 1987): 943.

216. Probably the major modern effort to deal with this challenge has involved attempts to apply something like John Stuart Mill's "harm principle": each of the individual mini-sovereigns can believe and live however he or she chooses but only so long as no harm is inflicted on the other mini-sovereigns. And yet Mill's idea does more to gloss over or conceal the basic difficulty than to resolve it. In the first place, the imposition of the "harm principle" as the governing rule to which everyone must conform seems in itself a violation of the basic right. Who says that an individual must exercise his or her right by defining a concept of existence and the universe that includes the harm principle? What if someone wants to define a concept of existence that does not include any such principle? Of even greater practical importance, however, is that upon examination the very idea of "harm" comes to seem utterly question-begging. If Linc complains of Zelda's conduct (even if that conduct consists of resisting some desire or action of Linc's), Linc is implicitly or perhaps explicitly asserting that Zelda's conduct causes harm to him. In *his* concept of existence and the universe, it seems, that assertion is true; and only by rejecting Linc's concept of existence can we say, "You think you are being harmed but you aren't." For elaboration, see Smith, *Disenchantment of Secular Discourse*, 70–106.

217. Greene, *How Rights Went Wrong*, xvii.

218. Greene, *How Rights Went Wrong*, xxxv.

219. See Trueman, *Rise and Triumph*.

220. Simon Feldman describes the idea: "the recovery of the true self is nothing less than the realization of a self that is uncorrupted and freed to act, morally and responsibly, in accordance with its own undistorted moral vision." Feldman, *Against Authenticity*, 107. See also Fukuyama, *Identity*, 32. "What Rousseau asserts, and what has become foundational in world politics in the subsequent centuries, is that a thing called society exists outside the individual . . . [and] is itself the chief obstacle to the realization of human potential, and hence of human happiness. This way of thinking has become so instinctive to us now that we are unconscious of it."

221. Lionel Trilling, *Sincerity and Authenticity* (Cambridge, MA: Harvard University Press, 1971, 1972), 11.

222. Trilling, *Sincerity and Authenticity*, 108.

223. Robert N. Bellah, Richard Madsen, William M. Sullivan, Ann Swidler, and Steven M. Tipton, *Habits of the Heart: Individualism and Commitment in American Life*, updated ed. (Berkeley: University of California Press, 1996), 55–56.

224. Bellah et al., *Habits*, 81.

225. Bellah et al., *Habits*, 82–83.

226. See Trueman, *Rise and Triumph*, 164. "The idea that we can be who or whatever we want to be is a commonplace today."

227. See generally Rossinow, *Politics of Authenticity*.

228. Eisenstadt v. Baird, 405 U.S. 438 (1972).

229. Griswold v. Connecticut, 381 U.S. 479 (1965). Although Justice Brennan merely joined the majority opinion in *Griswold*, his behind-the-scenes role in the case was significant. See Souter, 307.

230. Griswold v. Connecticut, 381 U.S. 479 (1965) at 486.

231. Eisenstadt v. Baird, 405 U.S. 438 (1972) at 453 (emphasis added).

232. Burton, *Strange Rites*, 10.

233. With respect to one particularly widespread spiritual-consumerist movement grounded in the idea of "wellness," Burton explains: "It's a theology, fundamentally, of division: the authentic, intuitional self—both body and soul—and the artificial, malevolent forces of society, rules, and expectations. We are born good, but we are tricked, by Big Pharma, by processed food, by civilization itself, into living something that falls short of our best life. Our sins, if they exist at all, lie in insufficient self-attention or self-care: false modesty, undeserved humilities, refusing to shine bright. We have not merely the inalienable right but the moral responsibility to take care of ourselves first before directing our attention to others. We have to listen to ourselves, to behave authentically, in tune with what our intuition dictates." Burton, *Strange Rites*, 94. See also ibid., 33. "Most of these new religions share ... the grand narrative that oppressive societies and unfairly narrow expectations stymie natural—and sometimes even divine—human potential."

234. Burton, *Strange Rites*, 167.

235. Burton, *Strange Rites*, 168.

236. Drutman, "How Hatred Came to Dominate American Politics."

237. See Patrick T. Brown and Rachel Sheffield, "U.S. Marriage Rates Hit New Recorded Low," United States Congress Joint Economic Committee website, Apr. 29, 2020, https://www.jec.senate.gov/public/index.cfm/republicans/2020/4/marriage-rate-blog-test.

238. See Elizabeth Wildsmith, Jennifer Manlove, and Elizabeth Cook, "Dramatic Increase in the Proportion of Births outside of Marriage in the United States from 1990 to 2016," *Child Trends*, August 8, 2018, https://www.childtrends.org/publications/dramatic-increase-in-percentage-of-births-outside-marriage-among-whites-hispanics-and-women-with-higher-education-levels.

239. See the Family Story website, https://familystoryproject.org/. See also Burton, *Strange Rites*, 157.

240. John Hillen, "Restoring Trust and Leadership in a Vacuous Age," *Law & Liberty*, April 27, 2021, https://lawliberty.org/restoring-trust-and -leadership-in-a-vacuous-age/. Yuval Levin cites studies showing that between the 1970s and today, public confidence in a whole range of institutions—public schools, the presidency, organized religion, hospitals—has declined precipitously. Confidence in Congress has plummeted from 42 percent of Americans in the 1970s to a shockingly low 11 percent in 2018. Yuval Levin, *A Time to Build* (New York: Basic Books, 2020), 29–30. See also Burton, *Strange Rites*, 48, 242.

241. Bruce Ledewitz, *The Universe Is on Our Side: Restoring Faith in American Public Life* (New York: Oxford University Press, 2021), xiii. For more recent evidence from a Gallup study, see, e.g., Madeline Halpert, "Trust in U.S. Institutions Hits Record Low, Poll Finds," *Forbes*, July 5, 2022, https://www .forbes.com/sites/madelinehalpert/2022/07/05/trust-in-us-institutions-hits -record-low-poll-finds.

242. Bellah et al., *Habits*, xxx–xxxiii.

243. In a revised edition of his book published in 2020, Robert Putnam noted that the loss of community documented in his book *Bowling Alone* had persisted. He explained: "My purpose . . . was to try to contribute to a 'revival of American community,' as the subtitle of *Bowling Alone* signaled. It is now perfectly plain that, in that sense, I have so far failed. . . . [The data] shows unequivocally just how how thoroughly America has continued to regress in the intervening twenty years—a downward plunge resulting not merely in fraying community ties but also in worsening economic inequality, greater political polarization, and more cultural individualism." Robert Putnam, *Bowling Alone: The Collapse and Revival of American Community* (New York: Simon & Schuster, rev. ed. 2020), 10.

244. Putnam, *Bowling Alone*, 6.

245. The quote in the subheading is from Walker Percy, *Signposts in a Strange Land* (New York: Farrar, Straus & Giroux, 1991), 314.

246. The celebrated skeptical philosopher David Hume looked attentively inside himself in search of his self and found . . . nothing. Or at least nothing unified and continuous that could answer to the label of the "self." "For my part," Hume reported, "when I enter most intimately into what I call myself, I always stumble on some particular perception or other, of heat or cold, light or shade, love or hatred, pain or pleasure. I never can catch myself at any time without a perception, and never can observe any thing but the perception." Instead of a unified self, there was "nothing but a bundle or collection of different perceptions, which succeed each other with an inconceivable rapidity, and are in a perpetual flux and movement." David Hume, *A Treatise on Human Nature*, 2nd ed., text revision and notes by P. H. Nidditch, analytical index by L. A. Selby-Bigge (Oxford: Clarendon Press, 1978), bk. 1, part 4, sec. 6, p. 252. Hume thus concluded that the self is a "fiction." Ibid., 255, 259.

247. The philosophical literature on the subject is vast. For some particularly probing reflections, see J. David Velleman, *Self to Self: Selected Essays*, 2nd

ed. (Ann Arbor, MI: Michigan Publishing, 2020); Derek Parfit, *Reasons and Persons* (Oxford: Clarendon Press, 1986).

248. The quote in the subheading is from Percy, *Signposts*, 384.

249. Trilling, *Sincerity and Authenticity*, 5.

250. See Velleman, *Self to Self*, 466. "Thus, [Harry] Frankfurt conceives of the self as an inner core or kernel comprising that *in* the person which really *is* the person and whose impact on the world is therefore his. The self so conceived underlies not just autonomy but personal identity as well."

251. Trilling, *Sincerity and Authenticity*, 25.

252. See Eisenstadt v. Baird, 405 U.S. 438 (1972); Planned Parenthood v. Casey, 505 U.S. 833 (1992); Lawrence v. Texas, 539 U.S. 558 (2003); United States v. Stevens, 559 U.S. 460 (2010).

253. Bellah et al., *Habits*, 84.

254. Feldman, *Against Authenticity*, 183.

255. Similar notions have supported movements for racial and sexual equality. A common rationale in equal protection and antidiscrimination law for prohibiting discrimination based on race or sex is that individuals have no choice over those features and no ability to change them; hence it would be deeply unfair for them to be disadvantaged in any way by these unchosen features.

256. See Trueman, *Rise and Triumph*, 340–41, which argues that although LGBTQ+ has proven useful as a political alliance, there is an inherent conflict in the movement because "both transgenderism and queer theory are predicated on a basic denial of the fixed nature of gender, something that the L and the G by contrast assume."

257. Mary Eberstadt, *Primal Screams: How the Sexual Revolution Created Identity Politics* (West Conshohocken, PA: Templeton Press, 2019), 8–9.

258. See Bellah et al., *Habits*, 55, which observes that "the nervous search for the self and the extravagant conclusions drawn from that search are probably relatively recent in our society." See also Taylor, *Sources of the Self*, 28: "Talk about 'identity' in the modern sense would have been incomprehensible to our forebears of a couple of centuries ago." See also Fukuyama, *Identity*, 35, which notes that "the concept of identity as it is now understood would not even arise in most traditional human societies."

259. See Trueman, *Rise and Triumph*, 78. "When personhood is seen as something connected to the sacred and transcending the merely material—say, as the possession of a soul or of the image of God—then the embryo is a person of potential and protected in, say, the Christian sacred order because she possesses the image of God from the moment of conception."

260. See Bellah et al., *Habits*, 82: "In most societies in world history, the meaning of one's life derived to a large degree from one's relationship to the lives of one's parents and one's children." See also Trueman, *Rise and Triumph*, 66–67: "In the past, a person's identity came from without, the result of being set within a fixed social hierarchy. One might perhaps say that belonging, or being recognized, was therefore a question of understanding one's place in that preexisting social hierarchy into which one had been born."

261. J. David Velleman, "Family History," *Philosophical Papers* 34, no. 3 (Nov. 2005): 357–78. For criticism of Velleman's argument, see Sally Haslanger, "Family, Ancestry, and Self: What Is the Moral Significance of Biological Ties?," *Adoption & Culture* 2 (2009): 91–122.

262. See Bellah et al., *Habits*, 83. "We talked to Christians and Jews for whom the self makes sense in relation to a God who challenges, promises, and reassures. We even talked to some for whom the word *soul* has not been entirely displaced by the word *self*. We talked to those for whom the self apart from history and community makes no sense at all."

263. Leeds, "A Life on the Court."

264. Stern and Wermiel, *Justice Brennan*, 4.

265. Stern and Wermiel, *Justice Brennan*, 8.

266. Stern and Wermiel, *Justice Brennan*, 16.

267. Stern and Wermiel, *Justice Brennan*, 3–25.

268. Stern and Wermiel, *Justice Brennan*, 23.

269. Stern and Wermiel, *Justice Brennan*, 3.

270. Leeds, "A Life on the Court."

271. Stern and Wermiel, *Justice Brennan*, 19, 25.

272. Bellah et al., *Habits*, 65.

273. Bellah et al., *Habits*, 63. See also Eberstadt, *Primal Screams*, 58, which observes that "the vote by much of Western humanity to live without a transcendental horizon removes one more way of answering the question *Who am I?* that religion traditionally supplied: *I am a child of God.*"

274. See Patrick J. Deneen, *Why Liberalism Failed* (New Haven, CT: Yale University Press, 2018), 50, which describes "the liberation of embedded individuals from their traditional ties and relationships."

275. Eberstadt, *Primal Screams*, 38. Eberstadt's book is a general exploration of this problem.

276. See Ratzinger, "Conscience and Truth," 39. "Nevertheless, retreat into self, however comfortable, does not redeem. The self withers away and becomes lost."

277. See Elena Renken, "Most Americans Are Lonely, and Our Workplace Culture May Not Be Helping," NPR, January 23, 2020, https://www.npr.org/sections/health-shots/2020/01/23/798676465/most-americans-are-lonely-and-our-workplace-culture-may-not-be-helping.

278. See, e.g., Maggie Fox, "Major Depression on the Rise among Everyone, New Data Shows," NBC News, May 11, 2018, https://www.nbcnews.com/health/health-news/major-depression-rise-among-everyone-new-data-shows-n873146.

279. Levin, *A Time to Build*, 12; Burton, *Strange Rites*, 163.

280. Aaron Kheriaty, "Dying of Despair," *First Things*, August 2017, https://www.firstthings.com/article/2017/08/dying-of-despair.

281. See "2020 We Are Donor Conceived Survey Report," We Are Donor Conceived website, Sept. 17, 2020, https://www.wearedonorconceived.com/2020-survey-top/2020-we-are-donor-conceived-survey/.

282. Velleman, "Family History," 359.

283. See Fact.MR, "US$ 3 Bn Genealogy Products and Services Market Driven by Surging Demand for DNA Testing: Fact.MR Study," GlobeNewswire, March 4, 2019, https://www.globenewswire.com/news-release/2019/03/04/1746055/0/en/US-3-Bn-Genealogy-Products-and-Services-Market-Driven-by-Surging-Demand-for-DNA-Testing-Fact-MR-Study.html.

284. Velleman, "Family History," 368.

285. See Michael C. Anderson, *Tribalism: The Curse of 21st Century America* (Jonesboro, GA: Simms Books, 2019); Burton, *Strange Rites*, 68, 79–80. See also R. R. Reno, *Return of the Strong Gods: Nationalism, Populism, and the Future of the West* (Washington, DC: Regnery Gateway, 2019).

286. See Fukuyama, *Identity*, 56, which describes the modern "crisis of identity" and asserts that "[t]his psychological fact lays the groundwork for nationalism."

287. Tara Isabella Burton observes: "Fandom, both as a practice and as a marker of identity, is at its core a kind of self-making: it's not just about *what we like* but *who we are*. Identifying oneself publicly as a fan—of a football team, of a pop star—is a public commitment to a tribe and a tribal identity." Burton, *Strange Rites*, 68. See also ibid., 64. "Severus Snape might not be an obvious choice for spiritual veneration. But, for more than a few of the women who call themselves 'Snapewives' or 'Snapefen,' Severus Snape was the closest thing they had to a god."

288. For a helpful discussion of how the commitment to conscience has evolved into identity politics, see Murphy, *Conscience and Community*, 280–83.

289. Rossinow, *Politics of Authenticity*, 343–44.

290. See also Carl R. Trueman, "Identity Politics, Opium of the People," *First Things*, April 29, 2021, https://www.firstthings.com/web-exclusives/2021/04/identity-politics-opium-of-the-people: "The one thing that binds all identitarian groups together is the human experience of wanting to belong and yet finding no place in contemporary society. The family is a mess. Religious institutions lack authority. The nation state is no longer a source of unity but a theater of conflict in which we fight about what is and is not America with much heat and little light. And yet that basic human need to belong persists, a need that is now being met by new identitarian communities—which I would argue are unstable and often illusory. Identity politics is in part a response to this tragic state of affairs."

291. Eberstadt, *Primal Screams*, 26.

292. The quote in the subheading is from Percy, *Signposts*, 309. Percy continued: "It is possessed by a sense of dislocation, a loss of personal identity, an alternating sentimentality and rage which, in an individual patient, could be characterized as dementia."

293. Walker Percy, *Love in the Ruins: The Adventures of a Bad Catholic at a Time Near the End of the World* (New York: Farrar, Straus & Giroux, 1971).

294. Percy, *Love*, 23. See Percy, *Signposts*, 375: "My ideal is Thomas More, an English Catholic—a peculiar breed nowadays—who wore his faith with grace, merriment, and a certain wryness."

295. Percy, *Signposts*, 249–50. More generally, as he put it elsewhere, Percy perceived in the modern world "the sickness of modern man, ... his homelessness

in the midst of the very world which, more than the men of any other time, he has made over for his happiness" (ibid., 252).

296. Percy, *Signposts*, 248–50.

297. Percy, *Love*, 50.

298. Percy, *Love*, 15, 112.

299. Percy, *Love*, 29.

300. Percy, *Love*, 29.

301. Percy, *Love*, 17–18.

302. Percy, *Love*, 18.

303. Percy, *Love*, 5–6. Was this feature prescient? Massimo Faggioli explains the severe divisions within the contemporary Catholic church and worries that "there is a risk here of becoming even more divided, cleaving into two different versions of Catholicism—not, as is legitimate, an assembly of Catholics with different ideas and spiritualities compatible with a vision of a pluralist church, a "big tent," but two distinct ideological identities of orthodoxy existing in a regime of mutual excommunication." Faggioli, *Joe Biden*, 131. See also Carl R. Trueman, "Arguments, Not Sound Bites," *First Things*, June 22, 2021, https://www.firstthings.com/web-exclusives/2021/06/arguments-not-sound-bites: "The polarization of American society finds its analogue in the polarization of the American church."

304. Percy, *Love*, 326. More opines at one point that America's mistreatment of blacks may be the original sin that dooms the country to destruction. Ibid., 56–57.

305. Percy, *Love*, 197–98; see also ibid., 216.

306. Percy, *Love*, 14.

307. Percy, *Love*, 212, 383.

308. Percy, *Love*, 112.

309. Percy, *Love*, 115. See also "the deep abscess in the soul of Western man" (ibid., 153) and "the dread chasm that has rent the soul of Western man" (ibid., 191).

310. Percy, *Love*, 157.

311. Percy, *Love* , 117.

312. Percy, *Love*, 214.

313. Percy, *Love*, 212.

314. Percy, *Love*, 109, 182.

315. Percy, *Love*, 47.

316. Percy, *Love*, 383.

317. Percy, *Love*, 58.

318. Percy, *Love*, 182–83.

319. Percy, *Signposts*, 312.

320. Percy, *Signposts*, 380.

Epilogue

1. Jacques Barzun, *From Dawn to Decadence: 500 Years of Western Cultural Life; 1500 to the Present* (New York: HarperCollins, 2000), xi.

2. See, e.g., Adrian Vermeule, "Liberalism and the Invisible Hand," *American Affairs* 3, no. 1 (Spring 2019): 172–97, https://americanaffairsjournal. org/2019/02/liberalism-and-the-invisible-hand/; Christopher A. Ferrara, *Liberty: The God that Failed* (New York: Angelico, 2012).

3. See, e.g., Rodney Stark, *Bearing False Witness: Debunking Centuries of Anti-Catholic History* (West Conshohocken, PA: Templeton Press, 2016), 135–67; Thomas E. Woods, Jr., *How the Catholic Church Built Western Civilization* (Lanham, MD: Regnery, 2005), 67–114.

4. See, e.g., Scott Hahn and Brandon McGinley, *It Is Right and Just: Why the Future of Civilization Depends on True Religion* (Steubenville, OH: Emmaus Road, 2020).

5. Tara Isabella Burton, *Strange Rites: New Religions for a Godless World* (New York: PublicAffairs, 2020). On page 10, Burton states: "From SoulCycle to contemporary occultism, from obsessive fan culture to the polyamorous and kink-based intentional communities of our new sexual revolution, from wellness culture to the reactionary-atavist alt-right, today's America is teeming with new claimants to our sense of meaning, our social place, our time, and our wallets." On page 25, Burton argues that "[a]t least half of America—and likely far more— is either a faithful None, an SNBR [spiritual but not religious], or a religiously flexible hybrid."

6. See Steven D. Smith, "One Step Enough," *Pepperdine Law Review*, special issue celebrating Robert F. Cochran, Jr., 47, no. 2 (February 2020): 549.

INDEX

STEVEN D. SMITH, winner of the 2022 Religious Liberty Initiative Scholarship Award, is the Warren Distinguished Professor of Law, co-executive director of the Institute for Law and Religion, and the co-executive director of the Institute for Law and Philosophy at the University of San Diego.